The Enigma of M

The Enigma of Meaning

Wittgenstein and Derrida,
Language and Life

GREGORY DESILET

McFarland & Company, Inc., Publishers
Jefferson, North Carolina

This book has undergone peer review.

ISBN (print) 978-1-4766-8982-1
ISBN (ebook) 978-1-4766-4961-0

LIBRARY OF CONGRESS AND BRITISH LIBRARY
CATALOGUING DATA ARE AVAILABLE

Library of Congress Control Number 2023000392

Front cover images: silhouette of Wittgenstein by Mark Durr and
Derrida silhouette artist reference image Photofest

Printed in the United States of America

*McFarland & Company, Inc., Publishers
Box 611, Jefferson, North Carolina 28640
www.mcfarlandpub.com*

Table of Contents

For John, Jackie, and Meredith
who gave so much in
the best of times and worst of times
at UC Santa Barbara.

Acknowledgments

As explained in the following Preface, I'm primarily beholden to John Macksoud (1933–2005) and Jacques Derrida (1930–2004) for motivation and insight in the creation of this book. They share much in their approach to language, but Derrida was able to fill out the approach into what is now famously known as deconstruction. I owe them more than what may be repaid in this book.

Further inspiration for this project arrived unexpectedly through the chance discovery that Wittgenstein's biographer, Professor Ray Monk, was in residence at the Santa Fe Institute conducting research for a biography of Robert Oppenheimer. Happening to be in Santa Fe at the same time, I contacted him and he kindly agreed to a meeting where he answered questions and sharpened my understanding of Wittgenstein. I benefited further from the opportunity to attend his presentation on Wittgenstein to the philosophy department at the University of New Mexico Albuquerque.

After Monk's talk, I met Professor Paul Livingston of the UNM Philosophy Department. Informing me he was teaching a class on Wittgenstein in the fall of that year, he generously agreed to my request to audit the class. His lectures and Q&A sessions took my understanding of Wittgenstein to another level. I remain indebted to him not only for the benefits of these class sessions but also for his friendly support for my work and for subsequent helpful email exchanges. Many thanks to you, Paul!

Also, I owe an exceptional thank you to Jan Sjabbo Helsloot of Amsterdam, another chance encounter. Jan volunteered to read the entire manuscript, chapter by chapter, offering valuable comments and suggestions throughout while also supplying French and German translation advice on passages in Derrida and Wittgenstein where precise translation proves difficult. I cannot thank Jan enough for his language expertise and his time and dedication in reviewing the manuscript and offering suggestions. Every author should be so fortunate to have a reader and commenter like Jan.

I also extend thanks to professors Martin Hägglund, Lee Braver,

Gary Zabel, Graham McFee, and Genia Schönbaumsfeld for helpful email exchanges. Their willingness to engage and answer questions was very much appreciated, and especially so on occasions of disagreement. Similarly, I thank Professor Ian Moore for our recent meeting in Santa Fe and for sharing his thoughts on the topic of the metaphysical roots of violence. Although we had no direct communication, I must also thank Professor Ralph E. Shain for inspiration for Parts II and III of the book, derived from his essay "Derrida and Wittgenstein: Points in Opposition" (2007). I'm also grateful for the comments of two anonymous reviewers whose suggestions independently converged on ways for refining the manuscript, suggestions that were incorporated into the final draft. And I thank Professor Briankle G. Chang of the University of Massachusetts Amherst for assistance in seeking qualified publishers.

At the beginning stages of this project I applied for an NEH grant to help fund the research and potential travel it would require. As part of this application, letters of reference were needed. I'm extremely grateful for the generous letters submitted in my behalf by the following professors: François Cooren of University of Montreal; Craig R. Smith of California State University, Long Beach; Michael J. Hyde of Wake Forest University; and Phillip K. Tompkins of University of Colorado Boulder. Unfortunately, this application failed to secure an award—not a surprising result considering opinions such as the following given by one of the panelists chosen to evaluate the application: "I'm not confident that the project has much intellectual significance or public appeal. It is striking that Derrida himself could not be bothered to carefully study Wittgenstein's writings."

Friend and colleague, Professor Emeritus Tompkins, must be further acknowledged for several lengthy discussions between us on the role of replication in the search for truth. Much substance on the role of replication in truth-seeking did not make it into the final draft of the book, but these discussions were nevertheless helpful overall in composing the chapter on truth in Part III. For those who may be interested in more detail regarding the role of replication in the context of truth-seeking in both the sciences and humanities, I recommend Tompkins' recent book *Open Communication and Replication as Methods for Finding Truth* (2021).

I'm grateful to Professor Emeritus Wes Morriston for his courses featuring Continental philosophers, which became part of my degree program at the University of Colorado Boulder. His excellent courses on Heidegger, Husserl, and Merleau-Ponty laid the foundation for easier entry into the study of Derrida's work. More recently, I thank him for informative discussions on broad philosophical issues, especially on infinity, which, as it turns out, is not only important in mathematics but also in language and metaphysics.

I'm also very appreciative of the information and encouragement given by Jackie Lohrke over the past decade relating to this and other endeavors focusing on events at UC Santa Barbara. And I thank longtime friend Michael Riberdy for numerous conversations on themes relevant to my research, for always probing and helpful questions, and for constant support for my writing projects.

Last but not least, I thank Christine Denning, my wife, whose expertise in psychotherapy met my philosophical preoccupations in countless engaging conversations. Thank you so much for your love and support and for your patience during this lengthy project.

Preface

This text has its origin decades ago when, as an undergraduate, I first encountered Professor John Macksoud at the University of California, Santa Barbara, circa 1970. By all accounts, Macksoud was a man of uncommon qualities, most especially his unparalleled skill in argumentation and his peculiar but winning sense of humor. Drawn by the title of his course, "The Limits of Language," I was surprised to discover it turned out to be entirely devoted to an exhaustive analysis of Ludwig Wittgenstein's *The Blue and Brown Books*. On the first day of class, Macksoud passed out index cards on which he requested each person anonymously write one question—a question he or she would like his course to address and possibly answer. He then collected the cards and began reading them aloud. He responded to a few cards by saying it was not likely persons interested in the given question would find what they were looking for in this particular course. He eventually read the question, "When using language, how do we know that we actually communicate?" He paused and asked, "Whose question is this?" When I raised my hand, he said, "It's likely you'll find this course to be of considerable interest." Questions concerning communication featured prominently throughout the course and, since then, these questions, along with Wittgenstein's work, have never left my horizon of interest. Although Macksoud is now deceased, I thank him greatly for his example, which has now inspired me for over five decades. Macksoud's writings, although not numerous, are unusually provocative and I recommend them, all of which are listed in the bibliography.

Years later, Jacques Derrida triggered a renewed interest in Wittgenstein during a visit with him at Irvine in 1993. He informed me that he regarded Wittgenstein's work to be of sufficient importance and complexity to require considerable time and effort to engage. However, he confessed he had not, to date, succeeded in finding the time needed for the task. As it turned out, he never found the required time before his death in 2004. In the years after his death, I felt an increasing sense of how unfortunate it was that he had not been able to give Wittgenstein's work the close reading he knew it deserved. Macksoud's influence prepared me for Derrida's deconstructive thinking and I began to see some possible ways Derrida might have responded to Wittgenstein's post–*Tractatus* published work. These thoughts led to imagining an extended exchange between the two, which eventually grew into this book project. I do not pretend to fully voice Derrida as he would have spoken, but I do believe this book counts as at least one well-considered response to Wittgenstein consistent with Derrida's approach to language. My debt to Derrida for his inspiration is, therefore, enormous and I thank him posthumously for sharing his time and thoughts with me on two separate occasions at Irvine.

In the current era of advanced information technology, language remains so constantly pervasive that its essential role in life often disappears through being taken for granted, much like the air we breathe. Similarly, communication through language and signs appears obvious since everyone routinely uses language and various signs in multiple daily pursuits including, especially, engaging with other persons. Nevertheless, communication, as the transport of meaning between conscious beings by way of material or audible signs, is a complex process challenging common assumptions. This book may be understood as a summation of decades of reading and research concerning questions of (1) the ground of meaning, (2) the manner and extent to which the use of language and signs may achieve communication, and (3) how communication may be explained, if and when it is achieved, and what cost such communication may impose— for no achievement comes without a price.

As will be more thoroughly addressed in the Introduction, Wittgenstein and Derrida emerge as prime candidates for the two most original and influential language theorists of the last century. Setting their views in dialogue with each other opens a perspective on the roles of language in human activities, yielding new insight for the possibilities of language and new appreciation for the importance of understanding the limits of language. No such dialogue between Wittgenstein and Derrida has thus far been adequately broached in a book-length offering. Two books appear to do so but fall short: Henry Staten's *Wittgenstein and Derrida* (1984) and Newton Garver and Seung-Chong Lee's *Derrida and Wittgenstein* (1994). Although not written explicitly as such, Part I offers a rebuttal of Staten's reading of *Philosophical Investigations* as consistent with particular features of deconstruction. And, concerning Garver and Lee's book, Ralph Shain remarks that their "critique [of Derrida] is vitiated by fundamental misunderstandings and confusions." I find Shain's assessment accurate. Garver and Lee offer a highly questionable comparison of Derrida and Wittgenstein and so I've declined to comment on their work in this book, although I do so elsewhere. Another book, written by Simon

Glendinning (1998), presents Heidegger in a three-way comparison with Wittgenstein and Derrida. This work, however, remains only tangentially related to the main line of inquiry conducted herein and its argument, for those who may be interested, is addressed in an essay presented on my site at academia.edu where my direct commentaries on Staten's and Garver and Lee's books may also be found. Among those who have published essay-length commentaries comparing Wittgenstein and Derrida, the more recent—those of Stone (2000), Wheeler (2000), and Livingston (2012)—also receive treatment on my site at academia.edu.

In the course of examining questions of meaning relating to the use of words and signs as these questions arise in the works of Wittgenstein and Derrida, this book features the later works of Wittgenstein and the early works of Derrida. Wittgenstein's *Philosophical Investigations* (1953, 2009) and *The Blue and Brown Books* (1958) and Derrida's *Speech and Phenomena* (1973), *Of Grammatology* (1976, 2016), and *Limited Inc* (1988) receive central attention. These works are among the most seminal in each philosopher's corpus relevant to philosophy of language and also among the most widely used in current undergraduate and graduate courses on the two philosophers. But wherever it may be judged to add helpful insight into the themes being considered, the discussion also draws on passages from other texts by Wittgenstein and Derrida.

However, even as the chapters herein direct attention to those aspects of the views of Wittgenstein and Derrida relevant to the use of signs and language in important philosophical contexts, the issues of language and meaning discussed also remain relevant to every language user. Although academic readers serve as the main demographic, this book is accessible to those who may not have extensive exposure to Analytic or Continental language philosophy. It restricts philosophical jargon to a minimum and provides context and examples necessary to make the lines of thinking open to readers with a broad range of different backgrounds and experience.

Concerning two of the primary texts, it should be mentioned that the original English translations of *Philosophical Investigations* (1953) and *Of Grammatology* (1973) have now been supplanted with updated versions published in 2009 and 2016 respectively. Since at this time the majority of existing English scholarship and commentary on these two texts draws on the original English translations and since I refer mostly to these commentaries, I have chosen, in nearly every instance of citation, to repeat the translations as provided in the first English publications. The one exception to this choice of translation occurs in Chapter 3 and the reason for it is noted therein.

Introduction:
The Life of Signs

Wherever one would care to look among the key occupations and preoccupations of contemporary life, language may be discovered to play a crucial role in processes enabling and governing the flow of activity. Digital media may be touted as game-changing technology, but humanity's first technology—language—still functions as the most potent and pervasive technology. No other technology can supplant the ascendant role of language in human affairs. In fact, the importance of language only increases with every new technological advance because communication becomes more critical in addressing the corresponding choices and complexities added to daily life. As the medium essential to all human activity and community, language can only be ignored at the expense of becoming the proverbial gorilla in the room. Whatever the life issue may be, these issues cannot be confronted without passing through the door of language. Everyone, from University Hill to Main Street, must confront language and negotiate its operations of meaning, whether through passive default or active effort. Due to the importance of language, the latter is the better option though likely an often deferred one.

However, the pervasiveness of language in human exchange in the form of communication and community-building combines with very real limits to its potential for aiding in these activities. These limits and their consequences have increasingly become all too evident in current times and are brought to the fore in striking locutions such as "no spin zone," "post-truth society," "fake news," "alternative facts," "legalese," "fact check," and a host of other expressions referring to various instances and sources of obfuscation and attempts to protect against them. These limits of language to reliably encode what some refer to as "plain truth" all too often instead aid and abet confusion, conflict, and violence—even deadly violence—condemning language to a double-edged role in human affairs.

The depth of such limits and their consequences are the primary focus and concern of this book.

Meanings routinely encountered in the words of a native language are not ordinarily understood as enigmas. Nevertheless, the greatest philosophers of the 20th century found themselves so intensely preoccupied with questions of meaning—emerging most directly and repeatedly in the use of language—that labeling meaning an enigma would not surprise them. The more their attention focused on language, the more the ground of meaning receded from clear understanding. The fact that abiding consensus regarding the ground of meaning still eludes the club of philosophers of language testifies to continuing unresolved challenges.

Among the most notorious philosophers of the 20th century, Ludwig Wittgenstein and Jacques Derrida also count as among the century's most provocative and influential *language* philosophers. However, no adequate extended commentary comparing or contrasting the work of these two philosophers on language currently exists. *The Enigma of Meaning* remedies this surprising deficiency by examining key differences in the philosophies of Wittgenstein and Derrida concerning the limits of signs and languages in conveying meaning and achieving communication. The importance of confronting and assessing the differences in their views has thus far been culturally and academically underestimated.

Constantly used by everyone every day, language acquires predictable assumptions about how it works. But as both Wittgenstein and Derrida explain, these assumptions often mislead speakers into believing language can do what is routinely expected of it. While both philosophers share certain understandings of language, each also emphasizes different limitations of language and sign operations in general and presents significantly different responses to these limitations.

Wittgenstein shows how to respond to particular limits in order to secure the ability of language to serve as a reliable means of communication. Derrida shows that precisely what enables words and signs to function as language also limits the reliability of communication. These differences regarding the limits of language hinge primarily on different assessments of the role of interpretation in the use and applications of words and signs.

Understanding the differences between these two seminal language philosophers and the choices in attitude toward language they present emerges as pivotal for developing a deeper understanding of the limits of communication. This increased understanding aids in navigating not only the uses of language but also the hidden ruses of language—ruses, which, if ignored, unnecessarily complicate and render more challenging many of the practices and routines of life. Increasing familiarity with specific limits of language in particular and sign operations in general emerges as not merely a helpful but, arguably, an essential step in successful management of communication and fostering of community. Increased familiarity with such limits by no means counts as a panacea for conflict but certainly belongs as a crucial measure in any effort to minimize the worst in human confrontations.

Stepping back a pace, it may well be asked: How can something as seemingly benign as language, regardless of whatever limits it may have, play a role—as suggested above—as instigator of confusion, conflict, and violence? The answer to this question is both simple and complex. The simple answer lies in the capacity of language and signs to promote ways of seeing. But as one of America's greatest language theorists, Kenneth Burke, once remarked, a way of seeing is also a way of *not seeing*. And failure of insight often lies at the root of conflict. But this simple answer belies deeper complexity. How does seeing/not-seeing through language occur?

The human addition of signs to life in the form of language gives names to the things of the world. But this addition merely adds a layer of signs to an already existing layer of signs. The word "apple," for example, is a sign for the object apple. The physical object, in addition to being an object, counts as yet another sign because it is recognized as only one instance of a class of objects. In fact, no species of animal, including *homo sapiens*, could have survived and evolved without the capacity, prior to any kind of language, to classify—as in distinguishing food from non-food and threats from non-threats. Gifted with language, humans have the means to add names to classified objects. The named object presents itself as but a single representative, a sign, of something beyond its unique singularity. But what is that *something*?

Philosophically, this something may be referred to as the *original*. In the word/object/original nexus, the word *apple* is a copy of a copy while the object named is but a copy of the original. If the object in the world is itself a copy, an instance of something conceived as the original, then only this original may count as the *true* object. But if objects in the world are but copies and not true objects, where may true objects, the originals, be found? Where may the ground of the truth and the meaning of what is real be found and reliably accessed in a world presenting itself as representations, as only copies and copies of copies?

This question lies at the core of the entire history of philosophy, not merely the history of language philosophy. Answers to it have generated a shifting ground of successive paradigms over many centuries. The early Plato famously answers that true objects may be found in a world of forms located outside the material/temporal realm. Alternative answers have since superseded Plato's, but these answers have all remained sufficiently in his debt to prompt Alfred North Whitehead's equally famous remark, "The safest general characterization of the European philosophical tradition is that it consists of a series of footnotes to Plato." Whether this world of forms, in varied theorizations, lies in the brain, the mind, the soul, or a noumenal sphere beyond any of these sources remains a perennial topic of contention at the base of philosophy—the level of metaphysics. This level is also referred to in the term *ontotheology*—the crossroads of metaphysics, ontology, and theology—which addresses the ground of what *is* or, to express it bluntly, the *really real*.

The really real, the world of originals or true objects, hides from direct perception, according to Plato, such that access to the real presents a constant challenge. But, in theory, when access is achieved, the form of a true object presents itself in pure and immediate presence. Its meaning manifests as *self-evident*. The sign drops away as intermediary when the initiate to the world of the true object interiorizes the pure presence in conscious awareness, dissolving division between word and object, subject and object, appearance and reality. Metaphysical systems from Plato to Descartes to Husserl, from realism to idealism to phenomenology, offer one version or another, one vision or another, of ontotheology.

One of the reasons so much Western philosophical tradition consists of a series of footnotes to Plato may derive less from Plato's genius, though rightly regarded as formidable, and more from the circumstance that later philosophers bump against the same metaphysical constraints of the really real—the obdurate but elusive enigma at the heart of meaning—for which Plato's theory of forms counts as a response. The combined nature of reality and the function of the sign presents and re-presents the same limits and accompanying conundrums regardless of what approach may be adopted. Attempts to overcome these limits, often regarded by philosophers as merely *apparent* limits, may be understood as continued expressions of thoroughly natural desires to acquire genuine knowledge and refine human communication. Nevertheless, confronting these limits and being turned away by them may induce a sense of existential angst, especially when considering the possibilities for genuine knowledge and communication appear to be acutely threatened by these metaphysical limitations. For this reason, it becomes important to examine and reexamine the nature of the consequences human community finds itself confronting when faced with these metaphysical limits, which may be seen as prefigured in the limits of language and the limits of the sign. At the metaphysical level, the question of these limits may also be understood as the problem of the one and the many.

The limits of language are exposed in a most dramatic way by staging a confrontation between the views of two of the 20th century's most seminal, yet also eccentric and provocative, language philosophers—the aforementioned Ludwig Wittgenstein and Jacques Derrida. However, true to disagreements between philosophers of language, it must be noted that while many academic professionals hail both Wittgenstein and Derrida as standout geniuses in the field of language philosophy, others call for their ostracism from the ranks of serious philosophers. Indeed, both have even been labeled obscurantist charlatans. This disparity of opinion ensures some degree of controversy attaches to discussions of their work. The potential for misunderstanding in their writings worried both philosophers and, true to their worst fears, controversies surrounding their work are often based on misreadings and misrepresentations. In this regard, Wittgenstein has, in more recent history, fared slightly better than Derrida, who continues to be a popular target of vitriolic attacks based on wrongful characterizations of his work.

Nevertheless, this book shares the point of view expressed in the *New York Times* by Williams College Professor Mark Taylor following Derrida's death in 2004: "Along with Ludwig Wittgenstein and Martin Heidegger, Jacques Derrida ... will be remembered as one of the three most important philosophers of the twentieth century. No thinker in the last one hundred years had a greater impact than he did on people in more fields and different disciplines." Similarly, regarding Wittgenstein, Ray Monk remarks in *The Guardian* in 2001, "*Philosophical Investigations* by Ludwig Wittgenstein ... is, in my view, the greatest philosophical book ever written." The opinion of Monk, as an award-winning biographer of Wittgenstein and an accomplished professor of philosophy at the University of Southampton, derives from considerable experience and study. The best lesson to draw from the disparities in judgment concerning the merits of the works of Wittgenstein and Derrida may be that prominent philosophers presenting new ways of thinking and new ways of doing philosophy rarely escape scorn and controversy in their lifetimes and well into the years thereafter.

Among philosophers of the 20th century conducting inquiries into language, few probed more deeply than Wittgenstein in the first half of the century or Derrida in the second half. The life experiences of Wittgenstein and Derrida contain noteworthy similarities. Both had troubled relationships with their countries of birth—for Wittgenstein, Austria, and for Derrida, Algeria. The families of each were Jewish and each suffered persecution as their countries fell under Nazi influence prior to and during World War II. Prior to the war, Wittgenstein emigrated to Britain and after the war Derrida emigrated to France. Wittgenstein became a naturalized citizen of Britain in 1938. Derrida and his parents were French citizens prior to the war but, along with all Algerian Jews, his citizenship was rescinded by the Vichy government and not fully restored until after the war. Although Wittgenstein and Derrida became citizens of Britain and post-war France respectively, they each felt a strong sense of residing both inside and outside membership in these national communities.

The experience of division between inside and outside deepened for Wittgenstein and Derrida due to their unusual relationships with the academic environments each found themselves attached to but never thoroughly at home within. Regarded as brilliant if not quite proper candidates for elite academic positions, both gained appointments at universities without having officially completed dissertations. Both traveled extensively, becoming more cosmopolitan than provincial, as much detached as attached to particular national and academic communities. The cosmopolitanism each grew into, perhaps more by circumstance than by choice, may account in some measure for the strong individualistic traits each developed, an individualism that, as Derrida was fond of reminding himself, must not be taken to imply indivisibility. Each in his own way experienced a strong sense of internal division—of being inside and outside, both self and other, through the various routines of life. At one point before meeting Bertrand Russell in 1911, Wittgenstein felt so internally lost and divided as to contemplate suicide—an act rightly regarded as an ultimate mark of self-abandonment. Two older brothers in his family had already committed suicide (1902 and 1904) and a third brother did so near the end of World War I in 1918.

Similarly, in interviews touching on aspects of his childhood, Derrida acknowledged having suffered from great shame and self-doubt as a result of persecution and ridicule at school for being a Jew. However, he later reevaluated this division that grew within him and transformed it into a revelation. He ultimately arrived at a new sense of himself, realizing, "I am not alone with myself, no more than anyone else is." He expressed this insight in an explicit way when he remarked: "I am not all-one. An 'I' is not an indivisible atom."

Wittgenstein and Derrida survived their early inner conflicts and self-doubts and developed, as a consequence of their experiences of division, an extraordinary capacity for seeing and experiencing from multiple points of view. This capacity aided greatly in their philosophical endeavors by enabling them to engage in deeply burrowing lines of questioning while gaining new ways of appreciating the repeating routines of ordinary language and ordinary life experience. But as will be seen in the following chapters, the similarities in the personal lives of Wittgenstein and Derrida did not ultimately succeed in generating substantially similar philosophical positions.

The differences between these positions unfold step by step in the chapters of Part I, ending in the Conclusion, which summarizes these differences and illustrates the significant metaphysical choices left for readers to contemplate and respond to in uniquely individual and perhaps also divided and conflicted ways. And yet, as will be argued, such conflicts need not be understood to advance division at the expense of cohesion and community. They may instead be seen to reflect difference and division as irreducible features of whatever unity may be seen to operate at the foundation not only of the self but also of all community—testimony to the enigma of the one and the many, the name and the named, operating at the foundation of the life of signs. Because of the pervasiveness and essential presence of language in everything human, both Wittgenstein and Derrida understood that heightened knowledge of the capacities and limits of language ought to become an essential feature of every person's ongoing preparation for and enhancement of life. Full appreciation of the inherent parameters of language, and signs in general, inhibits an array of counterproductive assumptions serving only to increase possibilities for widening and appropriating the distance between individuals and groups while, one the other hand, increasing the odds for expanding the quality of each person's life experience.

Moving to the structure of the book, Part I presents a direct comparison of the views on language in the work of the later Wittgenstein and early Derrida. These chapters highlight key differences, beginning with a short passage from Wittgenstein, following with discussion, and concluding with a Derridean response drawing on relevant passages from Derrida's work. Examining key moments of Wittgenstein's view of language alongside commentary suggesting how Derrida might reply to Wittgenstein's account, these direct comparisons between the two highlight their differences, which are argued to be more noteworthy than their similarities.

Building from this beginning, Part II shifts to examination of themes central to each philosopher's approach to language. These themes are combined in ways to illustrate differences and feature the following pairs: Private and Public, Family Resemblance and Dissemination, Games and Economies. These chapters prepare for Part III, which moves to the level of analysis containing the fundamental assumptions, the metaphysical decisions, grounding the most consequential differences between Wittgenstein and Derrida. This part examines the ways in which their opposing positions may be viewed through perennially puzzling philosophical themes such as: Other Minds, Metaphysics, Time, Truth, and Violence. The concluding chapter makes the case for deciding between the different paths taken by Wittgenstein and Derrida and the reasons for doing so.

Where the main text of the book focuses on exposition and comparison between Wittgenstein and Derrida, two appendices add more detailed commentary on particular lines of argument and counter-argument concerning the advocated readings of the two philosophers relating to the role of interpretation and the structure of oppositional relation in their work.

In conclusion, the differences between the positions assigned to Wittgenstein and Derrida are hopefully drawn out to where these differences may be better appreciated, debated, and realized among language users. Seconding the *New Statesman* (January 2019) motion to drag philosophy out of the "ivory tower and into the marketplace of ideas," philosophy must move to reappraise its role in society just as it must continue to reappraise the role of language in life. The importance of language to the quality of human culture and community insures the issues and insights concerning language highlighted in the works of Wittgenstein and Derrida merit attention and deserve to exert influence beyond the "ivory tower." Greater attention given to the life of signs will only enhance the signs of life in the lives of every language user.

PART I

Derrida in Response to Wittgenstein

1

Mind

It is misleading then to talk of thinking
as of a "mental activity" (BB, 6).

In the early pages of *The Blue Book* Wittgenstein targets a popular theory of meaning. This theory asserts meaning accompanies a sign as something like an image brought forth in the mind whenever hearing or seeing a given sign. Language-users find the meaning of a sign in a mental object existing alongside it. The prevalence of ostensive definition, as a means of learning language, fosters the inclination to look for a thing corresponding to the sign. The corresponding thing may not always be present, but the mental image may always remain present to the mind. To expose this inclination as misleading, Wittgenstein suggests substituting a painted image for the mental image and then asks, "Why should the written sign plus the painted image be alive if the written sign alone was dead?" He concludes that as soon as the painted image replaces the mental one, the mental image loses its *occult* property and suddenly stops giving life to the sign.

The occult nature of the mental process appears to give life to the sign when in fact it has no power to do so and instead conceals what actually occurs. For Wittgenstein, signs and sentences gain their significance from the system of signs, the language, to which they belong such that "understanding a sentence means understanding a language." He then makes the additional point that "whatever accompanied it [the sign] ... would for us just be another sign." The accumulation of signs and images, whether material or mental, does not serve to ground the meaning of a sign. Wittgenstein then summarizes this entire line of reasoning: "It is misleading then to talk of thinking as of a 'mental activity.' We may say that thinking is essentially the activity of operating with signs" (BB, 6).

Clarifying further, Wittgenstein explains the activity of thinking is performed by the hand when writing and by the mouth and larynx when speaking. But when confronted with the kind of thinking conducted

14

through signs or pictures in the imagination, Wittgenstein responds, "I can give you no agent that thinks." This remark might be thought to conceal a sentiment more like, "I *insist* there is no agent that thinks." But this is not his tone. Instead he says, "If then you say that in such cases the mind thinks, I would only draw your attention to the fact that you are using metaphor, that here the mind is the agent in a *different sense* from that in which the hand can be said to be the agent in writing" [emphasis added] (BB, 6–7).

Later in *The Blue Book*, Wittgenstein places a finer point on the issue by way of another analogy: "And it is as though we saw that what has pain must be an entity of a different nature from that of a material object; that, in fact, it must be of a mental nature. But to say that the ego is mental is like saying that the number 3 is of a mental or an immaterial nature, when we recognize that the numeral '3' isn't used as a sign for a physical object" (BB, 73). A mere similarity in grammar ought not to serve in itself as evidence for immaterial or metaphysical objects as analogous to material objects, as if such objects existed in a mental space like physical space only imperceptible to the five senses. On the first page of *The Blue Book* Wittgenstein issues a warning about such grammatical substantives: "We are up against one of the great sources of philosophical bewilderment: a substantive makes us look for a thing that corresponds to it." When this looking finds no appropriate corresponding object, it induces what Wittgenstein calls a *mental cramp*. As examples he cites relevant instances of the philosophical question, "What is X?" such as: "What is length?" "What is meaning?" "What is the number one?"—for which no objects of reference present themselves and for which answers of a defining nature do not immediately arise.

Similarly, looking for the agency corresponding to the word "mind" fosters illusions, not only about mind but also about language. For Wittgenstein, thoughts need not be imagined to occur in a medium called the "mind" which are then translated into language. Nor need thinking be conceived as prior or parallel to language. Thinking equates with the same process by which one person *communicates* with another. Learning language, learning to communicate with others, is also learning to think.

Wittgenstein understands that thinking as an operation independent of mental activity seems, at first, radically counter-intuitive. But equating thinking and operating with signs solves several problems—problems Wittgenstein views as giving rise to needless philosophical confusions, especially concerning communication. An operation is something performed and performance is *observable*. When thinking is understood to be operating with signs, the problem associated with mental constructs— namely, that they cannot be directly witnessed, assessed, and verified by others—is eliminated along with their potential for creating questions about the reliability of communication. If meanings are not hidden in a mental space behind words, then words need not be understood as inherently prone to misrepresent or conceal meanings.

Rhetorical theorist and Wittgenstein commentator John Macksoud labels Wittgenstein's characterization of thinking as "operating with signs" the *operational hypothesis*. Concerning the significance of this hypothesis Macksoud explains, "If Wittgenstein can show that, in a common case, what we describe as thinking is not independent of sign operations, he has demonstrated that a paradigm of thinking need not exceed sign operations, and by introducing a wedge that may be indefinitely expanded, he has shifted to any potential antagonist the burden of proof to demonstrate that *all* of the activities that we describe as thinking are not reducible to sign operations alone" (1973, 181).

This possible demonstration, however, as Macksoud notes, raises the intermediate question: What constitutes a sign? And, indeed, Wittgenstein asks, "What are signs?" But then he dodges full confrontation with this question when he replies: "Instead of giving any kind of general answer.... I shall propose to you to look closely at particular cases which we should call 'operating with signs'" (BB, 16). This approach strikes Wittgenstein as responsive rather than dismissive because he proposes to understand what a sign *is* by looking at what a sign *does*. Investigating examples of use, it would seem, cannot help but be informative. Macksoud suggests, however, that this approach ought to be questioned and one of the concerning problems with it will be addressed later below.

Wittgenstein overtly positions the claim that "thinking is essentially the activity of operating with signs" in the role of a hypothesis when he suggests testing the claim by conducting the following experiment: "Say and mean a sentence, e.g.: 'It will probably rain tomorrow.' Now think the same thought again, mean what you just meant, but without saying anything (either aloud or to yourself). If thinking it will rain tomorrow accompanied saying it will rain tomorrow, then just do the first activity and leave out the second" (BB, 42). In further illustration, he offers the analogy between thinking/speaking and melody/lyrics. If thinking is to speaking as melody is to lyrics then it should be possible to think the thought without the words just as it is possible to hum the melody without the lyrics.

Macksoud offers a critique of this experiment that may be paraphrased as follows: Suppose you say to Wittgenstein you performed his experiment and were indeed able to think the thought without saying the words. How will Wittgenstein respond? Can he say what you claim to have done is impossible? He must reject this kind of retort because it effectively annuls the results of the experiment and confirms there was no need to conduct it in the first place, since such a denial already concludes thinking *cannot* occur independent of saying.

Suppose, then, Wittgenstein merely suggests you must be mistaken and requests verification. How would you go about providing evidence of what you claim to have done? You could not, of course, point to your thought and say, "See, here is my thought and it is not a sign operation." No, there is no way you could *show* Wittgenstein your independent thought as a way of proving what you have done. To submit any manner of communicable response as demonstration introduces signs and thereby invites the rejoinder that the thought was actually just sign operations all along.

Macksoud's objections expose Wittgenstein's experiment as incapable of producing a *demonstrable* instance of thinking without saying. The experiment yields either a subjective confirmation of his operational hypothesis or a subjective disconfirmation. But if the latter remains incapable of persuading Wittgenstein of the falsity of his hypothesis, the former ought not to persuade him of its truth. The experiment requests an action the performance of which has no means of demonstration.

Macksoud acknowledges Wittgenstein does not overstate his hypothesis by proclaiming thought independent of sign operations to be impossible. Such a claim would needlessly transform an empirical question into an analytical insistence of the sort: "That cannot happen!" Wittgenstein's stance on this issue becomes clear when, for example, he proposes imagining a case where a man claims to *feel* the image of his visual field to be exactly two inches behind the bridge of his nose, for which he (Wittgenstein) offers this defense: "Should we say that he is not speaking the truth, or that there cannot be such a feeling? What if he asks us 'do you know all the feelings there are?'" (BB, 9). Similarly, in the case of thinking, what if Wittgenstein were asked: Do you know all the thoughts there are and that every such thought can only arise through the use of signs?

But despite the failure of his designed experiments in demonstrating anything conclusive, all is not lost with respect to the operational hypothesis. Wittgenstein presents another type of argument in PI#293. This section is part of a series on the use of pain terminology. Here pain terminology, as with all talk about sensations, may be understood to exemplify the problem encountered with inner states in general—which may include presumed mental contents such as thoughts—as private experience inaccessible to public observation. This famous passage, called The Beetle Box Analogy, is worth citing at length.

> Now someone tells me *he* knows what pain is only from his own case!—Suppose everyone had a box with something in it: we call it a "beetle." No one can

look into anyone else's box, and everyone says he knows what a beetle is only by looking at *his* beetle.—Here it would be quite possible for everyone to have something different in his box. One might even imagine such a thing constantly changing.—But suppose the word "beetle" had a use in these people's language?—If so it would not be used as the name of a thing. The thing in the box has no place in the language-game at all; not even as a *something*: for the box might be empty.—No, one can 'divide through' by the thing in the box; it cancels out, whatever it is.

In this analogy the personal experience of pain corresponds to the object in the box. This object could just as well be a thought or a mental image. In this defense of the operational hypothesis Wittgenstein does not suggest a subjective inner experience or thought correlate does not accompany saying. Instead he makes the stronger claim that such inner correlates, should they exist, lie outside the communication process. And, furthermore, if something like mental activity (as entirely separate from yet parallel to operating with signs) is superfluous in communication with others, it is then easier to see that it also may be superfluous as an accompaniment to the silent communication of thinking as talking to oneself.

Thus, not only is it the case that I do not know what "pain" is only from my own experience, I only *know* what "pain" is from my collective learning as an enculturated language-user. So long as a person demonstrates understanding of "pain" by using the word in expressions consistent with the grammar, the protocols, for pain behavior in the given community of language-users, then that person knows what pain is. The relevant criteria for *knowing* pain are public not private, and no one need "see" what is in, so to speak, the other person's box.

This defense of the operational hypothesis is more difficult to challenge. Doing so requires showing how thought and inner experience—beyond any form of operating with signs—are *not* superfluous to communication or to knowing. And in order to do this it would seem necessary to show that what Wittgenstein regards as outside the boundaries and therefore irrelevant to communication remains in some way consequential to it.

Return again to Wittgenstein's challenge to think the thought "It will probably rain tomorrow" without *saying* it. Imagine a farmer looking at the sky in the evening and thinking something equivalent to "It will probably rain tomorrow" without saying anything to himself or anyone nearby. Isn't it rather easy to imagine his thought, derived from years of experience looking at skies, arising outside of any need for language? And if someone nearby asks, "What are you thinking?" wouldn't it seem natural for the farmer to respond by "translating" his thought into the words "It will probably rain tomorrow"?

Consider another situation. You drive a car along a two-lane highway behind a slow moving truck. You pull out and attempt to pass only to realize an oncoming car approaches faster than anticipated. You brake hard and pull back, in time to avoid the oncoming car. Your passenger yells, "What were you thinking?" Well, you were thinking you had sufficient room to safely pass the truck because you thought the oncoming car was approaching more slowly. But did any of this "thinking" take place in the form of self-talk as you were driving along the highway? A verbal process certainly could have occurred but is clearly unnecessary to the task of driving the car, assessing the road conditions, and making decisions. Similar examples could be given in relation to any activity, such as planning and executing a watercolor painting, building a house, organizing a bookshelf, etc. The activity of using language arguably remains unnecessary for doing many kinds of activities that may easily be construed to involve forms of "thinking." Where thinking is understood as mental activity alongside the use of words, it seems that not only may words be used without parallel thought processes but that thoughts may also occur *without words*. How might Wittgenstein respond?

Thinking claimed to be associated with the above activities might be free of internal *discourse* but Wittgenstein may nevertheless count such activities as operating with signs. All such activities involve the trained reading of signs in various situations and environments and the use of these signs in processes of comparing, contrasting, judging, evaluating, etc. The claim that thinking is operating with signs entails that marks, symbols, images, pictures, charts, diagrams, perceptions, sounds, sensations—indeed, anything serving in any possible way as datum—may count as a sign. And now it may again be asked with new urgency: What is a sign? What are its limits? Is everything a sign?

Here it is worth pausing to note that some commentators on the work of Wittgenstein propose a narrower interpretation of his understanding of "thinking." For example, Brent Silby (1998) remarks, "Although Wittgenstein changed his mind and refuted his early work, there is a central claim in all of Wittgenstein's work. This is the claim that language is essential for thought. On Wittgenstein's account, Descartes' statement: 'I think, therefore I am,' seems to be wrong. Descartes should have said: 'I have language, therefore I think, therefore I am'" (1). Similarly, Derek McDougall (2008) ventures close to this view when he speaks of "Wittgenstein's need to find a new way of looking at things that has, as a consequence, the conclusion that the idea of the child who can think, only not yet speak, can have no application in a context in which language as both an empirical and a social phenomenon *is* the vehicle of thought" (52). On the contrary, Wittgenstein has no "need" to embrace the notion that language is the vehicle of thought because he argues, much more convincingly, that *signs* are the vehicles of thought. And signs include much more than the words of languages. For children, as well as adults who have learned a language, thinking may very well include sign operations beyond the use of words.

Furthermore, the claim that thinking is operating with signs seems much less newsworthy if every sense datum—any perception or sensation whatsoever—counts as a sign. Assuming as much, mere consciousness could be equated with thinking—precisely because conscious awareness involves modes of recognition that may be understood as the mode of operating with signs commonly called *reading*. If operating with signs constitutes thinking, then reading, as one form of operating with signs, also counts as a form of thinking.

Recall previously that Wittgenstein responds to the question "What is a sign?" by proposing to examine particular cases of operating with signs. Macksoud notes that this may satisfy the scientifically inclined but does not address the underlying import of the question, which is, "What is the mode of existence of a sign?" What *type* of entity is it? To this level of the question, the examination of particular cases is unresponsive. Macksoud explains: "Wittgenstein's answer is ... too vague (even perhaps self-defeating), precisely because there need be *just no* limits around the category of signs as Wittgenstein wishes to use it, for we have no way of knowing what counts as a *particular case* of operating with signs. Thus, signs might include all sensory impressions. For surely, *anything* can be a sign in *any* language." (1973, 181). In which case thinking as the activity of operating with signs suggests a "language" of signs exists in addition to the language of discourse in words and sentences. It would seem that merely to be conscious entails operating with signs.

As Wittgenstein appears to be using the term, anything may indeed be a sign. If Wittgenstein's arguments and examples imply as much, then it would appear his methodology exceeds an empirical approach and has moved very nearly in alignment with an analytical approach of the following sort: Whatever you choose to call "thinking" will be called "operating with signs." And in any instance where someone may want to assert, "Here is an example of thinking independent of signs," Wittgenstein may respond that only another instance of operating with signs has been identified. The notion of "sign" has become so broad and flexible that any apparent example of thinking without signs can ultimately be reduced to operating with signs.

In such a case of broad definition Macksoud does well to suggest this kind of tactical maneuver is "self-defeating" with regard to demonstrating his thesis. Given the troubles in providing a *demonstration* that thinking may occur independent of sign operations, it would seem this hypothesis remains incapable of confirmation. Any distinction between thinking and operating with signs reduces to an instance of competing definitions rather than competing hypotheses.

Nevertheless, at this point in his inquiry, Wittgenstein insists the notion of thinking as mental activity separate from sign operations—as an invisible process of the mind underscoring and supplying meaning to overt sign operations—serves more to mislead than to lead. When someone asks, "What are you thinking?" when sitting next to another person on the porch overlooking a horizon, Wittgenstein may identify the response "It will probably rain tomorrow" as a translation from one sign operation—reading the sky—into another sign operation—expressing in words. And this reading of the sky, just like the reading of script, need require no mental image as its correlate in order to understand the meaning it may present, namely, the likelihood of approaching rain. Whether called "thinking" or something else, Wittgenstein identifies all such reading activities as "operating with signs." And whether conducted inwardly or outwardly, silently or vocally, these operations remain in principle the same and may be regarded as *hidden* only insofar as they are not *expressed*.

Thinking includes more than the discourse of talk or self-talk. For example, in PI#354 Wittgenstein has his interlocutor express the following: "Experience teaches that there is rain when the barometer falls, but it also teaches that there is rain when we have certain sensations of wet and cold, or such-and-such visual impressions." A language of signs exists in relation to reading various elements of experience—including weather and all manner of phenomena. But Wittgenstein then follows the interlocutor's statement with a revealing series of comments. He acknowledges, "...sense-impressions can deceive us." Learning to read experience means learning the language of experience, but sensations, like words and symptoms, can be misleading. Wittgenstein then clarifies what manner of deception it is: "But here one fails to reflect that the fact that the false appearance is precisely one of rain is founded on a definition." Confusion may turn on the fact that other experiences may look like rain but it does not turn on the question of what rain is. Continuing in PI#355 Wittgenstein notes, "The point here is not that our sense-impressions can lie, but that we understand their language. (And this language like any other is founded on convention.)" Engaging this point further, he says, "For isn't it a misleading metaphor to say: 'My eyes give me the information that there is a chair over there'?" Eyes do not give the information there is a chair over there. The conventional grammar for the use of the word "chair" gives the information there is a chair over there.

Wittgenstein strives to point out the fact that a grammar of terminology exists that when breached promotes confusions—sometimes confusions initiating apparently profound philosophical questions. For example, in PI#357 he highlights the grammar of "speaking to oneself" by stating, "We do not say that *possibly* a dog talks to itself. Is that because we are so minutely acquainted with its soul? Well, one might say this: If one sees the behaviour of a living thing, one sees its soul." And in PI#359–360 he asks, "Could a machine think?—Could it be in pain?" In answer, he replies, "But a machine surely cannot think!—Is that an empirical statement? No. We only say of a human being and what is like one that it thinks. We also say it of dolls and no doubt of spirits too. Look at the word 'to think' as a tool."

For Wittgenstein, questions like "Can a dog talk to itself?" and "Can a machine think?" are not to be taken as empirical questions inviting investigation but rather as grammatically nonsensical questions. If the day comes when robots acquire sufficient human appearance and behavior to pass for nearly human, then humans may begin to say of these machines that they think. And if that day were to come, Wittgenstein would no doubt, without any philosophical laboring, assent to the proposition that machines do indeed think, because for him the issue is one of the current appropriate grammar for the word "to think" and not one of determining the philosophical essence of thinking. A new definition of thinking will follow a new grammar surrounding use of thinking terminology and this new definition will include certain machines.

But with this approach to these kinds of puzzlements it may well be asked whether Wittgenstein's grammatical solutions tend to cover over larger issues that do indeed have philosophical significance, such as: If humans do find themselves at some point in the future referring to certain machines as thinking machines, what does that imply for the natures of human beings and machines? And does not the answer to such a question give rise to further provocative ethical questions that might need to be pondered philosophically rather than grammatically? Perhaps so, but Wittgenstein's concern in relation to signs appears, at this point, to be focused on communication and clarity of communication, on how signs are in fact used rather than on how they ought to be used.

Before continuing, it is worth noting here again, in conjunction with the previous note above, that Wittgenstein's apparent preference for an empirical approach—examining particular cases of what he refers to as the grammar of the use of a word—leads to an analytical layer of definition residing in that grammar. For example, he answers "No" to the question "Is that an empirical statement?" in response to the statement "But a machine surely cannot think!" Determining whether a machine can think requires no intense examination of the workings of its parts in conjunction with each other. It requires only an examination of the grammar of the verb "to think" in the vernacular of the English language. Wittgenstein does not conduct an empirical investigation of the kind a linguist or anthropologist might. Nor has he conducted a survey. Instead, he relies on his own training, experience, and cultured sense of propriety with language to develop his conclusions and judgments regarding the grammar of common discourse practices.

Macksoud offers a summary of Wittgenstein's philosophical stance, which he calls, following Wittgenstein, *radical operationism*, for which he identifies two major planks: "Wittgenstein's program is to objectify language-using; the two central propositions of this program are that thought is radically sign-constituted and that language is radically convention-governed" (1973, 179).

The claim that Wittgenstein's program is to *objectify* language-using derives from his having shifted thinking and the locus of meaning from an inner mental activity to an outer sign operation—a performance open to observation. And the claim that, for Wittgenstein, language is radically convention-governed derives from his having shifted the meaning of signs from something inherent in the sign to the *use* of the sign—where the use of the sign gathers its utility from collective agreement in definitions as well as judgments.

This convention-governed practice, however, ought not be taken to mean that Wittgenstein's position corresponds to what surveys might reveal about the meanings of terms or that it fails to accommodate unconventional uses of language. As suggested above concerning ascription of the verb "to think" to machines, for Wittgenstein, rules of use are flexible and can change. Unconventional uses stretch the boundaries, but, as the rules stretch, the uses of signs remain coherent precisely through new uses that may be assimilated into new social practices. The complexity of Wittgenstein's position in this regard will come more clearly into view in the following chapters.

Expanding the radius of these concerns beyond Wittgenstein to Derrida, how would Derrida respond to the notion that everything is a sign? Derrida has become famous for his proclamation "*il n'y a pas de hors-texte*," (OG, 158) which *Of Grammatology* translator, Gayatri Spivak, translates as "there is nothing outside of the text [there is no outside-text …]." This translation has been removed from its context and fashioned into a general maxim attributed to Derrida by critics determined to show that he claims there is nothing outside of books and language—that the really real is discursive reality. But this interpretation of Derrida's words thoughtlessly impoverishes his text, both the English translation and the original French. *Hors-texte* more commonly translates as "inset," which then gives the translation "There is no inset." Images, pictures, photographs, drawings, or the like count as *hors-texte* or insertions into the text—often as unnumbered pages. Thus, Derrida's famous sentence suggests nothing may count as an insertion into the text because the text, any text, has no fixed boundary. Every text necessarily reaches beyond itself into all layers of context surrounding it—inclusive of physical and cultural environment, history, and world—and exclusive of which it not only remains inadequately read but cannot be read at all. The "text" cannot be limited to the sentence, the page, the book, the library, the community, the environment, the mind, or the world. As will be discussed in more detail in the following chapters, for Derrida the text cannot be explicitly corralled or contained, text and context have no natural or self-evident limits.

Nevertheless, Derrida approaches the question "What is a sign?" with the same caution as Wittgenstein. In *Speech and Phenomena*, Derrida remarks on Husserl's postponement of a direct answer to this question and his reasons for doing so, which are discussed in detail in the chapter on metaphysics. But Derrida believes the question ought to be confronted and, unlike Wittgenstein, he provides an answer rather than shelving the question as too metaphysical.

Derrida cites C.S. Peirce when discussing the nature of the sign. Here the difference between phenomenology and semiology squeezes down to the infinitesimal when Derrida paraphrases Peirce in claiming that which shows itself—the phenomenon—does not so much reveal a presence as make a sign. Derrida explains, "There is thus no phenomenality reducing the sign or the representer so that the thing signified may be allowed to glow finally in the luminosity of its presence. The so-called 'thing itself' is always already a representamen ..." (OG, 49). Here "representamen" equates with "sign" and the words "thing itself" may be understood to indicate any existent thing in the real world or any signified whatever. He then summarizes with this passage from Peirce, which he labels the *definition of the sign*. A sign is:

> Anything which determines something else (its interpretant) to refer to an object to which itself refers (its object) in the same way, this interpretant becoming in turn a sign, and so on ad infinitum ... [OG, 50].

Derrida understands this passage to mean that the sign, the representamen, "functions only by giving rise to an *interpretant* that itself becomes a sign and so on to infinity." Here "interpretant" is a response to a sign. And this response becomes itself a sign. The sign and its object form a relation through the interpretant, which is the meaning given the sign/object relation through the response of the sign-user or users. Without venturing too far into the depths of Peirce's semiology, the interpretant or response reproduces the initial sign/object relation. This reproduction itself constitutes an additional sign, in the understanding produced for the sign user—a sign with an understanding necessarily linking to other signs and to the whole of language. And, finally, the object plays a dual role in the signification scheme insofar as it not only serves as referent but also as yet another sign extending beyond its particularity to become the representative of a class.

For example, as soon as something in the world, say an apple, is grouped with like things by being assigned the word *apple* (Peirce's representamen), that thing (Peirce's object, the represented) becomes itself a sign as it represents the class or concept APPLE (Peirce's interpretant). Through language, the object, as representative of a class, becomes itself a sign, extending the sign/object/interpretant relation, which in turn generates further relations, and so on throughout different contexts in a community of language users. Derrida adds, citing again from Peirce: "If the series of successive interpretants comes to an end, the sign is thereby rendered imperfect." Expressed in another way, Derrida says, "The *represented* is always already a *representamen*.... From the moment that there is meaning there are nothing but signs. We *think only in signs*" (OG, 50).

The phenomena of experience function as signs and in this way phenomenology becomes semiology, as is explained in greater detail in Chapter 11. The claim that "we think only in signs" may also be understood to say that we perceive only in signs. As suggested in the Introduction, even before spoken or written language, even before *homo sapiens*, the world is a world of signs for living things. If this were not the case, the perceiver would be lost in an inchoate world, an unformed and chaotic landscape. The world is for every living thing a system of signs. The encounter with anything experienced only in its unique particularity, and therefore as something other than a sign, is experienced as an encounter with the unrecognizable, the alien, the monstrous. American philosopher, John Dewey, states a similar view in a memorable way when speaking of the relation between nature and experience: "Things in their immediacy are unknown and unknowable, not because they are remote or behind some impenetrable wall of sensation of ideas, but *because knowledge has no concern for them*" [emphasis added] (1958, 85–86).

Words referring to items that are not physical objects in the world require modifying the sign/object/interpretant model. The dominance of this model confirms Wittgenstein's observation of the strong tendency among language users to look for an object-like substitute for the physical object. The word "concept" inserts itself as such a substitute, but this operation then generates the need for distinguishing between concept and interpretant. One solution Peirce offers consists of distinguishing between interpretants. The dynamic interpretant corresponds to the effect a word achieves for a particular language user; the final interpretant corresponds to the full effect a word may be understood to have for any language user. The latter distinction aligns with what perhaps may broadly be understood in philosophical tradition as the "concept," whereas the former aligns with what may be understood as the particular interpretation operating for the language user or what may be called the subjective interpretation. As already suggested and what will be discussed more thoroughly in the following chapters, Wittgenstein draws into question the relevance of the dynamic or subjective interpretation in the communication agenda.

Peirce's interpretant, combining with word and object, invites the understanding of meaning as interpretation. But Peirce's interpretant must be distinguished from interpretation in the sense in which Wittgenstein uses the term. Only when theorized as a *process* intervening between signs and responses to signs does the mediating of interpretation constitute a system of meaning from which Wittgenstein would want to separate his views. Addressing the issue of interpretation more fully requires further development of the framework of Wittgenstein and Derrida's views of language and so this discussion is postponed until Chapter 3.

Thus far, Wittgenstein has been shown to offer a challenge to the traditional view of linguistic meaning as grounded in mental content with the claim that such content cannot serve as ground because it counts as merely another sign exposed to the same problems of meaning. The support for this claim, however, remains weak until Wittgenstein turns to the argument that mental content, even if it appears to play a role in securing meaning, need not only be unnecessary for meaning but may more justifiably be regarded as *irrelevant* to the entire process of generating meaning. In the place of mental content, he proposes that meaning may be adequately understood as arising simply by way of "operating with signs." This operational hypothesis builds further from the view that anything and everything may function as a sign—a view that finds support when introducing Derrida into the discussion. Derrida also shares with Wittgenstein the displacement of thought as central in grounding sign operations, but parts company by giving a definition of the sign whereas Wittgenstein declines to do so. Derrida's siding with Peirce's definition of the sign as including the interpretant opens a path, as will be seen, for separating the views of Derrida and Wittgenstein. Derrida's emphasis on the role of interpretation introduces a problem in aligning his approach with Wittgenstein on questions of meaning and communication.

However, Derrida meets Wittgenstein again in the claim, "We *think only in signs.*" When tied directly to the use of signs, thinking emerges from the noumenal realm of mind with its intangible contents and into the phenomenal realm of operations open to observation. Whereupon it may be imagined that language and thought might submit more to measures of empirical observation in investigation. But then complications arise.

2

Use

But if we had to name anything which is the life of the sign,
we should have to say it was its use (BB, 4).

When Wittgenstein begins to examine the meaning of a word, he immediately cites particular cases of use. He says, "We are inclined to forget that it is the particular use of a word only which gives the word its meaning.... The use of the word *in practice* is its meaning" (BB, 69). Taking him at his word, it would seem an encounter with a word in whatever may be its current instance of use ought to reveal its meaning. But, doubtless, everyone has come upon a word used in a particular instance whose meaning remains a mystery, and soldiering on to encounter more uses of the same word may yet leave the meaning obscure.

For example, you may not know the meaning of the word *laches*. Outside a courtroom one person says to another: "He got off easy. His attorney's laches defense worked." Do you now know its meaning? You may object that one sentence is not sufficient. As the conversation continues, you hear, "A laches appeal hasn't been seen around here for years" and, "Yeah, it's rare. I heard of a laches case last year in King County." Still, the meaning of "laches" escapes you. More context is needed. Suppose then you learn: "The defendant's attorney wore a brown suit with a red necktie" and, "The judge in the case seemed hard of hearing."

You may hear the word "laches" used repeatedly, learn of many other details of context, and still not understand its meaning. The trouble here quickly becomes apparent. Not only is more context needed but also the context must be relevant to the word's use. Overhearing the use of a word between those who know its meaning need not be sufficient to reveal its meaning. Insight into a word's meaning as it may be revealed through its use in practice seems likely to be insufficient in many cases.

At the beginning of *Philosophical Investigations*, Wittgenstein provides examples of language use in which the participants—for example, children learning a language—are taught the uses of words by pointing to an object and repeating a name. The meanings of these words are not learned through observing others' ongoing *uses* of the terms but rather through a *definition* of the terms—an ostensive definition. Wittgenstein here grants ostensive definition a crucial role in the learning of language in general as well as in learning the meanings of new words. Despite his emphasis on use, Wittgenstein allows for a significant role for definition in assigning meaning. After having introduced the notion of meaning as use in the opening pages of *The Blue Book*, he qualifies this notion in the following notable passage: "I want you to remember that words have those meanings which we have given them; and we give them meanings by explanations. I may have given a definition of a word and used the word accordingly, or those who taught me the use of the word may have given me the explanation" (BB, 27).

Here Wittgenstein acknowledges meanings are taught through explanations and he explains, "What one generally calls 'explanations of the meaning of a word' can, *very roughly*, be divided into verbal and ostensive definitions" (BB, 1). Without the initial instruction of a definition, users may circle around the meaning of a word with guesses and yet fail to grasp the relevant import of a word's use.

Identifying use as central in the meaning of words presents only part of a relevant account of meaning. Verbal definition as the translation of the meaning of a new term into known terms also plays a role, along with ostensive definition, in acquiring the meaning of terms. Nevertheless, Wittgenstein finds verbal definitions lack a quality he seeks: "The verbal definition, as it takes us from one verbal expression to another, in a sense gets us no further. In the ostensive definition however we seem to make a much more real step towards learning the meaning" (BB, 1). It might seem, then, that ostensive definition qualifies for Wittgenstein as the more preferred means for establishing the definition of a word.

When Wittgenstein says the meaning of a word is its use, he nevertheless understands that applications of words in particular cases may reveal only part of what is needed. He suggests every word has use value or currency in a given language and that any word used in a given instance performs work and serves a particular function relevant to its use value in that given instance. Words have many uses as tools have many uses and these uses can vary across contexts. For example, Wittgenstein says, "Think of the tools in a tool-box: there is a hammer, pliers, a saw, a screw-driver, a rule, a glue-pot, glue, nails and screws.—The functions of words are as diverse as the functions of these objects. (And in both cases there are similarities.)" (PI#11). Any tool, in order to be a tool, must have form *before* it can have function. Uses may be diverse but the tool must have a particular contour before it can be used for any particular purpose. Words as tools conform to the same principle. In the case of words, the definition provides the contour. Deriving meaning strictly from use places the cart before the horse. Yet this need not be taken to mean the cart has no influence on the horse.

Definitions may, nevertheless, fail to be definitive. Wittgenstein acknowledges definitions may prove "unsatisfactory." When a definition fails to mesh with all the accepted uses of a given term, users then seek the "correct" definition. But Wittgenstein admonishes that looking for a correct and complete definition may be a fool's errand: "Many words … don't have a strict meaning. But this is not a defect. To think it is would be like saying that the light of my reading lamp is no real light at all because it has no sharp boundary" (BB, 27).

Continuing with the analogy of words as tools, just as a tool can break and no longer serve to fulfill its function in a given task, so too words can break and fail to work adequately in specific instances. And, according to Wittgenstein, words most often break when used in contexts significantly outside the contexts they were initially devised to be used within. As examples of this kind of infelicity of word use, Wittgenstein points to words such as "soul" and "mind" used to designate an agency behind the activity of the body in the former or of thinking in the latter. As the hand draws a picture, so users are—Wittgenstein argues—led to speak as if the mind thinks (e.g., BB, 6–7). But he finds this to be a misleading analogy. And yet it would seem that words used outside their usual contexts, as when words are used metaphorically, can be very helpful.

Liberal users of language, such as poets, may caution not to forget that metaphors and analogies drive not only great poetry and literature but also creative thinking. And are not metaphors and analogies prime examples of terms used outside the contexts they were initially intended to be used "within?" Do metaphors and analogies, in Wittgenstein's view, pervert the use and meaning of words? This, of course, is demonstrably not the case. Wittgenstein adeptly employs numerous metaphors and analogies in discussing and illustrating his view of language. In fact, he uses metaphors to help indicate the limits of metaphor. For example, he describes misuses of words arising from uses outside their appropriate contexts by referring to instances of misuse as language "on holiday" (PI#38), producing a "mental cramp" (BB, 1, 59), or like an "engine idling" (PI#88, #132). Clearly, some metaphors and analogies lead astray while more carefully chosen ones lead aright. Examples of the latter include Wittgenstein's uses of "game" (discussed in Chapter 9) and "family resemblance" (discussed in Chapter 8).

Wittgenstein is not opposed to metaphor and the use of language in unconventional ways, but it remains unclear how he can defend the claim that there are times when words are "idling," as when gears move but do not engage other gears. It would seem, even by his own account, words always accomplish something, whether it be performing as expected, yielding communication and insight, or performing in unexpected ways, spreading mischief and confusion. But in cases of the sort where words mislead, the notion of the meaning of a word being its use takes on new meaning. If the meaning of a word is its use and the uses of words can be stretched in ways exceeding conventional use, then at what point does use pass from sense to nonsense? How may it be known when language is "on holiday," for surely just *any* use of a word does not rise to meaningful use. For example, do the words, "The purple grass sings a new algebra" count as meaningful because they have been used in what appears to pass for a grammatically correct sentence? In claiming the meaning of a word to be its particular use in practice, Wittgenstein still wants to distinguish between meaningful and nonsensical uses.

To avoid this problem, Wittgenstein argues that words have uses only within and because of the system, the language, from which they emerge. Language corrals and channels the ways in which words may be meaningfully used. The meanings of words originate within a given language and language is a *practice* organized around rules that must be learned. So when Wittgenstein says "The use of the word *in practice* is its meaning," he means something more like: The use of a given word in a given language— within the structure of rules and definitions of that language alongside the particulars of the immediate context of use—is its meaning.

Granting as much, the problem of unconventional use still persists. And Wittgenstein is admirably forthcoming in addressing this issue: "No sharp boundary can be drawn round the cases in which we should say that a man was misled by an analogy. The use of expressions constructed on analogical patterns stresses analogies between cases often far apart. And by doing this these expressions may be extremely useful. It is, in most cases, impossible to show an exact point where an analogy begins to mislead us. Every particular notation stresses some particular point of view" (BB, 28).

In light of these remarks, consider, for example, Wittgenstein's insistence that thinking is operating with signs and that the notion of mental activity accompanying these operations is unnecessary and even misleading. Why is the analogy between invisible operations of an agency called "mind" and operating with signs not useful rather than misleading? Again, when someone asks, "What are you thinking?" when sitting next to you on a porch overlooking the horizon, why is it not useful to suppose the answer, "It will probably rain tomorrow" occurred in a medium called the "mind" prior to any formulation in words and was then "translated," so to speak, into words?

Between alternative forms of expression, alternative choices of metaphor and analogy, what reasons may a speaker give for preferring one form of expression, one way of thinking, to another? In his thoroughness, Wittgenstein does in fact provide, at least obliquely, an answer. He responds, "Which form he prefers, and whether he has a preference at all, often depends on general, deeply rooted, tendencies of his thinking" (BB, 30). With this answer, he essentially concedes that his way of looking at language, consistent with the tool metaphor and centered in the operational hypothesis, likely accords with a deeply rooted tendency in his own thinking. And, as his point of view on language unfolds, it may well be asked repeatedly, "Why view language this way?" And Wittgenstein's answer must be kept clearly in view: "If ... we call our investigations 'philosophy,' this title, on the one hand, seems appropriate, on the other hand it certainly has misled people. (One might say that the subject we are dealing with is one of the heirs of the subject which used to be called 'philosophy.')" (BB, 28). His view of language professes to avoid the "mental cramps" he believes result from traditional philosophy and its prevalent dualisms of mind/body, interpretation/meaning, and rule/practice.

Wittgenstein views the history of philosophy as a long trail of metaphors which have crept into discourse but which are too far askew from the context they originally operated within to achieve anything more than the invention of increasingly extraneous pseudo-problems. Far from enlightening, he finds particular philosophical dichotomies, such as mind/body dualism, grounded in metaphors counterproductive to communication, which ultimately contributes to individual and collective confusion. But work remains, for readers of Wittgenstein, to determine the extent to which his warnings about particular misleading metaphors are indeed persuasive and justifiable.

Turning to Derrida, how would he respond to Wittgenstein's understanding of meaning as use? Since Derrida practices close readings, commencing a Derridean inquiry requires careful attention to the words Wittgenstein uses. Derrida might place emphasis on a particular word in order to highlight the point of view it signals.

For example, Wittgenstein says in *The Blue Book*, "If we had to name anything which is the life of the sign, we should have to say that it was its use." Here the word "its," even if understood in a metaphorical sense, is, for Derrida, a metaphor that misleads. A word is *and is not* an "it." A word, a sign, does not have the nature of a philosophically classic object, being, or presence. The identity, the "itness," of any word becomes problematic at the point of its origin. Word identity remains always divided, and necessarily so, due to what Derrida calls the *law of iterability*. For example, in a famous exchange with John Searle in 1977, Derrida remarks: "A standard act [speech act] depends ... upon the possibility of being repeated, and thus potentially ... of being mimed, feigned, cited, played, simulated, parasited, etc.... [T]he structure of iterability ... blurs the simplicity of the line dividing inside from outside, undermines the order of succession or dependence among terms, prohibits ... the procedure of exclusion. Such is the *law of iterability* [emphasis added]" (1977b, 234).

The iterability of words, the fact they may be used and re-used from one context to another, entails they retain features to carry recognition through new contexts as they also shed features sufficient to separate them from previous contexts. Without this internal division and tension, this opposition of retention and release through various contexts, signs could not function and would have no use at all.

The splitting, the rending of identity, transpires through the effects of context in two ways: the movement of context as the limitless capacity for expansion or contraction of circumference (spatial rending) and the movement of context as the inexorable passing of time (temporal rending). Derrida refers to this spatial/temporal rending as the differing and deferring of *différance*. This French word, spelled with an "a" rather than an "e," is a neologism designed as a place holder for the phenomenon of coming/going that remains difficult to name because it is not anything like an "it."

The way words may operate in any given *moving* context rests on the instability of formations as already *deformations* brought on through spatial/temporal rending. Derrida explains, "The self-identity of the signified conceals itself unceasingly and is always on the move" because *"What broaches the movement of signification is what makes its interruption impossible"* [emphasis in the original] (1976, 49). Iterability broaches the movement of meaning, which, unhalted, thereby also breaches meaning through what Derrida calls "repetition-with-a-difference." As a result, the operations of meaning cannot be controlled reliably, either on the side of the addresser or the addressee. A classic example presented by Derrida for the fractured identity of the sign appears in Plato's use of the word *pharmakon* in the *Phaedrus*, as well as in other dialogues, where this term, through various contexts, plays between meaning "remedy" and "poison" (1981a, 95–117).

It may be thought that key terms in a given text, such as *pharmakon*, present alternative meanings due primarily to semantic ambiguity in the term itself, as with words such as "lead" or "leaf" as in "He took the lead" or "She removed the leaf."

But the doubling of meaning to which Derrida draws attention does not arise from semantic ambiguity in a particular word but rather from a doubling of meaning as a result of the *syntax* of the text, the context within and through which the text weaves the use of the word. As Derrida notes, words manifesting dual effects such as *pharmakon* "…have a double, contradictory, undecidable value that always derives from their syntax, whether the latter is in a sense 'internal,' articulating and combining under the same yoke … two incompatible meanings, or 'external,' dependent on the code in which the word is made to function" (1981a, 221).

But to understand Derrida it is still necessary to go a bit further. His point is not that within the text a word such as *pharmakon*, means "remedy" in some instances of use and "poison" in other instances or that its meaning is obviated through ambiguity. The situation is as Derrida remarks, "Neither/nor, that is, simultaneously either *or*" (1981b, 43), which is also to say, in a sense, both/and—both meanings are always in play at every point of use such that it remains necessary to read the contradiction of these meanings as part of the essence of the text and an irreducible component of what it in effect says. This both/and structure introduces a new layer to the footing established by traditional philosophical ground. Derrida claims words functioning in the manner of words such as *pharmakon* "…admit into their games both contradiction and noncontradiction (and the contradiction and noncontradiction *between* contradiction and noncontradiction)" (1981a, 221).

This contradiction/noncontradiction between meanings, this spacing of the "between," exceeds even the separation of the semantic and the syntactic: "One no longer even has the authority to say that 'between' is a purely syntactic function…. Neither purely syntactic nor purely semantic, it marks the articulated opening of that opposition" (1981a, 222). Which is to say that the "between" of the interval separating opposing or different meanings belongs inseparably to the function of the given term in a particular text and is the generative opening Derrida points to with the term *différance*.

Doppelgangers beset words, leaving readers and writers in the position of being incapable of reading or writing *only* what may be intended. Derrida characterizes this circumstance as marked by the *undecidable*, where language fails to submit to a regimented calculation that would decide the issue of meaning on the side of univocal meaning. The language-user cannot simply *calculate* the meaning but must form a judgment based on an *incalculable* weighing of cues. Division in identity makes the production of meaning possible, but in a way that multiplies meaning beyond calculation through the unceasing influence and movement of context. Like Wittgenstein, Derrida resorts to metaphor to help illustrate: "Among other words, I have underlined *dehiscence*. As in the realm of botany … this word marks emphatically that the divided opening, in the growth of a plant, is also what, in a positive sense, makes production, reproduction, development possible. Dehiscence (like iterability) limits what it makes possible, while rendering its rigor and purity impossible. What is at work here is something like a *law of undecidable contamination* [emphasis added]" (1977b, 197).

This dehiscence, this splitting in the identity of terms, entails meaning cannot simply be a question of the particular use of a term. In each particular instance, use wraps within layers of *uses*, precluding the transparent assessment of a univocal use. Context and syntax impart meaning as they also fracture meaning. This structural division of meaning exceeds Wittgenstein's view, which accounts for different meanings of a word *across* a variety of instances of use while nevertheless minimizing routine diversity *within* particular instances of use.

Since context remains an unstable and unbounded component of meaning and yet an irreducible component, meaning depends in some measure on the way in which readers *choose*, whether by intention or by default, to contextualize a text. Some cues of meaning—what Derrida calls *restance* (often translated as *remainder* or non-present remnants)—trace forward from previous uses while other cues derive from the current context of use (Derrida, 1988b, 51–52). This tension between what attaches to and detaches from a word in its repetition across uses underscores the necessity for judgment yielding *interpretation*.

Restance is a neologism created by Derrida from the French *reste*, which translates as remainder or residue. However, the translation of *restance* as "remainder" is misleading because *restance* need not be confused with an abiding or permanent core preserved and remaining across repeated instances of use. It is not a minimum of idealization but rather a loose collection of traits extending from previous instances of use, which varies across the variety of future uses such that no single trait remains necessarily common to every instance. This feature of *restance* plays an important role in Derrida's view of language and is discussed in greater detail in Chapters 4 and 8.

This brief account of how Derrida would likely respond to Wittgenstein's highlighting of meaning as use might raise as many questions as it answers. Several detours into and around the issues raised need to be addressed and the following chapters explore these in greater detail. This initial sketch of a Derridean reply to Wittgenstein invites the rejoinder: How would Wittgenstein respond to Derrida?

Clearly, the issue of fractured identity at the core of signs entails, as already suggested, a manner of reading that may rightly be described as interpretation. In fact, as a counter to Wittgenstein's claim that the meaning, the life, of a sign is its use Derrida might be understood to reply: The meaning of a sign is its *interpretation*. For Derrida, the meaning of a sign cannot be merely its use because, once again, every instance of use fragments into *uses*—for which the question then becomes, "Which use or uses may predominantly be in play?" And this question may continue to be asked of a past use as it may persist in memory or in a written text over time, since, as time passes, the context of the given use continues to change. The next chapter examines Wittgenstein's understanding of the role of rules in the use of language. As will be seen, Wittgenstein presents a view of interpretation such that, if he were to respond, he would likely insist, contrary to Derrida: The routine use of words requires *no interpretation.*

3

Interpretation

When I obey a rule, I do not choose.
I obey the rule blindly. (PI#219)

Wittgenstein notes in PI#201 that a misunderstanding becomes clear regarding the use of the word "interpretation" (*Deutung*) from the mere fact that in the course of explaining a meaning "we give one interpretation after another, as if each one contented us at least for a moment, until we thought of another standing behind it." The infinite regress of one interpretation after another elicits from Wittgenstein the same response as physicists confronting infinities in quantum field equations: Something is wrong.

To draw Wittgenstein's concern to a finer point, consider an example. He suggests imagining an instance where "we give someone an order to walk in a certain direction ... by drawing an arrow which points in that direction" (BB, 33). He then proposes imagining this person be given the order to carry out the action in a sense *opposite* the first arrangement. The symbol providing the functional meaning of the arrow will now be another arrow pointing in the opposite direction. This added symbol, the second arrow, is what may be called the *interpretation* of the original arrow. This process is continued indefinitely until someone objects, "Every sign is capable of interpretation; but the *meaning* mustn't be capable of interpretation. It is the last interpretation" (BB, 34) Wittgenstein then counters, "Now I assume you take the meaning to be a process accompanying the saying, and that it is translatable into, and so far equivalent to, a further sign. You have therefore further to tell me what you take to be the distinguishing mark between *a sign* and *the meaning*" (BB, 34). Assuming every sign must be assisted by another sign in order for meaning to arise only delays the problem, which is: How does any sign *become* meaningful?

In PI#198 Wittgenstein discusses the issue of how a word may be properly applied in a particular context. He refers to the rightful application of a word as "following a rule." At the outset his imaginary interlocutor asks, "But how can a rule shew me what I have to do at *this* point?" Then the interlocutor adds a remarkable statement: "Whatever I do is, on some interpretation, in accord with the rule." On first reaction, this comment may seem oddly inappropriate. How could just any action accord with the rule?

Wittgenstein does not answer this question directly but responds to the interlocutor in this way: "That is not what we ought to say, but rather: any interpretation still hangs in the air along with what it interprets, and cannot give it any support. Interpretations by themselves do not determine meaning." The interlocutor then omits the word "interpretation" and repeats his previous comment in the form of a question: "Then can whatever I do be brought into accord with the rule?" Again, Wittgenstein does not answer the question directly, but instead provides a disarmingly simple yet provocative response: "What has the expression of a rule—say a sign post—got to do with my actions? What sort of connexion is there here?—Well, perhaps this one: I have been trained to react to this sign in a particular way, and now I do so react to it."

This response appears to match more directly the opening question of PI#198, where the interlocutor asks *how* the rule for application shows what to do in the particular instance. And the answer, apparently, lies not in any specific criteria for response provided by explicit rules but rather in the *training* every language user acquires in learning the native language. But the interlocutor hesitates at this response and objects, "But that is only to give a causal connexion; to tell how it has come about that we now go by the sign-post; not what this going-by-the-sign really consists in."

Apparently the interlocutor desires something more explicit, perhaps a formula for word use analogous to a formula in mathematics such as × + 1 for generating the series 1, 2, 3, 4 ... etc. Learning the use of words certainly involves training, as part of learning a language, but this training alone, arguably, provides no formula for applying words in different situations. But Wittgenstein replies, "On the contrary; I have further indicated that a person goes by a sign-post only in so far as there exists a regular use of sign-posts, a custom." Training accords with a custom, a social practice, in the use of words, and these practices lie embedded in the history of a language and the continuing behaviors of the people who use its words repeatedly in similar situations.

In PI#201 Wittgenstein explains further, "What this shews is that there is a way of grasping a rule [*es eine Auffassung einer Regel gibt*] which is *not* an *interpretation* but which is exhibited in what we call 'obeying the rule' [*der Regel folgen*] and 'going against it' [*ihr entgegenhandeln*] in actual cases." The phrase *Auffassung einer Regel gibt*, translated by Anscombe as "grasping the rule," suggests that in normal circumstances a word (a rule) triggers previous training to respond in a particular way when confronted with that particular word stimulus. *Auffassung einer Regel gibt* more literally translates as "view (or notion) of a rule," but Anscombe's translation effectively conveys the assimilation of a rule into actions sufficiently routine to bypass reflection.

In the remaining part of PI#201 Wittgenstein acknowledges, "...there is an inclination to say: every action according to the rule is an interpretation." But, in keeping with his distinction between grasping the rule and interpreting the rule, he then concludes, "We ought to restrict the term 'interpretation' to the substitution of one expression of the rule for another." Given his use of the phrase in PI#198, Wittgenstein means by "expression of the rule" the use of a word or a sign. And thus "the substitution of one expression of the rule for another" (*einen Ausdruck der Regel durch einen anderen ersetzen*) means the replacement of one word or sign by an equivalent word or sign—a variety of *translation*.

A passage from *The Blue Book* illustrates further and confirms the sense in which Wittgenstein understands interpretation as a species of translation. He begins by offering an analogy with pictures: "Now there are pictures of which we should say that we interpret them, that is, translate them into a different kind of picture, in order to understand them; and pictures of which we should say that we understand them immediately, without any further interpretation." He then compares this analysis directly with language and the procedure of translation: "If you see a telegram written in cipher, and you know the key to this cipher, you will, in general, not say that you understand the telegram before you have translated it into ordinary language. Of course you have only replaced one kind of symbols by another; and yet if now you read the telegram in your language no further process of interpretation will take place" (BB, 36).

But here an objection may be made concerning whether any given instance of sign use results in "grasping the rule" sufficiently to prevent confusion. Wittgenstein addresses this issue as well in another section of *Philosophical Investigations* where he again uses the analogy of a signpost to illustrate the operation of a rule: "Does the signpost leave no doubt about the way I have to go? ... where does it say which way I am to follow it; whether in the direction of its finger or (for example) in the opposite one?—And if there were not a single signpost, but a sequence of signposts or chalk marks on the ground—is there only *one* way of interpreting them?—So I can say that the signpost does after all leave room for doubt." [Note: this passage is cited from the 2009 Hacker/Schulte revised translation of *Philosophical Investigations* at PI#85 due to the important error correction—removal of "no"—in this last sentence, which in the

Anscombe translation reads "So I can say that the signpost does after all leave no room for doubt."]

At this point, Wittgenstein acknowledges the multiplicity of possible meanings, thereby seeming to grant a role for interpretation in sign reading. But then he imposes an important caveat when he immediately adds, "Or rather, it sometimes leaves room for doubt, and sometimes not. And now this is no longer a philosophical proposition, but an empirical one" (PI#85). Also compare, for example, where Wittgenstein says, "Now you might ask: Do we *interpret* the words before we obey the order? And in some cases you will find that you do something which might be called interpreting before obeying, in some cases not." (BB, 3).

Sign and response link by way of customary rather than causal or logical connection and the failure of a sign to function clearly in any given use results from a contingent, empirical failure rather than anything in the nature of signs and their use requiring they be interpreted. Interpretation may be needed only in cases where, due to an unusual factor in the circumstance, something encumbers the usual functioning of a sign creating a problem contingent on the unique situation.

"Grasping a rule" serves as a necessary requirement of Wittgenstein's operational hypothesis because it avoids what he regards as the fatal flaw of infinite regress initiated when admitting interpretation into the action of following or applying a rule. A rule is grasped, for Wittgenstein's purposes, when *automatically* followed in the accepted manner. This operationalization of meaning identifies training and custom as the factor sufficient to eliminate wayward responses.

Rules of use accrue through training and practice and accumulate as learned *conditionings of response* rather than immediate *procedures of reflection*. Language-using, in Wittgenstein's view, insinuates itself into daily routines to the point of becoming second-nature, where the application of terms requires only reaction without intervening action of translation. Wittgenstein likens interpretation to translation as the appropriate analogy for understanding why interpretation remains inessential to the use and reading of signs.

The absence of interpretation aligns with another significant consequence stemming from the operational hypothesis: "And hence also 'obeying a rule' is a practice. And to *think* one is obeying a rule is not to obey a rule … otherwise thinking one was obeying a rule would be the same thing as obeying it" (PI#203). Obeying a rule consists of the activity of observable operations and these overt operations then permit public acknowledgment of whether or not actions conform to the rule.

The absence of interpretation establishes language-using as distinctly overt, observable, and automatic—even to the point of being mechanical.

This view is nowhere more evident than in a passage from the *Brown Book* where Wittgenstein uses the example of a simple language game in which person B learns to bring a building stone on hearing the word "Column!" called out. Training establishes an association such that when the word is called out an image appears in B's mind and then a stone corresponding to that image is brought to the task at hand. But then Wittgenstein again questions the role of mental activity and whether the image in the mind must be a *necessary* feature of what has occurred. Wittgenstein asks, "If the training could bring it about that the idea or image—automatically— arose in B's mind, why shouldn't it bring about B's actions without the intervention of an image? This would only come to a slight variation of the associative mechanism." Where mental activity is found to be unneces- sary, any reflective process also disappears, and Wittgenstein concludes, "...this case is strictly comparable with that of a mechanism in which a button is pressed and an indicator plate appears. In fact this sort of mech- anism can be used instead of that of association" (BB, 89).

Mental images, like sample drawings or paintings, count as redun- dant and unnecessary for explaining the operation of meaning in commu- nication. And what Wittgenstein calls *reasons* for the choice in application of a word fall into the same category of redundancy as mental images. He clearly expresses this view in another example of rule following where he imagines someone assigned the task of finding a matching fabric from sev- eral bolts on a shelf. After having been shown the desired sample in an adjacent room, the subject then goes to the room where the bolts of fab- ric are kept and selects the correct one. Wittgenstein then asks how the desired material is rightly recognized. A cause for the correct selection might consist of a physiological or psychological explanation. But, Witt- genstein continues, "If on the other hand you ask for a reason the answer is, 'There need not have been a reason for the choice. A reason is a step pre- ceding the step of the choice. But why should every step be preceded by another one?'" (BB, 88).

Here, by way of the fabric analogy, Wittgenstein again speaks of the associative link between a word and its application as without reflection, interpretation, or reasoning. The training involved in learning language installs the mechanisms by which words may reliably be used. No rea- sons need be given because any reasons that could be offered count only as deferrals of the ultimate recourse to instruction and training as the explanation for why a given word applies in a given context. No reasons ground the connections between words and their applications due to the purely arbitrary and contingent nature of the training provided through a given person's native language. When asked why a particular word is used, the proper answer is: "This is simply what I do" (PI#217). But is this conclusion really where Wittgenstein intends to let the issue of interpretation rest?

Switching for the moment to Derrida, the picture of language becomes very different. Not only is it the case, in Derrida's view, that the addressee never "grasps" precisely what the addresser sends, but the message exceeds the intention and control of the addresser. For example, Derrida famously says that language "leaves us no choice but to mean (to say) something that is (already, always, also) other than what we mean (to say)" (1988b, 62). The difference from Wittgenstein's view of language becomes explicit when Derrida addresses the same topic of translation.

> In the limits to which it is possible, or at least *appears* possible, translation practices the difference between signified and signifier. But if this difference is never pure, no more so is translation, and for the notion of translation we would have to substitute a notion of *transformation*: a regulated transformation of one language by another, of one text by another. We will never have, and in fact have never had, to do with some "transport" of pure signifieds from one language to another, *or within one and the same language*, that the signifying instrument would leave virgin and untouched [emphasis added] [1981b, 20].

Wittgenstein's "grasping the rule" corresponds to what Derrida calls the "transport of pure signifieds." The exchange of signs between speakers of the same language proceeds, according to Wittgenstein, with a transparency precluding the need for interpretation. Derrida, on the other hand, clearly views the special case of translation from one language to another as misleading if viewed as fundamentally different in kind from the exchange of words between speakers of the same language. Wittgenstein highlights the *difference* between inter-language use and intra-language use in order to argue for the immediacy and transparency of intra-language use. Alternatively, Derrida highlights the *sameness* between inter- and intra-language use in order to expose the immediacy and transparency of intra-language use as an impression facilitated by familiarity with a native language. For him, this familiarity ought not to cloud recognition of the underlying process of interpretive choice as the salient model for language use inherent in both inter- and intra-language operations. Here his use of the word *transformation* signals *interpretation* and vice versa because all language use, whether in sending or receiving messages, *necessarily* initiates transformation. In Derrida's view, the "signifying instrument," the signifier, does not leave untouched the signified in communication within a given language as well as between different languages.

But Derrida's claims regarding interpretation would likely not convince Wittgenstein who would no doubt still question Derrida's understanding of meaning as interpretation. For Wittgenstein, a sign simply *means* and does not require any other sign or process for this meaning to operate. Otherwise, as previously queried, how does any sign *begin* to function in the capacity of a sign?

The question of importance for Derrida, however, is not how does a sign *begin* to function but rather how does it *stop*? Recall again the previously cited passage where he says language "leaves us no choice but to mean (to say) something that is (already, always, also) other than what we mean (to say)." Regardless of any distinction that may be made between meaning and saying, the use of signs, in any context whatever, results in expressions incapable of conveying *univocal* meaning, thereby establishing the necessity for interpretation. The law of iterability, discussed in Chapter 2, entails repetition-with-a-difference due to the shaping influence of a changing context, a moving spatial/temporal surround placing in motion the identity of the sign. If such were not the case, a sign would never begin to function as a sign because it would be frozen in place and in time and incapable of *repeatable* use and, thereby, incapable of any use.

On the contrary, for Wittgenstein, a sign cannot function as a sign unless, in ordinary circumstances, signifier and signified operate in something close to a stimulus and response connection. Lee Braver, for example, summarizes the importance of training in Wittgenstein's view of language: "We are habituated to react to orders or pictures or pointing in certain ways through a process much closer to Pavlovian conditioning than to discoursing in the Platonic Academy" (2012, 157). If interpretations were required in the use of signs, using language would be more like deciphering code and would result in cumbersome, time-consuming confusions. Derrida, however, would doubtless reply that convenient assumptions language-users all too often make in routine daily discourse invite misunderstanding of the limitations of language for providing transparent communication. These limitations obscure ways in which differences may intervene in unsuspected ways in human interactions such that what is called communication strides precariously along a seam between the possible and the impossible. In Derrida's view, differences intervening in the seam between the possible and the impossible of communication do not count as *potential* differences. Differences emerge inevitably from the iterable structure of language. This circumstance positions interpretation as *an essential feature of meaning*—a necessary entailment of signs—and not merely a contingent and occasional phenomenon arising in unusual circumstances.

Among the few who have written commentaries comparing Wittgenstein and Derrida, Ruth Sonderegger stands out as having sufficiently headlined and highlighted the role of interpretation as the crucial difference between the two philosophers. For example, in the first paragraph of her commentary she says, "If I am right, it can be shown clearly how Derrida's attempt to represent speaking and understanding as interpretation constitutes a significant advance beyond Wittgenstein" (1997, 183). Sonderegger, however, misses an important feature of Derrida's understanding of meaning as interpretation when describing the role of rules in Derrida's view. But discussion of this aspect of her analysis is reserved for the next chapter.

Both Wittgenstein and Derrida make claims about what is essential in order for signs to acquire meaning. These claims contradict each other on the point of interpretation. But who has the better argument? The next three chapters explore further the issue of interpretation and rule following and draw out the differences between Wittgenstein and Derrida in greater detail in the course of offering an answer to this question.

4

Rules

*Then can whatever I do be brought
into accord with the rule? (PI#198).*

Saul Kripke's reading of Wittgenstein on rule following has attracted considerable attention within Wittgenstein commentary due to its bold claims and incisive but controversial argument. This chapter, however, will skip the complexities of the critical commentary surrounding Kripke's thesis and instead use his reading as a springboard for venturing deeper into the issue of interpretation. Kripke's analysis of key parts of *Philosophical Investigations* serves this purpose admirably due to the clarity with which his mathematical illustration draws out the relevant issues leading to an appreciation of the ways in which the question of interpretation may ultimately resist clear resolution.

Kripke follows Wittgenstein in identifying a paradox in rule following relating to interpretation but does not follow him in finding this paradox to be easily set aside or dissolved. If remaining intact against its critics, the paradox noted by Wittgenstein, which will be cited shortly, leads to what is called *rule-skepticism*, whereby no rule may be rightly said to *determine* its applications. What may be called *rule-realism* opposes rule-skepticism. Although versions of rule-realism do not assert that rules determine applications, they do assert a highly reliable normative constraint across an indefinite number and variety of cases such that, when understood, rules, in practical respects, apply themselves. Where Appendix A explores in greater detail the relative merits of these opposing views in light of the notion of an "internal relation" between rules and applications, this chapter remains focused on the difficulties Wittgenstein raises regarding the activity of rule following and how Derrida's view may be contrasted with Wittgenstein's on this important but complex issue.

In *Wittgenstein on Rules and Private Language*, Kripke cites a key passage in *Philosophical Investigations* and claims it identifies the central problem addressed in this text. Here Wittgenstein reveals a paradox, giving rise, according to Kripke, to a new form of skepticism. Speaking of this new form of skepticism, he says, "Personally I am inclined to regard it as the most radical and original sceptical problem that philosophy has seen to date" (1982, 60). This is an extraordinary claim and deserves careful attention. Returning again to PI#201, Wittgenstein states the problem in the opening sentence: "This was our paradox: no course of action could be determined by a rule, because every course of action can be made out to accord with the rule."

This sentence is a reformulation of its expression by the interlocutor in PI#198 ("Whatever I do is, on some interpretation, in accord with the rule"). Since words are applied according to rules, there ought to be a means of confirming publicly, as mentioned in the previous chapter, whether a given rule has been followed. But in his reading of Wittgenstein, Kripke discovers this is not a simple matter. Drawing from Wittgenstein's deviant pupil example in PI#185, Kripke devises an illustration—a mathematical exercise—where a rule can be briefly stated and assessed as to whether it is followed or not.

Kripke imagines two persons, A and B, instructed to add together two numbers. To keep the illustration simple, he selects the numbers 68 + 57. For purposes of this illustration persons A and B are imagined in their past experiences to have never before added together numbers equal to or greater than 57. Person A adds the numbers together for a total of 125 and person B adds the numbers together for a total of 5. A total of 5? Further tests show their results agree on numbers added together when the numbers are less than 57. For person B, the addition of numbers equal to or greater than 57 always total 5 and that is just how "addition" works. For person A, that is not how "addition" works.

Person A's results may be described as following a rule mathematically expressed as $x + y = x + y$ while B's results follow a rule expressed as $x + y = x + y$, and if $x, y \geq 57 = 5$. The former counts as *addition* and the latter Kripke calls *quaddition*. Nevertheless, the computational results of A and B are indistinguishable for operations with numbers below 57. Kripke argues that until numbers of 57 or greater are used, no material facts can expose the difference between A using the rule of addition (plus function) and B using the rule of quaddition (quus function). This illustration, like Wittgenstein's pupil example, ought not to be dismissed based on its seeming unlikelihood. It deliberately falls short of the criterion of likelihood in favor of brevity, ease of description, and simplicity for purposes of illustration.

Continuing with Kripke's argument, his account becomes even curiouser. Neither A nor B can verify *for themselves* whether in the past they were using the plus or quus rule because such verification depends entirely on memory of a mental event. While in many cases memory may be checked by recourse to material evidence, in this case the memory is like the memory of a dream, which has no material trace and therefore remains inaccessible to means of verification. Prior to working with numbers of 57 or greater, person A can offer no proof (to self or others) for having possibly used the quus function in the past then having forgotten this and now started using the plus function. Similarly, B also cannot prove (to self or others) having possibly used the plus function in the past then having forgotten this and now switched to using the quus function. Neither memory nor observation can deliver demonstrative proof. In the absence of reliable verification, all are at a loss to settle the matter one way or the other.

Where overt behaviors are observed to be in concert, everyone assumes their actions accord with "the rule" when in fact, according to Kripke, different rules may have been followed. Until this difference manifests itself in observable, measurable ways, no one need suspect different rules are in use. This is the paradox Kripke claims Wittgenstein sees as a threat to communication and a potential justification for rule-skepticism. It threatens communication because, even where the "same" words or rules may appear to operate and "same" responses result, differences may be in play. And these differences may conceal subtle yet perhaps significant differences until such time as an unusual circumstance or new application suddenly makes visible these differences.

Taking a step back from this analysis, it should be noted that Kripke claims his example illustrates Wittgenstein's paradox that no course of action can be determined by a rule because every course of action can be made out to accord with the rule. But it may not immediately be clear why this conclusion follows from his example. Kripke speaks to the possibility the same outcome may result from following what are in fact *different* rules, whereas PI#201 clearly addresses the possibility that different outcomes may result from following the *same* rule. In the first case, the issue turns on *which* rule is followed while, in the second case, the issue turns on what *counts* as following a given rule. The former raises the question of criteria (What *is* the rule?) and the latter raises the question of judgment (What applications qualify as *following* the rule?).

Concerning Kripke's plus/quus illustration, it only appears the same results are generated by application of the same rule when, in fact, two different rules are in use. So long as no anomaly appears, the actors continue unaware of the different rules operating beneath the surface of their actions. B thinks he follows the conventional rule described as "addition," which, for unknown reasons, he understands to be x + y = x + y, and if x, y ≥ 57 = 5. He believes A to be mistaken. In his view, plus *is* what Kripke calls quus and A fails to correctly follow the rule when using numbers of

57 or above. And if A and B are operating in isolation from others, they may argue with each other endlessly, unable to achieve clear resolution about who is following the rule of "addition" correctly.

This circumstance raises the question whether there can be a *genuine* instance where following *one* rule yields significantly different applications. If such were the case, the model of rule following requiring no interpretation would then be brought into question by failing to exclude the model of rule following requiring interpretation. If operating with signs admits considerable latitude for what counts as operating—latitude for "following" the "same" rule—then the communication function of language begins to buckle under the weight of its own freedom.

As discussed in the previous chapter, latitude for interpretation of a rule throws a wrench into the machinery of the operational hypothesis. When admitting interpretation, the application of a rule—even when the conventional criteria for the rule are implicitly known and agreed on—may indeed yield unconventional results. In this case, a difference in results of application does not turn on the mistaken substitution of one rule for another rule but rather on differences in *how* the given rule is applied. For purposes of further illustration, consider this example of application of a rule offered by rhetorical theorist John Macksoud:

> Imagine that you come into my office and I invite you to sit down on a computer. You may be puzzled because, medievally, my office contains nothing which you would ordinarily recognize as a computer. Ever compassionate in the face of perplexity, I indicate an object and tell you that placing yourself upon it will constitute acceptance of my invitation. What? Is a chair a computer? What prohibits us from saying so? Computers must meet certain criteria. Let us specify them. First a computer must compute. My chair does so by being displaced more or less, and differently, at different moments, by your weight. It must have moving parts. In use, the parts of the chair move in relation to each other and to any fixed point. It must provide a readout of the results of its computations. That is what it does in the differences in its configuration and position after use. It must be electrically powered. And so it is: by the electrical charges of the cells within the muscles of your body [2009, 49].

Apparent deviancy in applying the word "computer" turns out to be a use that may, as Wittgenstein feared, be made consistent, "on some interpretation," with conventional criteria. This example shows that different results need not originate from different rules. They may instead derive from different *judgments* about how the criteria of a definition may be applied—judgments that may be justified through a stretching of boundaries the limits of which may prove as difficult to constrain as the limits of metaphor.

Thus, problems in communication may arise not only from mistakenly following a different rule while believing it to be the same rule as others follow but also from differences in application of what qualifies as the same rule. Wittgenstein records his full awareness of both difficulties in PI#242 when he says, "If language is to be a means of communication there must be agreement not only in definitions but also (queer as this may sound) in judgments."

Regarding the uses of words, it may seem, at times, that what links remarkably different uses of the same word in different contexts may be little more than that the same word is used. A question may then be appropriately raised as to whether different applications of the same word stem from following different rules or from different applications of the same rule. And this distinction may itself ultimately turn on a matter of judgment or preference about how to name the root of such differences. Granting as much, Wittgenstein's concerns about interpretation creating a situation of "anything goes" regarding rules, and thereby contributing to communication breakdown, gain credibility. Given these issues concerning rule following raised by Wittgenstein and highlighted by Kripke's illustration, the "if" in Wittgenstein's sentence "If language is to be a means of communication ..." looms ominously.

Is the communicative function of language defeated by rule skepticism? Wittgenstein clearly thinks not. His solution is revealed in the remainder of PI#242. But full appreciation of this solution requires recalling again the Beetle Box Analogy (PI#293), cited in Chapter 1. Here Wittgenstein claims that, for all practical purposes, the contents of each person's "box" (the rule each may be following) remains *irrelevant* so long as results in behaviors appear consistent with the practices of the linguistic community.

With this irrelevancy of possible rule following differences in hand, Wittgenstein's solution offered in PI#242 may be better understood. Introducing the example of measurement, he says, "It is one thing to describe methods of measurement, and another to obtain and state results of measurement. But what we call 'measuring' is partly determined by a certain constancy in results of measurement." The key phrase is "constancy of results," which may be taken to mean "sameness of results" across the applications of measurement made by different persons.

Wittgenstein further recognizes he must also confront the question of the "same," which itself is exposed to possible differences in judgments—as when his interlocutor asks in exasperation, "But isn't *the same* at least the same?" This is why Wittgenstein says in PI#225, "The use of the word 'rule' and the use of the word 'same' are interwoven."

Continuing similarly in PI#378, when a judgment of sameness has been made, Wittgenstein asks: "[H]ow am I to know that the word 'same' describes what I recognize? Only if I can express my recognition in some other way, and if it is possible for someone else to teach me that 'same' is the correct word here. For if I need a justification for using a word, it must also be one for someone else." Criteria for sameness operate as they do for all rule following—by way of sameness of results as measured by the ongoing accepted practices of the linguistic community. Constancy of results is the goal and so long as constancy is observed to be the case, then judgments require no justification and communication, for all appearances, flows smoothly.

In Derrida's view, however, it turns out that *every* instance of use—some more pronounced than others—presents fault lines around which different meanings, even opposed meanings, may be realized. Derrida is famous for identifying texts written by celebrated authors where selected words may operate with contrary meanings presenting undecidable alternatives. Among these examples are *supplement* as both addition and displacement (*Of Grammatology*), *pharmakon* as both cure and poison ("Plato's Pharmacy," in *Dissemination*), and *hymen* as both inside and outside ("The Double Session," in *Dissemination*).

In *The Politics of Logic* (2012), Paul Livingston explains the way in which Derrida undertakes "formalizing the undecidable" by stressing the role of syntax in generating the dissemination of meaning. In the case of particular words, Derrida notes, as mentioned in the previous chapter, that what produces contradictory layers of meaning "...is not the lexical richness, the semantic infiniteness of a word or concept." Instead, what counts here is the "formal or syntactical praxis that composes and decomposes it" (1981a, 220). This formal or syntactical praxis yields layers of signification creating *undecidability* between meanings. This undecidability arises through the operation of the words in syntactic *context* rather than exclusively through inherent or internal semantic *content*.

In the case of Mallarme's use of hymen, discussed in "The Double Session," Derrida remarks that this word could be replaced by other words such as "marriage," "crime," "identity," or "difference," and the effects would be the same due to the structure of the text. He remarks further that these effects, which present a "*double scene* upon a double stage," are not extraordinary *accidents* arising from unusual texts. These undecidable meanings present themselves repeatedly among wide varieties of texts: "Without reducing all these to the same, quite the contrary, it is possible to recognize a certain serial law in these points of indefinite pivoting: they mark the spots of what can never be mediated, mastered, sublated, or dialecticized." Granting as much, Derrida then returns to the scene of writing: "Is it by chance that all these play effects, these 'words' that escape philosophical mastery, should have, in widely differing historical contexts, a very singular relation to writing?" (1981a, 221). In Derrida's view, of course, the answer is "no."

The play of these effects derives from the structural or formal property of writing and of language in general and, consequently, may be consistently found in texts of every type. After reviewing these passages in *Dissemination*, Livingston concludes, "Thus, the point of emphasizing the ambiguous and even contradictory meanings of 'hymen' in Mallarmé's text is not to evince anything intrinsic to this word itself, but rather to show the way in which it (contingently and non-essentially) occupies a particular *position* in this text—the position, as we may say, of the undecidable, what the text itself, and the logic that governs it, does not give us—for *structural* reasons—the resources to decide" (2012, 115).

Livingston cites passages from "The Double Session" in an extensive account of the structural derivation of undecidability and the broader consequences of this undecidability, not only regarding the reading of texts but also in relation to the limitations and failures of limitation it imposes on every kind of system, including social systems ranging from the legal to the political.

Although essential to the meaning of a sign, context changes from one time to another and this change adds one or more vectors of meaning as it fails to preserve other vectors. Since context has no empirical limit, it requires a limit imposed by language-users—whether through active or passive choice—in order for a situation to acquire the contour to become a *situation*, to gain the definition necessary for practical functioning. This selective limitation also adds to or builds the function of the sign for the interactants, which need not be the same for each interactant. These points of potential difference, which affect the functioning of signs through repeated use, result in what Derrida calls repetition-with-a-difference, which is another expression for Derrida's term *iterability*.

Repetition-with-a-difference *opens* or *unlocks* the sign. Meaning is not contained in the mere presence of its material mark and instead opens itself to an absence to which it points. The sign is haunted by this absence to which it is attached but which projects no singular form, instead becoming the sign's point of otherness. The sign divides through meanings it repeats and meanings it creates within its new syntax/context. As noted near the end of Chapter 2, Derrida sometimes refers to this repetition as *restance* or remainder. But this remainder, as also noted in Chapter 2, must not be understood to constitute a minimal essential core persisting across different uses of the same word.

The description of this remainder is the point at which Ruth Sonderegger (1997), mentioned in the previous chapter, falters in her account of Derrida's interpretive view of language and rule following. Her discussion of how Derrida understands the operation of rules presents an opportunity for further clarification of Derrida's position in contrast to Wittgenstein's. She says, for example, "It is *Derrida's* claim that, in speaking, we assume that there is an explicable rule, or law, which all cases of application follow." She then responds, "[I]n fact there neither is nor can be such a rule." She understands Derrida appears, at times, to acknowledge as much but then, when speaking of concepts, he makes claims that would seem to clearly contradict this. Continuing, she explains that according to Derrida's model for what "we" do, "the common factor among the various occasions of the use of a sign is conceived as an idealization, as an idealized smallest common denominator ... the thread running through all uses ... thanks to which the various uses can be identified as uses of *a single* sign" [emphasis in original] (1997, 195). The "thread running through all uses" is an idealization conceived and taken for granted by language users, which they also "assume is explicable when they assume that what they say has a clear sense" (1997, 195).

In support of the claim that in fact a common thread does *not* run through all cases of the use of a given word, Sonderegger cites Wittgenstein describing the concept of *number*: "And we extend our concept of number as in spinning a thread we twist fibre on fibre." And the strength of the twine does not reside in the fact that some one fiber runs through its whole length, but in the overlapping of many fibers (PI#67; Sonderegger, 194). Thus, for Wittgenstein, the lack of a single thread running through all the uses of a given word suggests the uses reveal no corresponding concept of shared essence or absolute elemental boundary.

Sonderegger sides with Wittgenstein when he argues, in her words, "that the concepts of a particular group of speakers do not imply any ideal of absoluteness." Derrida, on the other hand, according to Sonderegger, makes an "avoidable metaphysical claim" when ascribing to speakers "a theoretically explicable ideal of exactness" (1997, 195–196). Derrida and Wittgenstein disagree on what they attribute to speakers as the underlying assumption concerning the rigor and exactness of concepts. Ultimately, Sonderegger believes Derrida unnecessarily assigns to language-users an underlying ideal of exactness and rigor regarding concepts in the use of language. This ideal, incapable of being attained, then sets in motion the aporia of an infinite regress of real life approaches or approximations that always fall short of the ideal and thus generate endless disappointment and frustration. But on this point Sonderegger misrepresents Derrida's position.

Derrida's "remainder" does not move from one instance of use to another while retaining even a *minimal* undisturbed and persistent core or "idealized smallest common denominator." Every element and aspect of meaning submits to the effects of iterability such that no essential core operates reliably across the various instances of use through time. Instead, the remainder consists of different fragments of use attaching to any given signifier through contingent iterations of previous uses sufficient to meet flexible expectations of "sameness" on the part of language users. The remainder is like a ball of leaves brushed up by wind as it moves along the ground, constantly losing some leaves and picking up others. While giving the appearance of being the "same" ball of leaves as it moves, constantly changing its elemental parts, this phenomenon merely functions as an "it" for particular practical purposes. Waves of water exhibit the same phenomenon of sameness/difference, while lacking an essential core. As Derrida says, "The remainder does not amount ... to the repose of permanence.... Ultimately, remaining and permanence are incompatible" (1988, 53–54). Like Wittgenstein, then, Derrida also believes no single thread runs through all uses of a word.

When Derrida suggests users assume the concept determines itself according to the exactness and rigor of "all or nothing," he does not directly challenge or refute this traditional metaphysical assumption of precision. In fact, he affirms this view, as Sonderegger notes, not only for others but for himself as well. But then, crucially, he explains that another "general logic" of concepts, a subtly different metaphysical ground, *supplements* the traditional ground and routinely slips past the awareness of users such that concepts present more than a singular determination. Concepts are divided at the core such that mind and body, for example, function as determined, separate, and singular but do so as the concept mind/body with inextricably entangled determinations. This is why, in his seminal essay "Différance," Derrida says of oppositions: "[O]ne of the terms appears as the différance of the other, the other as 'differed' within the systematic ordering of the same (e.g., the intelligible as differing from the sensible, as sensible differed; the concept as differed-differing intuition, life as differing-differed matter; mind as differed-differing life; culture as differed-differing nature)" (1973, 148). Derrida's position regarding oppositions, the boundaries of concepts, and idealization remains metaphysical in its seeming dialectical structure but this structure exceeds traditional metaphysics in its non-dialectical dialectic—a perplexing position examined further in the next chapter and explained in increasing detail through the progression of chapters in Parts II and III. For now it is sufficient to note that Sonderegger's characterization of Derrida's view of concepts remains misleading while nevertheless serving to point toward a key difference between Wittgenstein and Derrida.

While acknowledging the lack of an essential core or explicable rule running through all the applications of the same word, Wittgenstein must be separated from Derrida in the way in which he assesses the consequences of this circumstance. Derrida finds these consequences generate complications for meaning and communication, whereas Wittgenstein finds these complications to be mostly inconsequential. In his view, when they become consequential, they may be empirically dealt with on a case-by-case basis. When confronting such "trembling of meaning" (to use Derrida's expression), Wittgenstein explains what he believes dissolves both the complications of rule following paradoxes as well as complications stemming from any apparent need to interpret a rule before acting on it.

For Wittgenstein, the solution traces to the uses to which words and sentences are put, and these uses, as it turns out, arise from the *activities* of people and communities working together for various purposes. Apart from shared activities and purposes, these words and sentences lose their force and utility and become, in Wittgenstein's expression, idling gears. He refers to the activities and purposes for which words are devised and to which they are connected as *forms of life*. Particular words and linguistic routines coordinate with forms of life and these routines he calls *language games*. He uses the word "game" strategically to suggest that these routines, like games, manifest a specific structure aligning with specific situations. He discusses many such routines, for example: giving orders, reporting events, describing objects, using measurements, constructing stories, telling jokes, asking, greeting, thanking, requesting, wishing, and hundreds more. Wittgenstein explains, "Here the term 'language-*game*' is meant to bring into prominence the fact that the *speaking* of language is part of an activity, or of a form of life" (PI#23). The *intimate* relation between life and language prompts his remark, "...to imagine a language means to imagine a form of life." Language itself grows out of forms of life and these life activities ground the meanings of terms in the purposes and practices to which they are used and applied.

However, when words evolve in the context of one language game and are then imported to a different language game, confusion may result, according to Wittgenstein, sufficiently misleading to cause a "mental cramp." He explains, "Our investigation is therefore a grammatical one. Such an investigation sheds light on our problem by clearing misunderstandings away. Misunderstandings concerning the use of words, caused, among other things, by certain analogies between the forms of expression in different regions of language.—Some of them can be removed by substituting one form of expression for another; this may be called 'analysis' of our forms of expression, for the process is sometimes like one of taking a thing apart" (PI#90).

In this passage, Wittgenstein's *analysis* may be thought to resemble Derrida's *deconstruction*. But what Wittgenstein derives from his notion of *grammar* contrasts with the previously mentioned effects Derrida assigns to *syntax*. The two actions are guided by different assumptions concerning the limits of language. Deconstruction, as Derrida practices it, may broadly be understood as a process of examining texts to discover ways in which the textual structure presents fractures, providing the basis for a division of key terms between alternative readings—readings that may not merely be different but also seemingly contradictory. In contrast, Wittgenstein's analysis serves to expose the ways in which key terms may mislead due to their placement in a context or language game starkly alien to the language game from which they derived their original use and grounded meaning. Wittgenstein's analysis serves to resolve or dissolve an anomaly of use by noting the language game appropriate to a given word whereas Derrida's deconstruction serves to expose and confirm an anomaly for which a repair cannot be guaranteed.

In defense of his approach, Wittgenstein finds language games tied to forms of life, to activities generating trained performative capacities and routines within a community of persons bound together by these shared practices. The practical meanings of words and of language and language games are not hidden in formulas such as would require philosophical excavation in order to discover. The meanings of all words, including even those giving metaphysicians the most trouble (such as being, time, truth, absolute, etc.), remain open to clear view as these meanings emerge in the non-philosophical language games structuring their use in concrete situations and practices corresponding to the circumstances from which they arose and are most commonly used. Philosophers look for meanings in an occult space accessible only through mental exertion when in fact these meanings may be accessed through an inspection of the language of everyday routines. Many philosophical puzzles may be adequately clarified by sorting word uses into the language games to which they properly belong. When this sorting is successful, meanings become clear—or at least rise to the level of clarity necessary for them to operate without generating seemingly deep and crippling confusions and paradoxes.

Derrida would likely find Wittgenstein's account of language and meaning admirable in its attention to the subtle features of context brought forth in the study of language games and the importance of the role of context in meanings. But he would also likely find this account insufficient in the extent to which it ultimately *underestimates* the role of context in the generation of meanings. To claim, as Wittgenstein does, that the question of meaning can, in normal cases, be cleared up by aligning use with the appropriate language game would not be acceptable to

Derrida. Instead, he would likely respond by pointing out that the discernment of *which* language game and form of life may operate in particular contexts remains an issue itself in question and by no means routinely obvious. Examination will show that more than one language game may be found to operate. Inability to rule out simultaneous overlapping of different games permits different applications and interpretations between speakers within the same context of use. Derrida thoroughly explores such difficulties in his essay "Signature, Event, Context" (1977a).

For example, in particular utterances is the language game in play a threat or a promise? Sarcasm or sincerity? Compliment or criticism? Hint or ruse? Command or reminder? Wish or whim? Statement or citation? Offense or defense? Confession or plea? In any given context, the words in use may easily be recognized but their relevant meaning requires interpretation regarding the manner of their use and the motivations involved, even in the most mundane situations. Understanding use requires framing the context in which the words are used, which requires an assessment of the relevant features of the endlessly expansive context of what is said, when it is said, where it is said, and who is saying it. As Derrida repeatedly argues, reading relevant context is no simple task in human interactions because crucial elements of context may remain unobserved or unexpressed in particular situations.

Consider this example: When getting ready to leave the house, the owner may say to a visitor, "Please close the window." The visitor closes the window and communication appears successful. But the owner does not notice that the visitor also locks the window after closing it because, for the visitor, "close the window" means what for the owner "close and lock the window" means. This difference does not seem trivial when the owner and visitor return later to discover the key to the house has been lost and the window normally used as an emergency entrance is now locked. Whereupon the owner sighs and complains to the visitor, "I asked you to 'close the window' not 'close and lock' the window!" Had the visitor been a close friend, sufficient context may have been available to know that the owner never locks the "emergency access" window. Or had the owner understood the visitor's different training and propensity for house security, sufficient context would have been available to prompt the modified request, "Please close the window but do not lock it." The request, "Please close the window," conveyed meaning but, as it turned out, was not sufficiently mean-ing*ful* because elements of context were lacking for which the owner had no reason to suspect were necessary for the visitor.

Even where communication appears to occur, iterability insures a play of differences. These differences may manifest in deferred consequences sufficiently delayed in time to obscure the connection back to the problematic communication—as, for example, when the owner loses the house key several weeks later and, having not touched the window in that time, discovers it is locked and cannot recall that it got that way when he asked the visitor to close it. This simple example illustrates the tenuous nature of communication at every turn in daily discourse. The play of differences yields *consequences* that may or may not always be traced to their triggering origins.

Shifting to the question of rules operative in reading intentions, again Derrida and Wittgenstein may appear to be in agreement. Wittgenstein's stance against mentalism leads him to argue that intending, as with all inner processes such as feeling, wishing, pretending, expecting, and the like, is mistakenly understood when characterized as not only a parallel accompaniment to speech but as also providing the *essence* of the meaning of the associated speech acts.

For example, when referring to an unspoken intention to deceive someone, Wittgenstein has his interlocutor say, "My intention was no less certain as it was than it would have been if I had said, 'Now I'll deceive him.'" To which Wittgenstein then responds, "But if you had said the words, would you necessarily have meant them quite seriously? (Thus the most explicit expression of intention is by itself insufficient evidence of intention.)" (PI#641). Henry Staten cites Derrida noting the same difficulty: "No criterion that is simply *inherent* in the manifest utterance is capable of distinguishing an utterance when it is serious from the same utterance when it is not (*Ltd Inc*, p. 208)" (cited in Staten, 1984, 118). Both Wittgenstein and Derrida acknowledge the difficulty in reading intention from the manifest utterance.

However, Wittgenstein and Derrida each assign different roles to intention understood as a mental process. Wittgenstein does not deny there may be mental processes of intention but sweeps aside any such hidden processes as *irrelevant* to the activities of speaking and communicating. In the extent to which intention remains relevant, it may be read from what manifests observably in the circumstances and actions surrounding utterances. In Wittgenstein's view, observable cues accompany and betray intention for the careful observer of behavior. In other words, intention for Wittgenstein relevantly resides not in mental processes but in manifest operations. For example, he comments in PI#647: "What is the natural expression of an intention?—Look at a cat when it stalks a bird; or a beast when it wants to escape." In his approach to language, Wittgenstein merges, but does not equate, intention and expression, folding inner into outer. And here "expression" may be taken to include all non-verbal behavior accompanying linguistic expression. Everything *relevant* remains open to view. Whatever part of intention may lie hidden from view falls within the scope of Wittgenstein's general remark concerning his investigations, "For what is hidden, for example, is of no interest to us" (PI #126).

By contrast, Derrida folds outer into inner, as in "there is nothing *outside* of the text." But here "inner" must be understood as having nothing to do with the privacy of the mental or subjective. For Derrida, technically speaking, there is no outside; nothing qualifies as purely "outside" since as soon as meanings come into being they become "inner," become part of the *text* within boundless con-*text*, not only for humans but for all life forms engaged in reading their world. This folding of the outer to the inner differs from varieties of subjectivism because, for Derrida, both the subject and the object of traditional metaphysics are effects of *différance*—which is Derrida's term for what may be understood to account for the generation of differences. Subject and object form an entangled set of differences such that the subject no longer remains locked within itself in a solipsistic bubble—as some commentators believe to be the fate of the subject in Cartesian metaphysics. Instead, the subject emerges as open and other to itself, incapable of separation from the object world and the generative "othering" effects of *différance*. Wittgenstein's shift from inner to outer makes it possible, in his view, for signs to be read. Derrida's shift from outer to inner makes it *both* possible and impossible for signs to be read. The generation of differences through the action of *différance* initiates an entanglement between sameness and difference opening signs to the dispersion of the more radical relationality of dissemination—a consequence more thoroughly discussed in Chapter 8.

At this point, it is worthwhile to pause and consider, from another angle, the difference between Wittgenstein and Derrida concerning the theme of inner and outer, understood as mind and body or as psychological and physical. Defenders of Wittgenstein's critique of Cartesian metaphysics (e.g., McGinn, 2013) argue that Wittgenstein displaces the mind/body distinction with the living/nonliving distinction and, in doing so, relieves philosophical problems associated with the mind/body distinction such as the problem of other minds and skeptical challenges arising from the inaccessibility of inner or mental states. For Wittgenstein, the body objectifies the soul. Derrida may be seen to align with this view but, for Derrida, this does not relieve challenges in reading behavior because behaviors present themselves as *signs*. In Derrida's approach, the difference between the signifier and the signified is not altered or sidelined by the living/nonliving distinction. The behaviors of living beings manifest as signs and therefore conform to the laws of signs including most especially, in Derrida's view, the necessity for the interpretation of signs. Wittgenstein grants that any ultimate reading of the soul of another human being remains beyond reach. But this is the case, in his view, because of the inaccessibility of the complete history of any one human being by another rather than irreducible difficulties relating to the interpretation of behaviors as signs.

Wittgenstein's solution to the misunderstanding surrounding the notion of interpretation in the context of reading signs, consisting of the distinction between "interpreting" and "grasping the rule," may in many ways appear adequate. But if the situation were as Wittgenstein indicates, it would seem that "grasping the rule" would, owing to its automatic or near automatic nature, also yield pronounced clarity and consistency in the application of words. If so, this entails, as Sonderegger argues, rigorous boundaries for words and concepts. And yet Wittgenstein acknowledges such clear boundaries are not widely the case in the ordinary use of language. But then, granting as much, how does he align this admission with the view that using words ordinarily requires no interpretation?

By contrast, Derrida subscribes to rigorous distinctions between words and concepts while also making the case for the pervasive role of interpretation in rule following. But then, granting as much, how does he align his view of rigorous distinctions with the admission that using words requires interpretation? Clarification of these apparent contradictions comprises the subject of the next chapter.

5

Limits

You still owe me a definition of exactness (PI#69).

Wittgenstein's concern regarding clarity in communication appears prominently in PI#133: "For the clarity we are aiming at is indeed *complete* clarity." This declaration reveals much about the motives driving not only *Philosophical Investigations* but also Wittgenstein's entire career. He strives for clarity concerning concepts, communication, method, and metaphysics. Concerns about linguistic practices and confusions surrounding them are puzzles he attempts to dissolve in order to bring peace, in the form of clarity, to philosophy. The next sentence in PI#133 leaves no doubt regarding the breadth of his agenda for clarity: "But this simply means that the philosophical problems should *completely* disappear." However, Wittgenstein's whistleblowing on the scandal of needless confusion and uncertainty in philosophy need not be read to suggest all ambiguity and indistinctness count as part of the problem. He takes a more clever approach for dismantling doubt in the use of language.

In PI#99 Wittgenstein voices an interlocutor who insists that, despite occasional openings for misunderstanding, sentences "must nevertheless have a definite sense.... An enclosure with a hole in it is as good as none." In response Wittgenstein asks: "But is this true?" He answers by suggesting concepts are as exact as they need to be. Fuzzy boundaries do not indicate lack of clarity but instead present the *measure of clarity* needed for the operations involved. If clarity falls short of requirements for certain purposes then a sharper boundary may be drawn. Wittgenstein's account of the specific requirements for clarity is worth quoting at length: "If I tell someone 'Stand roughly here'—may not this explanation work perfectly? ... But isn't it an inexact explanation?—Yes; why shouldn't we call it 'inexact'? Only let us understand what 'inexact' means. For it does not mean 'unusable.' . . Am I inexact when I do not give our distance from the sun to the nearest foot? ... No *single* ideal of exactness has been laid down" (PI#88).

Boundary haziness need not preclude functional clarity in the use of language. Wittgenstein concludes, "It is clear that every sentence in our language 'is in order as it is.' That is to say, we are not striving after an ideal, as if our ordinary vague sentences had not yet got a quite unexceptionable sense, and a perfect language awaited construction by us" (PI#98). Lack of clarity exists only in relation to an ideal of exactness and this ideal results from speculative philosophy irrelevant to the routine use of language in particular practical applications. Thus, Wittgenstein explicitly challenges the notion that "an indefinite boundary is not really a boundary at all" (PI#99).

Wittgenstein's challenge contrasts sharply with Derrida's admission, made famous in his "Afterword" in *Limited Inc*: "I confirm it: for me ... unless a distinction can be made rigorous and precise it isn't really a distinction" (1988b, 126). Wittgenstein and Derrida appear to differ sharply on this issue and it is not obvious why Derrida makes such a claim, especially given his numerous statements in apparent contradiction to it. For example, Derrida says, "Iterability blurs *a priori* the dividing line that passes between ... opposed terms ... 'corrupting' it if you like, contaminating it parasitically, qua limit.... The line delineating the margin can therefore *never be determined rigorously*, it is never pure and simple [emphasis added]" (1977, 210).

On the one hand, Derrida claims a distinction is not really a distinction unless it can be made "rigorous and precise" and, on the other hand, he claims the dividing line between opposed terms can "never be determined rigorously." When comparing these two claims, it would appear, to borrow Wittgenstein's metaphor, language has, for Derrida, gone "on holiday."

Sorting out this seeming contradiction requires exploring the broader context of Derrida's view of language. In another passage Derrida adds further weight to his claims about the rigor associated with the use of concepts: "Every concept that lays claim to any rigor whatsoever implies the alternative of 'all or nothing' ... Even the concept of 'difference of degree,' ... is, qua concept, determined according to the logic of all or nothing, of yes or no: differences of degree or non-difference of degree. It is impossible or illegitimate to form a philosophical concept outside this logic of all or nothing.... To this oppositional logic ... without which the distinction and the limits of a concept have no chance, I oppose nothing, least of all a logic of approximation" (1988b, 116–117).

But with these remarks Derrida appears to dig the hole even deeper for himself. The wording he uses, cited previously, of a "blurred" dividing line between opposed terms would seem compatible with the notion of "difference of degree." Blurred edges separate by virtue of degrees rather than sharp lines. Claiming the dividing line is "all or nothing," "yes or no," admits of no degrees.

In the next sentence, however, Derrida presents what may someday rival Wittgenstein's PI#201 passage as one of the most commented on in twentieth-century philosophy: "Rather I add a supplementary complication that calls for other concepts, for other thoughts beyond the concept and another form of 'general theory,' or rather another discourse, another 'logic' that accounts for the impossibility of concluding such a 'general theory.' This other discourse doubtless takes into account the conditions of this classical and binary logic, but it no longer depends entirely upon it" (1988b, 116–117).

This cryptic passage requires considerable deciphering. Derrida calls for "other concepts," "thoughts beyond the concept," another form of "general theory." And these calls lead to "another discourse," another "logic." He claims this other logic "takes into account" the classical binary logic, which means it does not simply replace this classical logic but instead *supplements* it. Derrida presents a contrast between classical discourse and another discourse, and yet this supplement does not, he argues, constitute a mere repetition of classical binary logic in the difference between supplement and traditional logic. Rather than standing in full opposition to each other, these two irreducible discourses appear to form a tension between each other.

When Derrida finds it impossible or illegitimate to form a concept outside the logic of all or nothing, he speaks of what he calls the "philosophical concept," which is to say the notion of concept understood within the context of the history of philosophical discourse. By this he means the framework imposed by classical philosophical binary logic, where concepts emerge through binaries such as essence/accident, good/evil, true/false, love/hate, etc. Even everyday concepts may be placed in accordance with this philosophical binary logic, such as table/non-table, chair/non-chair, tree/non-tree, etc. Derrida does not attempt to directly challenge or discard this philosophical binary structure. Instead, he shows how a supplemental logic necessarily accompanies this classical logic and challenges it *from within*.

In order to see the logic of this challenge and how it works in linguistic systems, it is helpful to do as Wittgenstein often does and illustrate the point by way of an analogous phenomenon in the realm of images. Consider, for example, what are called *stereograms*. A stereogram presents one picture in one glance and another picture in another glance. Stereograms flip between two-dimensional and three-dimensional images. The dual effect is often stunning, since the image data remain unchanged yet the image radically changes. The two images exist in superposition. Each can only be viewed one at a time and yet both images are "there" simultaneously. As discussed in the previous chapter, Derrida provides demonstrations of how such dual effects also figure prominently in language.

The analogy between stereogram images and words renders Derrida's view of the boundary issue surrounding concepts more intelligible. Consistent with this stereogram experience, it makes sense to say that concepts have a kind of "all or nothing" quality just as it makes sense to say that each image in a stereogram is clearly present. The two images are discrete and "rigorous" and yet each contaminates the other, since the "same" data produce both images. This is the sense in which Derrida uses the word "blurs" with respect to the "margins" of a given term, producing what he calls a "corruption" of one image by the other. The stereogram, the data field within the frame, gives rise to "blurring" effects because within it the two images inextricably merge and yet nevertheless appear, in alternating views, determined, discrete, and intelligible.

With this explanation in hand, it becomes possible to see that for Derrida concepts retain determinate rigor while the sign (the word) evoking them flips between alternative readings corresponding to different concepts. These concepts remain highly determined within the context of their writing but also exist in destabilized superposition through alternative readings of words—as in the example of *pharmakon*, which, in its embedded syntax, evokes more than one concept. These alternative readings each remain coherent, following rules of semiotic intelligibility, and consequently present instances of the *undecidability* mentioned in the previous chapter. Which reading ought to be favored becomes difficult to decide on the merits of the evidence of the text. This circumstance of superposition presents readers with alternating either/or and both/and experiences.

For Derrida, imagining concepts as indefinite or indeterminate tends to mislead. Instead, it remains more helpful to imagine concepts as having all the precision and rigor it is *possible* for them to have. It turns out that problems concerning rigor derive from the word, the signifier type, for concepts. The word cannot hold the concept. Only through words may concepts be articulated and explicated. But since words and the law of iterability to which they submit impose structural limits on explication, concepts cannot be fully articulated and yet do display the rigor sufficient to establish differences. This state of affairs, however, need not be taken to necessitate the view that ultimate meaning resides in an idealized noumenal realm of abstraction. Concepts (signifieds) and signifiers cannot ultimately be disentangled. As will more thoroughly be discussed in the chapters that follow, Derrida clearly forsakes recourse to classic versions of idealism to repair what might appear to be holes in the fabric of language.

The determinations of concepts are called upon through signifiers, the words and signs, which cannot preclude containing within them the seeds of their own deconstruction. No signifier remains immune to the potential flipping of alternative discretely different determinate meanings and concepts in any given context of use.

Some commentators on Derrida (e.g., Plotnitsky, 1994, 209–223), however, discuss the ways in which his tendency on particular occasions (e.g., Derrida, *Limited Inc*, 148–149) to separate the use of the word "indeterminacy" and "undecidability" may promote confusion. The flipping of meanings between alternative readings in particular contexts of use may justifiably be understood to qualify as a kind of indeterminacy. In these cases, meaning is not univocally determined. Nevertheless, Derrida is right to insist these cases are not adequately described as indeterminacy in the sense of vague approximations. The flipping phenomenon is a distinctly different kind of indeterminacy for which Derrida wants to reserve the word "undecidability"—to indicate the emergence of determined, different, viable alternatives. With adequate understanding of these distinctions, Derrida's use of "indeterminacy" and "undecidability" need not promote confusion.

Wittgenstein displays thorough awareness of the phenomenon of flipping, which he calls *changing of aspects*. He devotes many pages to a discussion of it in section xi of Part II of *Philosophical Investigations* (pp. 193–229). He understands it presents a significant problem for his way of viewing language and dwells on it because he sees it threatens the line he draws between rule following requiring processing (interpretation) and rule following requiring no processing.

Biographer, Ray Monk, explains, "It is [Wolfgang] Köhler's *Gestalt Psychology* (1929), and especially the chapter on 'Sensory Organization,' that Wittgenstein has in mind in much of his discussion [of the dual aspect phenomenon]" (1990, 508–509). The Gestalt view of perception proposes the perceiver organizes discrete sensory data into patterns. Monk provides the following example: "...we do not, for example, see three dots on a page; we form them into a triangle and see them as a whole, a Gestalt" (1990, 509). Köhler's work initiates not only a *dynamic* (as opposed to passive/receptive) theory of perception but also, on the basis of this perceptual understanding, a dynamic theory of human psychology. Monk explains further that this theory "...blurs the distinction between a physical object and a mental construct (an idea, etc.), and results in a rather confused notion of a somewhat shadowy *thing*" (1990, 512).

This "shadowy thing" is precisely what exasperates Wittgenstein because it challenges the way he posits language-users receive and respond to the meanings of words. The Gestalt theory grants a constructive role to the reading of sensory stimulation. For example, the model of perception consistent with different reactions by different individuals to the same visual stimuli provides the foundation for the Rorschach psychological test. This test has proven useful through the updated Holtzman inkblot technique as a diagnostic tool used by many psychologists in sorting personality and psychological differences among clients. Although the perceptual constructions of different persons may be manifestly similar in many respects, the element of construction insures a measure of diversity in perception as well. This measure of diversity signals what may be called a *cognitive* contribution in perceptual organization—the kind of "mental activity" or processing Wittgenstein views as routinely unnecessary in reading signs.

Due to the apparent challenge to his position posed by the Gestalt model, section xi of *Philosophical Investigations* addressing the dual aspect issue counts as a crucial part of the book. In this section, Wittgenstein struggles to defend his view. As Monk notes, "He did not ... find it easy to formulate a felicitous description of aspect-seeing that removed the confusions."

A careful examination of the differences between Wittgenstein and Derrida concerning the dual aspects phenomenon reinforces the contrast in their views of language. For purposes of illustration of the dual aspect, Wittgenstein makes use of the famous Jastrow duck-rabbit figure. At the outset he states there are "two uses," two different grammars, of the word "see." On the one hand, there is "seeing" and, on the other hand, there is "seeing as." The former counts for Wittgenstein as *response* and the latter as *interpretation*. Someone shown the Jastrow illustration and asked, "What is it?" might reply, "A picture-rabbit" or "A picture-duck." Wittgenstein stresses the point that viewers are not likely to respond, "I'm seeing it as a picture-rabbit" or "I'm seeing it as a picture-duck." Seeing is a response, seemingly involving no interpretation, whereas the "I'm seeing it as ..." formulation indicates an action involving processing.

To clarify this point Wittgenstein poses a simple question: Does the "now I am seeing it as ..." formulation make sense when, if in sight of a knife and fork, someone were to say "Now I am seeing this as a knife and a fork." This expression makes no more sense than to say "Now it's a fork" or "It can be a fork too." In summary he concludes: "One doesn't '*take*' what one knows as the cutlery at a meal *for* cutlery; any more than one ordinarily tries to move one's mouth as one eats, or aims at moving it" (PI, 195). Everyday "seeing" simply appears as seeing without the hesitation or qualification conveyed in the expression "now I am seeing it as...."

In summary, in section xi, Wittgenstein defends his position in two ways. First, instances of the flipping of meaning, the radical play of meaning, count as special cases of picture figures or figures of speech in which the combination of unusual internal features and contextual organization creates the potential for "noticing aspects"—seeing the same figure differently. These Jastrow type features are not, in Wittgenstein's view, part of the integral structure of *every* picture, concept, and text as they are in Derrida's view. And, second, even in the case of dual aspect images, the person looking at the image "sees" it immediately one way or the other rather than confronting a vague image, processing the data, and then "seeing it as" one way or the other. The seer may later see the dual aspect and thereby learn this image has more than one interpretation, which then merely qualifies it, in Wittgenstein's view, for inclusion in the class of images that are special cases. Only in certain cases may objects or scenes induce some confusion and require interpretation or explanation, but in most cases dual aspects are not in play. Regarding figures or pictures of the Jastrow type, Wittgenstein asks, "Do I really see something different each time, or do I only interpret what I see in a different way? I am inclined to say the former. But why?—To interpret is to think, to do something; seeing is a state" (PI, 212).

The situation is analogous in the case of applying words or reading signs. So also Wittgenstein distinguishes between thinking and seeing. *Thinking*, as used in this context, entails a process, a doing, whereas seeing happens. But Wittgenstein acknowledges this difference does not always readily present itself in the case of seeing aspects: "Here it is *difficult* to see that what is at issue is the fixing of concepts. A *concept* forces itself on one. (This is what you must not forget). For when should I call it a mere case of knowing, not seeing?—Perhaps when someone treats the picture as a working drawing, reads it like a blueprint" [emphasis in original] (PI, 204).

Nevertheless, as already noted, Wittgenstein was not content with his analysis of the aspect problem and continued to have doubts about his position. For example, Monk cites Wittgenstein admitting his difficulties to his friend Maurice Drury: "Now you try and say what is involved in seeing something as something. It is not easy. These thoughts I am now working on are as hard as granite" (1990, 514). With this admission Wittgenstein makes a significant concession to Derrida's position.

Turning to Derrida, every sign not only invites but also requires interpretation and every use of language records an act of interpretation. This does not mean that in every situation solicitation or oscillation of meanings necessarily consciously appears to language-users, but nevertheless reading signs always involves interpretation, even when it does not seem so. Signs present contextually embedded data, which cannot manifest in a univocal pattern due to the dynamic nature of perception (reading) in reaction to moving (differing and deferring) contexts.

What for Wittgenstein counts as an exemplar of a special case—the Jastrow image—counts for Derrida as another exemplar of the essential, irreducible consequence of the structural constraints befalling all material images and signs. The stereogram effect, the Jastrow effect, the flipping phenomenon, exists not only in special cases in language but *necessarily* in every case, as a consequence of the law of iteration, an essential structure of all sign systems.

Although the notion that image-signs or word-signs can be read without intervening interpretive processing in any given context of use emerges as a notion thoroughly challenged and repudiated by Derrida, for Wittgenstein nothing could be more necessary and certain than that interpretation of this kind does not take place in the ordinary use of language. Without this necessity, the process of communication slides into doubt and the threat of miscommunication remains present in any and every instance of the use of signs. This state of affairs regarding communication presents a primary obstacle Wittgenstein's work aims to dismantle and yet for Derrida nothing could be more inevitable. And, as will become clearer in the chapter on time, nothing, in Derrida's view, could be more desirable. In this respect, Wittgenstein and Derrida operate with fundamentally different *attitudes* toward language and communication, which also correspond to very different underlying metaphysical orientations, as is explored in detail in Chapter 11.

Whether a given use is conventional or unconventional, the meaning of the word or text is, for Derrida, not simply clear or partly clear, vague or less vague. Instead, meaning is *divided*. Meaning exists in superposition, which may present sense in significantly different readings supported by context. This division is potentially subject to transformation as context changes, as when the duck aspect of the duck/rabbit figure readily emerges after the figure is presented alongside the written word "duck." A change in context may alter a particular dual aspect of the figure but such changes cannot render the data immune to dual effects and may also introduce new dual effects. Such effects may be overlooked but not eliminated.

Given these differences between Wittgenstein and Derrida on the issue of interpretation, a crucial question emerges: What means may exist for resolving differences regarding an act of naming or the application of a word in a particular context where the naming or the application carry with them significant but different consequences? For both Wittgenstein and Derrida, rules and concepts cannot be made fully explicable in discourse (even though, for Derrida, this assumption frames the idealization of concepts). But do their respective philosophical positions regarding language establish an understanding of meaning in such a way as to adequately prepare for *justification* of the application of words? This question is explored in the next chapter.

6

Justification

I don't know, it just looks like a yard (BB, 11).

The expression "This is what we do" occurs often in commentaries on Wittgenstein's work in relation to discussions of the issue of rule following. The expression has gained favor as a shorthand way of referencing the substance of Wittgenstein's famous "my spade is turned" metaphor introduced in PI#217. In this section the word *justification* (*Rechtfertigung*) also makes an important appearance: "'How am I able to obey a rule?'—if this is not a question about causes, then it is about the justification [*Rechtfertigung*] for my following the rule in the way I do. If I have exhausted the justifications [*Begründungen*] I have reached bedrock, and my spade is turned. Then I am inclined to say: "This is simply what I do."

Here the words *Rechtfertigung* and *Begründungen* are used interchangeably and are each translated by Anscombe as "justification." In other places in *Philosophical Investigations* the word *explanation* (*Erklärung*) is used in an equivalent sense. The substance of Wittgenstein's orientation toward justifications regarding the use of words and the following of rules traces back to his methodological grounding of the learning of meaning through the act of presenting examples. Teaching by means of examples alone would seem to be only a partial method of teaching, one leaving a learner to fill many gaps. Wittgenstein's imaginary interlocutor objects in PI#209, "But then doesn't our understanding reach beyond all the examples? ... is that *all*? Isn't there a deeper explanation; or mustn't at least the understanding of the explanation be deeper?" Wittgenstein, in the role of the trainer, replies, "Well, have I myself a deeper understanding? Have I got more than I give in the explanation?" This response reinforces his view expressed in PI#208, "I shall teach him to use the words by means of *examples* and by *practice*.—And when I do this I do not communicate less to him than I know myself."

Here Wittgenstein dispenses with the notion that beneath examples lies a bedrock understanding and that such bedrock provides an ultimate layer of justification for how a rule of use is taught and followed. The bedrock, such as it is, relies on training, practice, and custom rather than the logic of reasons. The reasons that may be offered present superficial layers merely deferring rather than providing justification. This much Wittgenstein makes clear in PI#211: "How can he know how he is to continue a pattern by himself—whatever instruction you give him?—Well, how do I know?—If that means 'Have I reasons?' the answer is: my reasons will soon give out. And then I shall act, without reasons."

Much of the discussion in Chapter 3 also relates to this issue along with the notion that following a rule is much like that of a "mechanism" where "a button is pressed and an indicator plate appears" (BB, 89). Where something like a mechanism operates, it makes as much sense to ask for justifications or reasons as it does to ask why someone reports seeing the color blue when looking at the sky.

The passages from *Philosophical Investigations* cited above concerning justifications and reasons, however, may appear inconsistent with a line of argument delivered several sections later in the text. When Wittgenstein continues the assault on the role of mental activity in signification by exploring examples of sensation terminology, he simultaneously introduces a different slant on the notion of justification. This shift regarding justification occurs in the series of sections, beginning at PI#258, relating to the example of a diarist who wants to make a written record of the occurrence of a particular sensation he repeatedly experiences.

The diarist cannot give the sensation he wants to monitor an adequate discursive definition so he gives it a kind of ostensive definition by writing the sign "S" while concentrating on the sensation. He then writes this sign in his diary every day he has the sensation. In this way he forms a connection between the sign and the sensation and in doing so constructs what would appear to be a *private* code for tracking the experience, for no one else knows the meaning of "S."

Wittgenstein then launches a critique of this "S" code in PI#261 and this is where his shift in the need for justification appears. "What reason [*Grund*] have we for calling 'S' the sign for a *sensation*? For 'sensation' is a word of our common language, not of one intelligible to me alone. So the use of this word stands in need of a justification [*Rechtfertigung*] which everybody understands." When Wittgenstein says "everybody," this also includes the diarist for reasons that will become apparent.

This assertion appears to contradict what Wittgenstein says elsewhere about justification. At one point no justification is found to be necessary in the use of words and now, in this circumstance, justification is necessary. Understanding what has changed requires placing this remark in greater context.

If the diarist chooses to label what he wants to keep track of as a "sensation," then Wittgenstein sees the need for "justification which everybody understands." And this need for justification would not change if the diarist prefers not to label what he wants to track with a notation as specific as "sensation." Choosing any other word leaves the same problem, as Wittgenstein notes in PI#261: "And it would not help either to say that it need not be a *sensation*; that when he writes 'S,' he has *something*—and that is all that can be said. 'Has' and 'something' also belong to our common language." But then Wittgenstein may be asked why, when using a word in a *private* diary, would there be the need for a justification everybody understands?

If the diarist intends for his record to be intelligible only to himself and were to use an invented mark unlike anything in any known language or code, then it would seem he might succeed in creating a thoroughly private code. However, according to Wittgenstein, the necessity for justification remains, because every code must have a means of verification, otherwise, through failure of memory, it may lapse into incoherence. Wittgenstein says that where justification is needed "it must also be one for someone else" (PI#378). And this will be the case because, according to him, "...justification consists in appealing to something independent" (PI#265). And independent justification will serve to justify use for the diarist as well as *all* users.

The notation, like any sign—whether it is invented or taken from a common language—must be *potentially* accessible (discernable) to *all* in order to be accessible to *any*. If this were not the case, the notation could not serve as an accessible record even to the keeper of the diary because in the same way the sign remains open and functional to the keeper so also it remains potentially open to everyone else. Also, if it were possible for the diarist's record to remain truly private, to be a "private language" that "no one else understands" (PI#269), it would have no avenue of justification apart from the diarist himself, which is to say his memory. But the diarist's memory, with its possible lapses, is precisely what the system of notation is devised to overcome.

Using another example, Wittgenstein explains the growing difficulty of justification in a further exchange with his imagined interlocutor: "Let us imagine a table (something like a dictionary) that exists only in our imagination. A dictionary can be used to justify the translation of a word X by a word Y. But are we also to call it a justification if such a table is to be looked up only in the imagination?—'Well, yes, that is a subjective justification.'" This is where Wittgenstein interjects to say, "—But justification consists in appealing to something independent." His interlocutor, however, is not convinced: "But surely I can appeal from one memory to another. For example, I don't know if I have remembered the time of departure of a train right and to check it I call to mind how a page of the time-table looked. Isn't it the same here?" But Wittgenstein shows why this is of no use: "—No; for this process has got to produce a memory which is actually *correct*. If the mental image of the time-table could not itself be *tested* for correctness, how could it confirm the correctness of the first memory? (As if someone were to buy several copies of the morning paper to assure himself that what it said was true.)" (PI#265).

The diary keeper may apply common words like "sensation" in the course of recording and tracking "something" but that "something" will not *reliably* count as "something" even to the diary keeper without a way of assessing it independent of one person and one memory. And making a mark or a note to himself as a way of reminding himself of what the notation in the diary means is itself subject to the same difficulty as the diary notation. As Wittgenstein remarks in PI#202, "And to *think* one is obeying a rule is not to obey a rule." The diarist may *think* he is tracking his "something" accurately and reliably but he may be in error and not realize it. Without a way to test for correctness independent of his own judgment, the diarist cannot be assured of the reliability of the notation.

For independent confirmation to be possible in the case of the diarist, the tracked sensation must also have an observable behavioral component, other than the report, "I am having this sensation." In other words, in order to acquire meaning (for the diarist or for anyone), the sensation must itself have a component that is also of the nature of a sign, which is to say an expression that is of a piece with the sensation and observable to others. Where there is nothing to read, there can be no justification for naming. And where there may be signs to read for one person, such as a sensation, but no corresponding public symptoms of the sensation, then there also can be no justification for naming. For the reasons Wittgenstein provides, subjective judgment is not sufficient for sustaining meaning.

Of the two uses of justification discussed, the first use occurs in demonstrating that following rules for which one has been trained calls for no justification because what justification there may be only exists in the form of a native language and the training in its use. The second use of justification occurs in demonstrating that the practice and grammar of rule following, even when conducted privately, implies and requires a *public* test for rule following. Without reliable justification, which Wittgenstein defines as independent of subjective assessment and therefore as publicly accessible and verifiable agreement in rule following, a private language or code must collapse.

Consistent with this conclusion, which entails that signs are no more inherently private than keys to locks, Wittgenstein's analysis leads to the further conclusion that the privacy of any purported "private language" or "secret code" remains only *contingently* private rather than *structurally* private. A language or code understood only by one person is contingently private. A language or code capable only *ever* of being understood by one person is logically or structurally private and it is this kind of system that would appear to be impossible, which is to say, functionally useless as a code even to its user. A sign's usefulness as a sign requires a means of justification or verification open to inspection by anyone and everyone. These issues concerning the question of private language and private rule following are explored in greater detail in Chapter 7.

Returning to justification, Wittgenstein's approach may be summarized as follows:

1. Ordinarily justification in the use of terms is unnecessary because language is a public exchange and language-users operate from training not reasoning. This is how we are all trained, so this is what we do. (e.g., see *BB*, p. 11)

2. In attempts at private use of terms, including privately invented terms, justification becomes necessary because the use of a private code still requires independent tests for rule following in order for the inventor to know that the code invented is being reliably used (e.g., see PI#258 and surrounding).

Wittgenstein elaborates on this first use of justification when, in a passage from *The Blue Book*, he requests the reader consider the process of estimating a length by the eye. He stresses the importance of realizing there are many different processes that might be called "estimating by the eye" and lists four examples where in each case a different length is being estimated. In the first instance someone estimates the height of a building by supposing a story to be about fifteen feet and concluding it is sixty feet high because it has four stories. In the second case, someone estimates a length from a distance by claiming to know what a yard looks like at that distance and thereby concludes the length in question to be four yards. In the third case, someone imagines the height of a tall person reaching to a certain point and then concludes the length in question must be about six feet above ground. In the fourth case, someone looks at the length in question and simply says, "I don't know; it just looks like a yard." Concerning the last response, Wittgenstein remarks: "This last case is likely to puzzle us. If you ask 'what happened in this case when the man estimated the length?' the correct answer may be: 'he looked at the thing and said it looks one yard long.' This may be all that has happened" (BB, 11).

In the first three cases, explanations are provided for the estimated length, but what is the point of the last case? It would seem justifications given in the preceding cases count as ornamentation inessential to the act of naming and that the last case shows all that remains sufficient for naming. Again, this passage illustrates Wittgenstein's insistence that no interpretation, calculation, or reasoning processes need *necessarily* intervene between words and their application. Looking, seeing—scanning, naming—this set of events need be all that occurs.

In the use of justification, as given in point #2 above, justification functions as the means by which any language or code, once established by a person for their private use, acquires reliability. In other words, a private language that remains entirely private is not a viable language. Every language, in order to remain functional, must necessarily be public or available to a public if the language users want to insure consistent and reliable use. Since a reliable and structurally private language appears impossible, then justification in that instance becomes irrelevant. Thus, every language is fundamentally public and the routine use of a public language requires no justification.

Despite his explanation, Wittgenstein's account of justification may ultimately seem unsatisfying, leaving the impression that it differs little from the case of the man who buys "several copies of the morning paper to assure himself that what it said was true." Ought the notion that justification remains unnecessary in the public use of language serve as the basic description of the structure for acts of naming? The rhetorical theorist, John Macksoud, suspects Wittgenstein's line of thought underlying his examples leads to the "…penetrating epistemological question whether there need be *any* justification for the process of naming" (1973, 186). And Wittgenstein consistently answers through his examples: No justification necessary.

Consider another instance. Wittgenstein presents an example in the *Brown Book* where a person "B" is shown a fabric sample and then asked by person "A" to bring a matching bolt of fabric from among several bolts in another room. Wittgenstein then imagines several possibilities for how B might accomplish this task and these all involve using a "memory image" of the fabric. (He then lists another case, which he numbers 14c): "B goes to the shelf *without a memory image*, looks at five bolts one after the other, takes the fifth bolt from the shelf." And the fifth bolt, it turns out, is the correct fabric. Wittgenstein's interlocutor wonders how, by what process, this correct selection happens: "But surely in case 14c) B acted entirely automatically. If all that happened was really what was described there, he did not know why he chose the bolt he did choose. He had no reason for choosing it. If he chose the right one, he did it as a machine might have done it."

Considering a possible alternative explanation, Wittgenstein then asks, "Now what would such a reason which justified his choice and made

it non-automatic be like?" He answers that the opposite of automatic comparing would be having before the mind's eye a "memory image" and then
having a "specific feeling" of not being able to distinguish between the
memory image and the fabric on the fifth bolt. This specific feeling connects the memory image and the sample and provides the "reason" for
the choice. Then Wittgenstein asks, "But if so, what connects this specific
experience with either?" In other words, how is this non-automatic experience, this feeling, this connection, distinguished from automatic recognition? In some particular cases a hesitation or a thought might occur (such
as, "Is this right?"), but does that necessarily change the choice from automatic to non-automatic? And Wittgenstein concludes, "...the distinction
between automatic and non-automatic appears no longer clear-cut and
final as it did at first."

The non-automatic alternative corresponds with the notion that
something like decision actually occurs, involving processes like thinking, evaluating, and having reasons. Wittgenstein does not deny that in
some particular cases something like this may occur, but his illustrations
are intended to show that it is superficial and unnecessary in accounting
for what happens in ordinary cases. Asking again, "How has he recognized
it [the fifth fabric bolt] as the right one?" Wittgenstein answers, "There
need not have been a reason for the choice. A reason is a step preceding the
step of the choice. But why should every step be preceded by another one?"
(BB, 87–88).

In response to Wittgenstein's line of thought, Macksoud asks the
logical next question: "If at the end of the chain of justification, we seem
to have no justification, what need have we for it at the beginning of the
chain?" By grounding meaning in use and by grounding use in the training or conditioning of "automatic" responses, Wittgenstein appears to
have dismantled the chain of justifications to the point where Macksoud
suggests the chain might as well end with this: "We need not name or judge
by criteria *at all*" (1973, 187). Instead, we may say, "This is what we do."

If the application of words transpires in ordinary circumstances by
way of automatic associations between rules and applications, then such
mechanization effectively sidelines the need for reasons in acts of naming. Even though Wittgenstein admits in the discussion of the fabric bolt
example that the distinction between automatic and non-automatic choice
appears "no longer clear-cut and final as it did at first," he then uses this
cloudiness to press for the conclusion that the non-automatic process
remains ornamental and, like an idle gear, functionally inert. Therefore, it
may be dismissed as irrelevant to the normal use of words.

At a reductive level, it's possible to appreciate the force of Wittgenstein's reasoning. I see an object in the room, a chair, and request of

another person, "Please sit in the chair." Without hesitation he sits in the chair. But to see the potential problems inherent in this automatic model of word use, recall Macksoud's example cited in the previous chapter: "I invite you to sit down on a computer." Aside from illustrating limits to the automatic model, this example illustrates the point that even were it the case that training in the use of words involved learning and using conventional criteria, anomalies in *applications* of criteria, as Macksoud admonishes, "cannot be settled simply by stating the criteria" (2009, 45). Here Wittgenstein might respond with what he says in PI#242: "If language is to be a means of communication there must be agreement [*Übereinstimmung*] not only in the definitions but also (queer as this may sound) in judgments [*den Urteilen*]." But can training through the use of a limited number of examples insure agreement in judgments across multiple future uses of words, even routinely used words?

For example, consider the phrase "reasonable doubt" as used in courts of law. These are two very common words most people encounter regularly and, when placed together, their meaning, it would seem, ought not to raise reasonable doubt concerning the meaning of "reasonable doubt." Despite instructions from a judge on how to understand this phrase, despite even a written list of criteria, members of a jury may differ in their judgments about how to apply the criteria. Perhaps they are instructed that "guilty beyond a reasonable doubt" means: "no other logical explanation can be derived from the facts of the case except that the defendant committed the crime." Suppose then the jury requests criteria for "logical." They are then provided a list of synonyms such as "sensible, rational, practical, plausible, possible," and the like. Some members of a jury may then read "logical" as "possible" such that it is possible another explanation can be derived from the facts, so it is therefore reasonable to conclude the defendant is not guilty. Other jurors may disagree and arrive at a different understanding by reading "logical" as meaning "plausible" and conclude no other plausible explanation can be derived from the facts, so the defendant is guilty. Still others may find the distinctions between "possible," "plausible," and "practical" confusing and of little help. Another juror when asked how he applied the principle of reasonable doubt might respond by saying, "I don't know. I just did it.'"

Regarding Wittgenstein's account of the relationship between rules and applications, definitions and judgments, Macksoud advises that Wittgenstein's examples serve as, "...a wedge to introduce the notion that although we like to think we have reasons for behaving (in this case naming) as we do—that we are rational—we may be, in common cases, linguistic automata" (1973, 188). But Macksoud advocates for the attitude that to whatever extent humans may indeed be or become linguistic automata, nothing in language or the learning of language need enforce that outcome, that the necessity of any such thing is largely an illusion supported by all too easy habits of thought and attitudes toward language use.

As a rhetorical theorist attentive to the uses of language to appeal, persuade, entertain, and inform, Macksoud extolls the deep resources of language: "...external circumstances need not *necessarily* limit the ways in which we name our perceptions" (2009, 45). Macksoud continues to this conclusion: "...conventions don't apply themselves ... there is choice within the conventions ... it is we, and not the rules, who choose, no matter how we may try to blind ourselves to the fact of choice" (2009, 51). And if such were the case, it would seem the role of justification would remain highly relevant.

Similarly, Wittgenstein also subscribes to the view that nothing in context, including overt expression of criteria, can *guarantee* a particular application of a sign (the rule following paradox). But here he differs from Macksoud in the belief that the training, which creates the routine link between rules and applications, largely displaces the need for justification in the ordinary use of language. For Macksoud, ordinary uses of language—whatever "ordinary" might here mean—constitute precisely where vigilant attention to the need for justification must very often be focused. Where such attention is not focused, behaving like an automaton becomes automatic and someone else's justifications, whether automatic or calculated, impose themselves in ways and in contexts they perhaps should not.

For Macksoud, the interesting question concerning the problem of naming is not "whether there *is* justification in fact for an act of naming, but whether we *ought* to look for and generate justifications and where and how we ought to look for them." The crucial question is axiological rather than analytical or empirical. Macksoud explains further:

> Even if Wittgenstein's argument is flawless in reasoning and solidity on the grounds on which it rests, even if his examples are correctly extrapolated from our ordinary experience and are paradigmatic of the use of all language, one may still hold that.... Wittgenstein has missed the meaningful question of language-using. Even if we are deceiving ourselves that it [generating justifications] makes a difference ... this is an illusion that serves us well if we but consider the alternative attitude. Ought we really to allow jurors ... to conclude [their work] ... without at least some deliberative process in which justifications are generated so that their judgments will be of an order different from "I don't know, I just think so"? [1973, 189].

While it may be the case that not every instance of naming carries a weight similar to that of a jury in deliberation, situations in the course of daily life do often require acts of naming exceeding anything like Wittgenstein's model of automatic application. Did someone just lie to me, or did they forget what they had done? Was what he said an insult or a joke? Did he just make a promise or a threat? Should I think of her actions as cooperative or competitive?

Judgments (applications) rather than definitions are constantly in question and agreement in judgments with others often far from what can be anticipated. Wittgenstein may largely be right when he says in PI#241 that speakers in the same language "agree in the *language* they use" in the sense that they understand basic rules of use for words (their definitions) but he is not largely right when he says, as in PI#242, that if there is to be communication there must be agreement in judgments if this is taken to indicate that agreement in judgments is to be expected and communication to be routine. Communication may fail due to different judgments, perhaps more often than it succeeds, and it may in many cases not be possible in the immediate situation to precisely know the difference. Concerning the question of communication, Ruth Sonderegger appropriately remarks, "In this respect communication is an expression of the fact that we cannot start with the assumption that we agree (in every respect) when we use the same language.... The contention that interpretation is not a significant part of our linguistic behaviour constitutes a variant of the thesis that understanding is always already present, and variations in it trifling. It is as though only the shared parts of understanding constitute language" (1997, 197–198).

Turning now to Derrida, how would he respond to Wittgenstein on the question of justification and to Macksoud's critique of Wittgenstein? To begin, returning to the question of interpretation, Derrida responds to critics who fasten on his badly understood expression "there is nothing outside of the text." Extending to the metaphysical level, Derrida remarks: "That does not mean all referents are suspended, denied, or enclosed in a book, as people have claimed, or have been naïve enough to believe and to have accused me of believing. But it does mean that every referent, all reality has the structure of a differential trace, and that one cannot refer to this 'real' except in an interpretive experience" (1988b, 148). To repeat: All references to the "real" transpire through an *interpretive* experience, which means, for Derrida, the real experienced *as signs*. And it would be expected that an account of language as invariably interpretive aligns with the attitude that no use of signs ought to be regarded as inherently exempt from the need for justification. Derrida's understanding of signs precludes responding to their applications with: No justification necessary.

As would be predicted, Derrida confirms the importance of justification throughout his work and does so prominently in his discussion of sovereignty in *Rogues* when he says, "As soon as I speak to the other, I submit to the law of giving reason(s), I share a virtually universalizable medium, I divide my authority" (2005, 101). For Derrida, "giving reasons" to the other—justification—rises to the level of a "law" rather than polite deference or refined protocol because the other, as person, emits a call just as does the other of the divided identity of the sign. Leaving the call unanswered obviates the structure of interaction as it does the structure of the sign. In an interview conducted in 1993, Derrida emphasizes the importance of giving reasons and of justification in the broad context of public life:

> I insist on these two motifs, *the public space* and the *principle of reason*, as I have often done. The media and academia have the duty to respect, as their conditions, the duty and the right on which they are founded, the principle of reason and the spirit of the Enlightenment ... which is to say among so many other things, their *public* destination, as Kant used to say, their belonging to the public sphere where one is required to give one's reasons, to justify one's discourse, to present an argument, and so on [1995, 427].

However, Derrida and his deconstructive practice are often accused of undermining the basis for justification of any and every use of language because the "play" of signifiers championed in deconstruction leads to the consequence that "anything goes." But Derrida responds, "I have never accepted saying, or encouraging others to say, just anything at all" (1988b, 145).

Deconstruction embraces the full range of what can be considered relevant to justification by way of opening context as broadly as possible, beyond "the book" and into the world. This opening of and openness to context is consistent with the view that language-users must be prepared to assign justification a prominent role in discourse, discussion, and conversation. Affirming justification accords value to the other by acknowledging the call of the other and, similarly, assigns value to truth by acknowledging its call. Derrida's remarks in the following passage illustrate the value of truth in tension with the "other" of context: "The value of truth is never contested or destroyed in my writings, but only reinscribed in more powerful, larger, more stratified contexts ... within interpretive contexts" (1988b, 146). Derrida's and Wittgenstein's views on truth are discussed in greater detail in Chapter 13.

For Wittgenstein, however, the call for justification ought instead to be viewed as a symptom that something is wrong. In most such cases the solution to the puzzle may be found through an examination of the language game in which a confusion may have arisen requiring justification. And this process remains consistent with one of Wittgenstein's most prominent maxims: "We must do away with all explanation, and description alone must take its place" (PI#109).

But can it really be the case that in his complex and thoughtful works Wittgenstein marginalizes explanation, as if cases of difficulty in applying and reading signs rarely arise and, when they do, are easily resolved by recourse to description? For example, consider Wittgenstein's argument in this passage, which presents the justification for the use of a name and, once again, begins with an exchange with an imagined interlocutor:

> Suppose I give this explanation [here the German word is *erkläre*, in which case this phrase may be read as, "Suppose I declare"]: "I take 'Moses' to mean the man, if there was such a man, who led the Israelites out of Egypt, whatever he was called then and whatever he may or may not have done besides."— But similar doubts to those about "Moses" are possible about the words of this explanation (what are you calling "Egypt," whom the "Israelites" etc.?). Nor would these questions come to an end when we got down to words like "red," "dark," "sweet."—"But then how does an explanation [*Erklärung*] help me understand, if after all it is not the final one? In that case the explanation is never completed; so I still don't understand what he means, and never shall!"— As though an explanation as it were hung in the air unless supported by another one. Whereas an explanation may indeed rest on another one that has been given, but none stands in need of another—unless we require it to prevent a misunderstanding. One might say: an explanation serves to remove or to avert a misunderstanding—one, that is, that would occur but for the explanation; not every one that I can imagine [PI#87].

In cases where the reason why a word is applied may not be clear, Wittgenstein grants that an explanation or justification may be useful. But notice that he says, "Nor would these questions come to an end when we get down to words like 'red,' 'dark,' 'sweet.'" Apparently, such common words and their uses may similarly fall prey to the endless explanation regress. The meaning of any word as used, including quite common words, can be doubted, but once such doubts enter, an explanation free fall begins, which Wittgenstein regards as ultimately pointless. He halts this regress by asserting of explanation: "…none stands in need of another—*unless we require it to prevent a misunderstanding*" [emphasis added]. But the kind of misunderstanding requiring such explanation will not be a normal occurrence:

> It is only in normal cases that the use of a word is clearly prescribed; we know, are in no doubt, what to say in this or that case. The more abnormal the case, the more doubtful it becomes what we are to say. And if things were quite different from what they actually are—if there were for instance no characteristic expression of pain, of fear, of joy; if rule became exception and exception rule; or if both become phenomena of roughly equal frequency—this would make our normal language-games lose their point [PI#142].

Language-games begin to lose their point for Wittgenstein to the extent explanations and justifications become routinely necessary; this necessity then emerges as a symptom of lack of agreement in judgments.

However, the problem Derrida brings to attention, as drawn out in previous chapters, resides not so much in language games losing their point but rather in determining *which* language game or language games may be in play in any given situation. The notion of language games evolved for Wittgenstein through a progressive examination of the most primitive kinds of language interactions, such as those built up around teaching and learning a language and in giving and following simple commands. These interactions, which Wittgenstein calls "primitive language-games," serve as his models for understanding the workings of more complex language games. However, as a result, Wittgenstein routinely accords to language games a discrete quality rendering unproblematic not merely the question of boundaries between them but also rendering unproblematic the potential overlap and partial convergence of different language games within any given speech act.

Determining which language games are in play and which words naturally fit within which games appear to be rather simple, automatic determinations for Wittgenstein. But if anything can be learned from Derrida, it would be that identifying the local context (what Wittgenstein refers to as the language game) is, in any given instance, more complex than assumed. This complication raised by Derrida throws a wrench into the machinery Wittgenstein understands as the grasping of non-interpretive meaning and, consequently, the accompanying presumption of the irrelevance of the need for justification in ordinary language use.

For Derrida, the ordinary remains potentially extraordinary insofar as what passes for the ordinary may conceal the extraordinary in the otherness always haunting the repetition of signs. Against Wittgenstein's view that confusions wrought by words used outside the grammar of the appropriate language game may be remedied by returning the use of such words to their domestic grammar, Derrida demonstrates that such confusion may not so easily be relieved because the language game in play cannot present itself as merely self-evident. Furthermore, the notion of a domestic grammar to which words belong belies the metaphoric substrate, the see-this-as structure, of word use. For Derrida, words do not have a home grammar to which they inherently belong. Instead, they have only a network of differences within which they operate and around which users develop varying levels of acumen and agility in conveying and assigning sense and meaning.

For Derrida, the issue of communication is also not confined merely to clarity and clarification. Different expressions and readings betray different judgments and different judgments align with different perspectives. Different perspectives may intentionally or unintentionally advance one agenda over another. As both Wittgenstein and Derrida agree, no use of language is neutral. Consequently, judgments may not be well received if justified by expressions such as "This is what we do," for it may well be asked, "Who is 'we'?" And in many cases it may be difficult to separate "this is what we do" from "this is what I insist we do." The potential for slippage into the fallacy of argument from authority gains salience when considering the extent to which it may be impossible to exclude social, political, ethical, and aesthetic factors from communication.

Returning to the issue raised at the end of the previous chapter, the relationship Wittgenstein sees between use and justification leaves little doubt that in his modeling of language the role of justification recedes to a degree warranting concerns about how well this general orientation may promote an attitude toward sign operations sufficient for optimal performance of these operations. And Wittgenstein's modeling of language and the role of justification may also promote an attitude inadequate for anticipating the routine capacity for these operations to fall short of desired performance, leading language-users into difficulties that may range from the relatively mundane to the thoroughly catastrophic. For these reasons, Derrida's approach presents itself—due to its deeper admonitory insights—as a more proficient approach to language-using and sign operations in general. His approach advocates a kind of doubt about communication cutting across this or that instance to include vigilance toward language and the use of signs permeating down to the fundamental structure of communication. This kind of doubt need not be confused with forms of nihilistic abandonment and despair regarding communication. Instead, it ought to be understood as the deepest affirmation of communicative processes because, without this penetrating doubt prompted by the fundamental structure of communication, there would be, as Derrida has demonstrated, no possibility for communication at all. Further potential benefits and insights deriving from Derrida's approach come more fully into view through the discussions in the chapters of Parts II and III.

PART II

Wittgenstein and Derrida in Contrasting Terms

7

Public and Private

Philosophical Investigations presents what has come to be known as the Private Language Argument. Wittgenstein identifies what counts for him as a "private language" in PI#243 when he asks, "But could we also imagine a language in which a person could write down or give vocal expression to his inner experiences—his feelings, moods, and the rest—for his private use? … The individual words of this language are to refer to what can only be known to the person speaking; to his immediate private sensations. So another person cannot understand the language."

The wording, "so another person cannot understand the language," suggests a language not *possible* for anyone else to understand. For such a language to be radically private in the sense of being beyond decryption, it must have a certain feature. This is why Wittgenstein imagines this language as existing only within the sphere of reference to private sensations or what may be called private objects. Unlike physical objects, so-called private objects have no point of shared contact or shared accessibility. Code breaking may only be achieved when there is shared access to both words and objects of reference. A code devised by one person and referring only to private sensations offers no point of adequate access for deciphering, assuming these sensations or inner experiences are given no outward expression apart from the signs used to reference them. As such, the private language Wittgenstein imagines is not merely contingently private. He imagines a structurally private language—one incapable of decoding by another person.

Probing deeper, Wittgenstein asks in PI#256: "Now, what about the language which describes my inner experiences and which only I myself can understand?" He answers in a manner consistent with the Beetle Box Analogy of PI#293 when he says, "The essential thing about private experience is really not that each person possesses his own exemplar, but that nobody knows whether other people have *this* or something else." No one knows what may be inside anyone else's "box." And so Wittgenstein adds, "The assumption would thus be possible—though unverifiable—that one section of mankind had one sensation of red and another section another." This circumstance then invites the response he offers in PI#274: "It is as if when I uttered the word ['red'] I cast a sidelong glance at the private sensation, as it were in order to say to myself: I know all right what I mean by it." In which case he wonders whether, in the example of the word "red," "everyone should really have another word ... to mean his *own* sensation of red" (PI#273). But then a question yet remains concerning the extent to which the connections between words and referents in such private referencing may be reliably meaningful even for its creator.

At the point of PI#243, Wittgenstein has already established a position regarding what he calls "obey[ing] a rule 'privately'" by providing a compelling reason for the inadmissibility of such when he says in PI#202: "Hence it is not possible to obey a rule 'privately': otherwise thinking one was obeying a rule would be the same thing as obeying it." The combination of PI#202 and PI#243 makes the argument that if using a language requires following rules and it is not possible to obey a rule privately, then a structurally private language is not possible. But is it true that a rule cannot be followed privately, especially a rule relating signs to personal sensations?

In private rule following, the rule follower becomes the sole arbiter of whether words are used correctly and reliably. In such a case, obeying a rule cannot be distinguished from thinking one obeys a rule. For Wittgenstein, however, this situation affords no possibility for verification of rules being followed. As he notes in PI#265, whether a rule has been followed "consists in appealing to something independent." Independent of what? Independent of *subjective* judgment—as, for example, when accessing sensations or the contents of memory. If thinking one follows a rule cannot count as following a rule, then what Wittgenstein means by "independent" must exclude any form of subjective assessment. Granting as much, the possibility of a reliable, structurally private language referring to the private sensations of the language creator must be ruled out. But is the ground for such a conclusion consistent with the idea of a private language?

At this point in analyzing the possibilities for the existence of a private language, the experiment, discussed in Chapter 1, becomes instructive again. Here Wittgenstein challenges the reader to try thinking a thought, such as "It will probably rain tomorrow," without the words, as if humming the melody of a song without singing the lyrics. In response, it was suggested that this experiment fails because no demonstration of successfully accomplishing this feat could be offered other than the subjective response, "Yes, I did this. Now what?" The case of a private language presents an analogous situation. The claim there can be no such thing as a private language may be met with the response, "But I use a language every day, which no one else can understand, for tracking my inner experiences and sensations and I am confident I use it consistently and accurately." How may Wittgenstein prove this claim to be false? In defense of such a claim, his own analysis may perhaps be used against him. Compare two lines of reasoning he presents in PI#246 and PI#258.

In #246 Wittgenstein says, "It can't be said of me at all (except perhaps as a joke) that I *know* I am in pain. What is it supposed to mean—except perhaps that I *am* in pain?" He then concludes, "The truth is: it makes sense to say about other people that they doubt whether I am in pain; but not to say it about myself." Here Wittgenstein appears to grant that each person serves as the arbiter of the presence and quality of particular experienced sensations and that it makes no sense to use the grammar of "know" in expressions such as: "Does he really *know* if he is in pain?"

Shifting to PI#258—the example of the diarist who wants to note in a calendar the recurrence of a certain sensation—the diarist may form "a kind of ostensive definition" by concentrating his attention on the sensation, "and so, as it were, point to it inwardly" and then select a sign and record it in the diary. But then Wittgenstein asks, "But what is this ceremony for? for that is all it seems to be!" Continuing his interrogation of this process, he voices his interlocutor: "A definition surely serves to establish the meaning of a sign.—Well, that is done precisely by the concentration of my attention; for in this way I impress on myself the connexion between the sign and the sensation." But Wittgenstein is not impressed with this explanation as he then questions the process supposedly creating it: "But 'I impress it on myself' can only mean: this process brings it about that I remember the connexion *right* in the future. But in the present case I have no criterion of correctness." In the absence of any suitable criterion, Wittgenstein concludes, "[W]hatever is going to seem right to me is right. And that only means that here we can't talk about 'right.'"

Well, yes, but that depends on the criteria used to assess what is "right." And here it may be reasonably asked: Why should the reliability of a *private* language used to record *private* sensations be assessed by the rules applying to *public* verification? Recall again the passage from *The Blue Book* cited in Chapter 1 where Wittgenstein defends the assertion made by the man who claims to feel the image of his visual field to be exactly two inches behind the bridge of his nose: "Should we say that he is not speaking the truth, or that there cannot be such a feeling? What if he asks us 'do you know all the feelings there are?'" (BB, 9). Similarly, the private linguist may ask, "Do you know all the knowings there are?"

In assessing private sensations and the consistency of private signs referring to them, what warrant exists to favor criteria borrowed from public verification?

When comparing PI#246 and PI#258, it seems curious that in the former case it makes no sense for persons having a sensation, such as pain, to doubt whether they are in pain whereas in the latter case the presence of an impression, which is also a sensation, must be brought into doubt. Wittgenstein may object that this doubt does not concern the diarist's sensation but whether the current sensation is the *same* as previous occurrences. He may insist the question is one of judging the *sameness* and not merely the presence of a sensation.

But, once again, what warrants the claim that the presence of a *sensation*, such as pain, need not be doubted in one's own case while the presence of an *impression of sameness* ought to be doubted? Is it reasonable to count the difference between a "sensation" and an "impression" as crucial in these cases? In other words, why does the *impression of sameness* between two sensations not count as an inner experience that, like the sensation of pain, ought to be admitted as beyond doubt by the person having this experience? Cannot the diarist's experience of the sameness of two inner sensations be equally as authoritative as would be his claim that he is in pain? Why, suddenly, is a "criterion of correctness" of a public nature necessary? Here a criterion for what is "right" imposes itself from a *public* language game into a *private* language game.

In the case of the private system of notation for sensations no outstanding reason exists to criticize the notion that whatever is going to seem right is right. What other notion of "right" could be brought into operation without thereby altering the system into an essentially public notation? It is as if one asked for payment in coin from a machine dispensing currency. The demand for a public criterion for correctness concerning another person's private system of notation seems like an illegitimate demand.

Nevertheless, a stubborn Wittgenstein proponent may still want to ask advocates of a reliable private language for their sensations how they can be certain in claiming they use their invented terms for their sensations correctly and consistently over time? In response, the answer could be as simple as: "I trust my memory." The objection that no one's memory is infallible may be met with the further response: "How do you know my memory of inner sensations isn't infallible?" And this question has no adequate logical or empirical answer—no test that could refute it. And, in fact, persons with a condition called hyperthymesia have been able to demonstrate astoundingly accurate recall of past details of every day in their lives.

What has been called Wittgenstein's Private Language Argument—thought to demonstrate the impossibility of a private language—seems not so much an argument as instead a marker showing the point at which argument cannot even begin. Or it must be understood as a definition of verification. For Wittgenstein, it seems genuine verification cannot occur apart from a community of others. Or, to express the point in a Wittgensteinian manner, it would seem he claims the grammar of the word "verification" rightly belongs in the same language game as the word "public." But, as argued, denial of the possibility of a private language may be challenged. While socially dependent verifications may constitute the ground for rule following in the public sphere, these conditions may not comprise the limits of grounding for the subjective or private sphere.

The subjective/objective distinction belongs to the same class of metaphysical errors Wittgenstein undercuts in his dismissal of Cartesian mind/body dualism. As discussed, he offers a solution to one aspect of this dualism in his various illustrations of the non-relevancy of the subjective for communication. But care must be taken in noticing that sidelining the subjective does *not* necessarily resolve the issue of meaning skepticism. By contrast, the way in which Derrida undercuts Cartesian dualism preserves the difficulties for communication raised by meaning skepticism while explaining why these difficulties are inherent in the possibility for communication.

The potential for "hidden" differences in meaning between subjects as agents makes subjectivity troublesome for communication as well as for claims concerning the public nature of language. But these troubles trace their roots, in Derrida's view, to *différance* rather than subjectivity. What is called "subjectivity" counts as another effect of *différance*. This latter term functions as Derrida's placeholder for the endless effects of differences made possible by and through the iterability of traces in play across temporal and spatial contexts. Wittgenstein asserts that these differences, if hidden, may just as well stay hidden. But, as Derrida insists, these hidden differences remain relevant to communication—due to the circumstance that they everywhere place its success in peril.

Having said this, it remains necessary—for the sake of clarification of Derrida's position—to backtrack to a point of intersection between Wittgenstein and Derrida and then move forward again. Henry Staten, for example, argues that in "Signature Event Context" Derrida fully supports the view that it is not possible for there to be a private code or language, because such a possibility exceeds the nature, the being, of the sign:

> It is true that we can speak to ourselves, but we can do even that only because language is structurally open to the understanding of other human beings: "There is no code ... that is structurally secret" (*Margins*, p. 315). In holding

that a code must in principle be capable of being understood by someone other than the originator of the code, Derrida is arguing along lines parallel to Wittgenstein's argument against the possibility of a "private language." For Wittgenstein as for Derrida, a language or "code" must be such that it can be learned and practiced by someone else; Derrida's way of putting this is to say that signs or marks must be capable of being "repeated" or "iterated" by "any possible user in general" (*Margins*, p. 315). [1984, 120].

Wittgenstein and Derrida appear to be in agreement, in Staten's view, in concluding that signs and language are public. Signs can at best only be private as a secret, which is to say only contingently private.

However, unlike Wittgenstein, Derrida makes the additional point that the public nature of language need not entail the full *transparency* of language. The repeatability of the sign—the quality enabling it to be read and thereby serve as a means of communication—also undermines the readability of the sign, opening communication to rupture, distortion, misreading, ambiguity, and every type of obstacle to communication. The narrative inviting the conclusion that any given language cannot be *fully private* tells only part of the story and, as argued above, even this part may be challenged since the possibility of a viable private language can neither be confirmed nor denied. Another part of the story, an equally important part, reveals how language fails to be *fully public* in the sense of ever permitting the possibility of what could be classified as full, reliable communication or clear and complete expression of intention. In what sense can language be said to be fundamentally public if it cannot guarantee communication?

In "Signature Event Context" Derrida discusses what he calls the "inevitable consequences of these nuclear traits of all writing" that *everywhere and always* threaten the possibility of communication (here Derrida again uses the word "writing" to include all written *and* spoken sign operations). He presents a list of four moments threatening the traditional conception of communication.

   1. the break with the horizon of communication as the communication of consciousnesses or presences, and as the linguistic or semantic transport of meaning;
   2. the subtraction of all writing from the semantic horizon or the hermeneutic horizon which, at least as a horizon of meaning, lets itself be punctured by writing;
   3. the necessity of … *separating* the concept of polysemia from the concept I have elsewhere named *dissemination*, which is also the concept of writing;
   4. the disqualification or the limit of the concept of the "real" or "linguistic" context, whose theoretical determination or empirical

saturation are, strictly speaking, rendered impossible or insufficient by writing [1982, 316].

Point #1 challenges the notion of the transparent transport of sense from one consciousness to another. Point #2 challenges the notion that understanding a sentence means understanding a language such that language cannot guarantee a shared background against which words and sentences may be capable of conveying transparent meaning. Point #3 challenges the notion that a genealogical hermeneutic search may retrieve and present a transparent sense of the meaning of any word or text (explained in greater detail in the next chapter). Point #4 questions the notion that context, both linguistic and non-linguistic, can manifest accessible pragmatic boundaries for purposes of constraining the use or meaning of words to the point of guaranteeing communication.

If communication is always and everywhere in question, then doubt remains structurally inseparable from any particular instance of language use. And if doubt compromises the transparency of communication, then it also compromises language as structurally public. For Derrida, the truth about communication lies in the metaphysical entanglement of the public/private and the possible/impossible pairs.

An adequate understanding of the sign confronts division and difference as co-original with any measure of sameness, not only at the origin of language but also at the origin of everything that is—at the origin of the trace of being. This division and difference, arising from the moment of origin, presents the difficulty of assigning a name to what seemingly cannot be named without thereby also initiating a misunderstanding. Facing this risk, Derrida resorts to inventing the neologism *différance* as a placeholder for the generating principle of the being of the trace and the paradoxical nature of resulting contrasts and oppositions. Each side of an opposition penetrates the other to the core and renders it structurally incapable of functioning in a pure and autonomous form. No idealization of either is possible. This is also why at times Derrida refers to the term *différance* as a "nonconcept," because it does not operate with merely the dualistic boundaries (X, non–X) of a traditional philosophical concept. The entanglement of opposites implicit in *différance* supplements or exceeds such traditional boundaries while not eliminating them. Consequently, Derrida may say on the one hand that no code is structurally secret while also acknowledging that meaning is everywhere contaminated by *différance*. This circumstance entails that the difference in use that every user of a code necessarily generates insures that this use contains non-transparent elements and is therefore neither fully public nor fully private. Doubt and meaning are inextricable.

Given to iterability and the pervasive effects of *différance*, every reading of signs contains something new as well as something old in an incalculable mix. Derrida is clear on the radical consequences of this structural state of affairs, which he expresses in this passage: "Such a *différance* would at once, again, give us to think a writing without presence and without absence, without history, without archia, without telos, a writing that absolutely upsets all dialectics, all theology, all teleology, all ontology" (1982, 67). No oppositional pairings remain intact with their classical structure, including the public/private pair. Nevertheless, the mitigation of all manner of beings (writing, history, dialectics, etc.) into traces does not inaugurate a nihilism of futility in pursuing ideals; it merely changes the attitude toward ideals, an adjustment explained in detail in the chapter on metaphysics.

The effects of *différance* expose all sign operations to circumstances beyond the exclusive control of individuals *and* publics, pressing the dialectic of oppositions into what may more broadly be viewed as a deconstructive *economy* of differences. The nature of this economy is explored in Chapter 9.

8

Family Resemblance
and Dissemination

In the early pages of *Philosophical Investigations* Wittgenstein presents an exchange on the question of the essence of language. His imaginary interlocutor complains to him that he has talked about all kinds of language games but has not said what the essence of a language game is and, consequently, has not said what the essence of language is. He has left untouched the question of what is common to all such activities that makes them language. Wittgenstein responds by saying he is guilty as charged. He has not identified any one thing these activities have in common justifying use of the word "language" for all of them. In his defense, however, he argues that everything called "language" has "no one thing in common" (PI#65) and that all such activities are "related" to each other in many different ways. Instead, these relationships and their network account for the use of the same name.

For further illustration, he fixes on the word *game*. Rather than beginning by assuming all games have something in common it would be better to "look and see" whether any such common thing can be found. From board games to card games, some common features disappear while others remain. The same continues to be true when adding ball games, Olympic games, dice games, and so on. This examination of various games shows a complex weave of "similarities overlapping and criss-crossing" (PI#66) with no one trait or set of traits remaining common to all. Describing this state of affairs, Wittgenstein concludes, "I can think of no better expression to characterize these similarities than '*family resemblances*'; for the various resemblances between members of a family: build, features, colour of eyes, gait, temperament, etc. etc. overlap and criss-cross in the same way.—And I shall say: 'games' form a family" [emphasis added] (PI#67).

After introducing the notion of family resemblance, Wittgenstein turns to the concept of number where he finds a similar family situation. But now he begins to talk of a close association between family resemblance and the fuzziness of boundaries around concepts. When discussing the concept of number, he adds that boundaries for any concept can be rigid or not: "For I *can* give the concept 'number' rigid limits ... but I can also use it so that the extension of the concept is *not* closed by a frontier. And this is how we do use the word 'game'" (PI#68).

In routine practice words like "game" are not rigidly well defined (see also "wishing" in BB, 19). And this results from the circumstance, as discussed in Chapter 5, that concepts remain usable *without* clear boundaries. For Wittgenstein, not knowing the boundaries of a concept is not a matter of ignorance: "We do not know the boundaries because none have been drawn. To repeat, we can draw a boundary—for a special purpose. Does it take that to make the concept usable? Not at all!" (PI#69).

The weave of similarities and relationships among the various uses of a given word form a family of uses for which there appear to be no rigid boundaries but which nevertheless loosely tether the uses around the same word. Following the analogy given in the notion of family, the threads of the weave of uses might be traced and mapped like a genealogical record. One kind of use inseminates and thereby imparts certain traits to another kind of use in another context. But only a partial trait or set of traits continue in the new use, since this passing on, similar to insemination, falls short of imparting a full repetition or record of the original, as would be the case, for example, in cloning. This insemination, or partial passing on, then mixes with new uses, new contexts, resulting in the creation of a new family member.

The notion of family resemblance and the entire process of the passing on and spreading out of meaning implicated in it align—up to a point—with Derrida's understanding of the way in which meaning propagates. But although this notion moves in the right direction, it falls short of being radical enough to account for what happens in the use of language. What Wittgenstein describes with the notion of family resemblance relates to what Derrida understands in the term *polysemy*. In contrast to this term Derrida offers *dissemination*. The way in which he distinguishes these two terms illustrates another significant difference between his view of language and Wittgenstein's view.

Polysemy, in Derrida's use, refers to a multiplication of meaning in a word or phrase over time and through various contexts, the diversity of which may be traced by way of the science of lexical semantics that would track and present these meanings. As a concept, then, polysemy accords with a process of insemination, the imparting of traits that may be traced to previous word uses and sources. However, instead of multiplying or dispersing meanings through inseminations, disseminations fracture and fragment meaning across time and context such that notions of source or origin become meaningless. In his discussion of writing as arche-writing in *Dissemination*, Derrida likens this to a particular kind of dispersion when explaining, "To write means to graft." Furthermore, *grafting* is not something befalling or disrupting an originally proper meaning or thing. In this regard, for Derrida, "There is no more any thing than there is any original text." Grafting does not merely affect the grafted text but "radiate[s] back toward the site of its removal, transforming that, too, as it affects the new territory" (1981a, 355).

Over time, following insertion into other contexts and alteration by these new contexts, "the scion [the graft] inevitably comes to be grafted onto itself. The tree [of meaning] is ultimately rootless," composed of nothing but grafted shoots. And yet, although rootless, "everything is a root, too, since the grafted shoots themselves compose the whole of the body proper" (1981a, 356).

Derrida then switches to another metaphor, describing the act of reading as analogous to scratching the surface of a painting only to discover another painting beneath the surface: "All this requires that you take into account the fact that, in scratching upon this textual matter, which here seems to be made of spoken or written words, you often recognize the description of a painting removed from its frame, framed differently, broken into, remounted in another quadrilateral which is in turn, on one of its sides, fractured. The entire verbal tissue is caught in this, and you along with it. You are painting, you are writing while reading, you are inside the painting ..." (1981a, 357).

"You are inside the painting" while all the while painting. The frame fails to constitute a border within which some "thing" will have been shown. The stasis of a meaningful "thing" amounts to an illusion similar to the frozen contents of a photograph, in relation to which the video and its moving image is only a slight improvement with regard to the effects of framing. Everything in the frame, including the framer and the frame itself, remains in play, in constant motion and transformation. For Derrida, this results in the writer/reader existing on "the edge," aware of the paradoxical nature of the border itself: "You are not settled outside, since the absolute outside is not outside and cannot be inhabited as such; but you are forever being expelled, always involved in a process of expulsion, projected outside the column ... through its force of rotation, yet also pulled in by it" (1976, 358).

Insofar as everything counts as a sign, dissemination explains why there is and can be no "outside" to the text, the world, the cosmos. The outside that remains inside suggests an elastic boundary, re-circumscribing every attempt to escape it. The attempt to find a transcendent vantage, a comprehensive overview, results in a recontextualization arriving at *another* context rather than an ultimate or absolute context or an absolute outside.

The understanding of communication shifts considerably when viewed through the trope of grafting and re-grafting of dissemination. In the essay "Signature Event Context," Derrida explains these effects as effects of "general writing" and that the consequences of these effects insure that communication does not occur as a "transport of sense" or an "exchange of intentions." Consciousness, presence, speech, meaning, and truth are all effects of this general writing: "The semantic horizon which habitually governs the notion of communication is exceeded or punctured by the intervention of writing, that is of a *dissemination* which cannot be reduced to a *polysemia*. Writing is read, and 'in the last analysis' does not give rise to a hermeneutic deciphering, to the decoding of a meaning or truth" (1982, 329).

When Derrida says "writing is read," he means "read" to be understood within his broadened sense of writing/reading as "general writing," as "arche-writing," encompassing all sign operations beyond mere inscription. Reading in this sense becomes a kind of writing insofar as reading must also be seen as a form of grafting onto any given text, altering and transforming the text as it deciphers it. Reading, like writing, recontextualizes, imparting a new frame through which meaning shifts and slides.

In the 1971 interview with Jean-Louis Houdebine and Guy Scarpetta, Derrida provides one of the better discussions of the consequences of dissemination and how this way of understanding the use of signs differs from polysemia. Polysemia and polythematism represent progress in repealing the traditional rule of monothematic writing or reading, whereby the latter approach always seeks a singular dominant referent or signified as its meaning. He then adds the qualification that, nevertheless, "polysemia, as such, is organized within the implicit horizon of a unitary resumption of meaning, that is, within the horizon of [a] ... totalizing dialectics that at a given moment, however far off, must permit the reassemblage of the totality of the text into the truth of its meaning." By contrast, "the force and form of ... [dissemination's] disruption *explode* the semantic horizon." Producing an endless number of "semantic effects," dissemination cannot be followed to a simple origin or a final presence of meaning. "It marks an irreducible and *generative* multiplicity," foreclosing the possibility of "a saturating taxonomy of its themes, its signified, its meaning" (1981b, 44–45).

Undermining every manner of genealogical connection, no tracing of "family traits" through the uses of given terms remains intact and relevant throughout the operations of dissemination. The graftings, regraftings, self-graftings, the tracings and erasings of arche-writing, sever, cross, mix,

double, divide, and re-draw all lines and lineages such that the hermeneutic or exegetic "reassemblage of the totality of the text into the truth of
its meaning" emerges as a delusional goal. However, contrary to the com-
plaints of many of Derrida's critics, this dissemination, even in its apparent radicality, not only still permits meaning to arise but signification
would be *impossible* without these uncontrollable effects.

As Derrida explicitly distances himself from notions of family resemblance and genealogy as adequately descriptive of operations of signification, he does so also with respect to apparent family resemblances in
the textual themes addressed by authors and theorists often associated
with his own work. Derrida clearly indicates this in his lengthy preface to
Lacoue-Labarthe's *Typography*.

> What I share with Lacoue-Labarthe, we also both share, though differently,
> with Jean-Luc Nancy. But I hasten immediately to reiterate that despite so
> many common paths and so much work done in common, between the two of
> them and among the three of us, the *experience* of each remains, in its singu-
> lar proximity, absolutely different; and this, despite its inevitable impurity, is
> the secret of the idiom. The secret: that is to say, first of all, the *separation*, the
> without-relation, the interruption. The most urgent thing—I will try to work
> on this—would be to break here with the family resemblance, to avoid gene-
> alogical temptations, projections, assimilations, or identifications [as cited in
> Peeters' 2013, 372].

The language of this passage cannot help but prompt the question whether
Derrida intends here to make reference to Wittgenstein's use of the phrase
"family resemblance" and its implications of genealogical hermeneutics.
But regardless of whether that is the case, this passage must be taken as yet
another indication of the necessity for separation of the views of Derrida
and Wittgenstein.

Granting as much, the question must still be asked: What practical
difference does it make to view language through the lens of "dissemination" rather than "family resemblance"? Has not Derrida acknowledged
polysemia represents "progress" in the right direction with respect to an
adequate approach to understanding language and word use? Could it be
that he attempts to put too fine a point on the dispersions and iterations of
meaning? For example, might not the difference between polysemia and
dissemination be seen as analogous to the difference between Newton's
and Einstein's theories of gravity? Newton's theory was good enough to
get astronauts to the moon and back. Would not the notion of polysemia
be more than good enough to get people through the day's speech routines
and conversations by acknowledging and illustrating the potential for various threads of meaning?

Here Wittgenstein's discussion of exactness comes to mind again.

Consider another of his expressions of this problem: "An indefinite boundary is not really a boundary at all. Here one thinks perhaps: if I say 'I have locked the man up fast in the room—there is only one door left open'—then I simply haven't locked him in at all; his being locked in is a sham. One would be inclined to say here: 'You haven't done anything at all.' An enclosure with a hole in it is as good as *none*. But is that true?" (PI#99). The notion that family resemblance is too imprecise a notion for handling the ordinary exigencies of language will likely meet Wittgenstein's question: "But is that true?"

Nevertheless, Derrida might likely respond to the claim that his notion of dissemination is too exacting for ordinary language use with the same question: "But is that true?" Derrida's extensive investigations of the everyday notions of justice, hospitality, gift, forgiveness, friendship, terrorism, democracy, and numerous other commonly used terms reveal the extent to which these notions submit to a trembling and solicitation consistent with the radical rupturing of meaning deriving from dissemination. These investigations succeed in raising the question: Do we really know what we are talking about when we use such words even though we may use them every day? Here the word "know" shoulders considerable stress, perhaps much like the word "exact." If you are asked whether you know the distance of the Earth from the Sun, will it be necessary to ask what time of year, what unit of measurement, and to what points of reference on the Earth and on the Sun? There can be no responsive response without inquiring about the context of the question—which triggers all the factors discussed in Part I standing in the way of plain meaning and simple answers to simple questions. Assuming communication to lie in between the possible and the impossible serves better to prepare language-users for appreciating the very real limits language imposes on the many uses to which it is put. The next chapter pursues this theme of the limits of language through the concepts of game and economy as used by Wittgenstein and Derrida.

9

Games and Economies

In *The Blue Book* and in *Philosophical Investigations* Wittgenstein explains, in incremental steps, the relevance of the metaphor of *game* in relation to language. He begins with examples where one person, having taught another the meaning of a word by ostensive definition, issues a command to move the named object to a specific location. From these simple uses of language—similar to how "a child begins to make use of words"—Wittgenstein moves to more complex examples. These more complex examples, nevertheless, retain key features of the simple examples and exhibit an extension of words grounded in the practical origin of their use. Wittgenstein expresses the benefits of this transition from simple to complex uses in *The Blue Book* where he says, "When we look at such simple forms of language the mental mist which seems to enshroud our ordinary use of language disappears. We see activities, reactions, which are clear-cut and transparent.... We see that we can build up the complicated forms from the primitive ones by gradually adding new forms" (BB, 17).

Just prior to this paragraph, Wittgenstein assigns a name to these simple forms of uses from which the full complexity of language systems emerges and extends into everyday practices: "I shall in the future again and again draw your attention to what I shall call language games.... Language games are the forms of language with which a child begins to make use of words. The study of language games is the study of primitive forms of language or languages."

Consider a specific example of a primitive language Wittgenstein provides at the outset of *Philosophical Investigations*: "Let us imagine a language ... meant to serve for communication between a builder A and an assistant B ... [T]here are blocks, pillars, slabs and beams. B has to pass the stones ... in the order in which A needs them. For this purpose they use a language consisting of the words 'block,' 'pillar,' 'slab,' 'beam.' A calls them out:—B brings the stone which he has learnt to bring at such-and-such a call. Conceive this as a complete primitive language" (PI#2).

A few sections later he refers back to this language game: "We can also think of the whole process of using words in (2) as one of those games by which children learn their native language. I will call these games 'language-games' ... And the process of naming stones and of repeating words after someone might also be called language-games" (PI#7). However, unlike in the passage cited from *The Blue Book*, Wittgenstein then expands the notion of language-game: "I shall also call the whole, consisting of language and the *actions* into which it is woven, the 'language-game'" [emphasis added]. A few sections later he names the "actions" into which language-games are woven: "Here the term 'language-*game*' is meant to bring into prominence the fact that the *speaking* of language is part of an activity, or of a *form of life*" [emphasis added] (PI#23). And just as he finds many language games within language, so also he finds many forms of life, many structured activities, grounding language games within the whole of language. If asked how many kinds of language games there are within language, Wittgenstein answers "countless kinds." The number of such games is not fixed. New ones come into use and others fade away.

As in the case of the word "sign," Wittgenstein provides no definition of "game" and instead approaches an understanding of the concept through examples. But his examples indicate that, like language itself, games are prominently rule-governed activities. The rules derive from the human agents who participate in these activities and, as Wittgenstein acknowledges, these agents exercise agency by adding, dropping, or changing rules. A form of life is itself a game through and around which may be woven a corresponding language game. The concept of "game," then, serves as a root metaphor by means of which Wittgenstein seeks to illuminate and characterize the sum of all the processes linking language and human activity with the surrounding world.

Turning to Derrida, the sprouting of language and of meaning submits to the rupturing of multiple roots and multiple grafts. He references the grafting feature of language with terms such as dissemination, *différance*, supplement, etc.—to which can also be added the word *economy*.

The term "economy" commonly refers to systems exhibiting structured exchanges—transitions, transactions, and transformations among and between elements composing the system. Mathematical renderings of exchanges in the natural world—for example, Newton's F=ma and Einstein's $E=mc^2$—illustrate what physicists call a *conserved* economy—a balance of exchange indicated by the mathematical concept of equation. The conserved economy of Newton's physics configures the relationship between mass and motion (acceleration) as *calculable* force. Conserved economies present orders of exchange as highly predictable events.

However, the limitations of the notion of a conserved economy as adequately descriptive of complex physical systems became evident in the 20th century when constraints on predictability emerged as a notable feature in quantum microcosmic economies as well as information economies. The term *entropy* describes an essential feature of such economies. High predictability of events in an economy yields an economy of low entropy whereas low predictability yields an economy of high entropy. For example, a coin toss presents a system of high entropy because a predicted outcome will be correct roughly 50 times out of 100 tosses. A conserved economy exhibits the low entropy of a closed system wherein events may be predicted with considerable reliability.

Inspired by the work of French polymath Georges Bataille (1998) and his use of a key distinction between a *general economy* and a *restricted economy*, Derrida (1978) adapts these terms for use in the context of sign systems. A restricted economy corresponds to what has been described as a conserved economy and Derrida's use of the term conforms to the way in which Wittgenstein describes language games with regard to the high predictability (low entropy) of meanings in routine exchanges between language users. Derrida contrasts such restricted economies with general economies. A general economy presents events of transformation and exchange with notably less reliable predictability and, consequently, higher entropy. In Derrida's view, the use of signs in communication exchanges achieves a status of high entropy as a result of the *underdetermination* of signs. [Note: Here the word "underdetermination" is used analogously with its use in scientific explanation as it refers to the situation where available evidence remains insufficient to prompt a clear decision between two or more competing theories, each accounting for all the available evidence].

While lower predictability may not appear to feature prominently in anticipated verbal or written exchanges in communication, increased entropy manifests in the *meanings* of such exchanges—the alternative ways in which exchanges may be intended or read. The play introduced by underdetermination into the constraints of the communication exchange may also yield effects of both underreading and overreading—on the one hand overlooking or sidelining particular elements of the exchange and on the other hand reading too much into the exchange. In this respect, a general economy reflects exchanges *exceeding* measures of control and recuperation characteristic of a restricted economy.

Philosopher, mathematician, and literary theorist Arkady Plotnitsky (1994) explores Derrida's use of general economy alongside parallel developments in physics, specifically in the work of Niels Bohr. The theoretical base of Bohr's work constitutes a "dislocation" of classical assumptions in physics by way of the "general economic character of complementarity as a theoretical matrix." Similarly, this character of complementarity, according to Plotnitsky, is "codetermined by the irreducible loss—and thus indeterminacy—in the process of representation and by the equally irreducible heterogeneous multiplicity of all representations that such a matrix generates and employs" (1994, 10). The play of movements (events) in a given system qualifying as a general economy exhibits a degree of event unpredictability inherent to the system rather than as merely a consequence of limitations of scale or measurement. As in the case of information theory, the more unpredictable and random the point of loss in event repetition the higher the entropy in the system.

A further notable difference between restricted and general economies arises from the structure of oppositional relation implicit in each of these systems. A restricted or conserved economy imposes a structuring principle establishing a strong polarity of opposites with evident boundaries of difference. The structural tension in a restricted economy between opposites such as true and false or fact and interpretation operates with a clarity facilitating either/or alternatives and simplified, calculable decision-making. In a general economy, however, these restricted oppositions submit to a dislocation or displacement. This displacement involves a reconfiguration of the dynamic play between opposites. For example, Plotnitsky explains, "All general economies deal with arrangements (between and within the configurations they consider) that are *complementary* in the broad sense of being heterogeneous but interactive—heterogeneously interactive and interactively heterogeneous" [emphasis added] (1994, 10–11). Here Plotnitsky uses the term "complementary" in a "broad sense" and that is how the term is used herein—indicating a differing pair where each cannot be reduced to the other and yet each cannot exist apart from the other. Later in his text, Plotnitsky develops a distinction between complementarity and undecidability while granting that even this distinction may be best understood as complementary in nature, such that complementarity, undecidability, and even indeterminacy often function in tandem (Chapter 5 offers a more detailed accounting of indeterminacy in relation to undecidability).

Following Derrida, Plotnitsky expresses the displacement of the traditional oppositional tensions characteristic of restricted economies using as key examples the tensions between signifier and signified, description and reality, interpretation and that which is interpreted. Plotnitsky emphasizes that these displaced tensions illustrate an important difference between the terms *absolute* and *radical*. He says, for example, there cannot be "an absolute difference between an account and that which is being accounted for in a general economy. Once difference is absolute [between any set of classic opposites], *it is not radical enough* for a general economy.

Absolute difference or exteriority of that type would always lead to a restricted economy, repressing the radical—but again never absolute—difference defined by and defining the field of general economy" [emphasis added] (1994, 22). A general economy displaces discrete and essential difference between opposites with a new structure presenting a complementary tension between elements both essentially separate yet essentially combined, each irreducible one to the other yet inextricable one from the other.

The quantum view of matter and energy presents an example of a general economy due to the necessity for replacing prediction with probability in the transition from Newtonian mechanics to quantum mechanics. Similarly, deconstructive semiology conforms to the greater entropy of a general economy as a result of the inability to strictly limit or halt the dissemination of meaning. The principle of complementarity applied to any oppositional pair yields a structure in which the two sides of the opposition penetrate and include each other in every manifestation such that no pure instance of either obtains. This type of oppositional structure exhibits what Derrida calls a *law of universal contamination*.

Derrida also uses the term *autoimmunity* as another way of illustrating universal contamination. The concept of immunity describes the process whereby the immune system of an organism uses antibodies to turn against an agent identified as threatening and terminate or expel it. In the orthodox understanding of autoimmunity, the immune system malfunctions and recognizes an element of its own constitution as an antigen and effectively turns against itself to destroy a part of itself. This results in harmful effects on the body. However, as Michelle Jamieson (2017) adeptly explains, Derrida uses the term "autoimmunity" with a more subtle and contemporary meaning consistent with the notion of complementarity between self and other. In this use of the term, the more orthodox stark dualism of self and other submits to a displacement whereby self and other are shown to be entangled together in a complex ecology or economy of self-identity in constant motion over time. This economy warrants, according to Jamieson, a new model of disease and, consequently, a modified understanding of the notions of allergy and autoimmunity.

Jamieson explains that the early twentieth-century Austrian pediatrician Clemens von Pirquet coined the term "allergy" as a combination of "Greek *allos*, meaning 'other, different, strange' and *ergon*, meaning 'activity, energy, work" (14). Pirquet never intended for the word to suggest a rigid division between domestic and foreign, self and other. Instead, it was meant to suggest the ongoing work of negotiation between self and adaptation to environment. Such negotiation, obviously, does not result in collapse of the distinction between self and other but instead emphasizes the potential for successive changes and accommodations in relation to the nature of the boundary between self and other. The precise nature of this boundary is extremely important to understand, as Pirquet's research on allergy responses revealed. The organism's response to an antigen never occurred as either supersensitivity (disease) or immunity (protection) without the subject having previously been exposed to the antigen, *having it already present in the body*. The question of disease response is, thus, one of quantity and quality of exposure over an interval of time—as would be the case with any substance, even sugar and salt—and the current composition and disposition of the body and its surroundings. "The organism is always already infected," Jamieson explains, "and the antigen always already incorporated" (22).

This understanding of allergy and autoimmunity ought also to be applied to Derrida's use of terms such as "parasite" and "contamination." The boundary between self and other is in constant motion rather than fixed. Each side of this opposition entangles in the traits of the other, manifesting not necessarily as an overt observable blend but as a flipping of faces or features depending on current conditions. Immunity and autoimmunity, therefore, need not accord with degrees of mixture or gradations of difference. Instead, they conform to what has been discussed in previous chapters as *superposition*—a paradoxical simultaneity of both continuity (irreducible dependence) and discontinuity (irreducible separation). Derrida's use of metaphors such as economy and autoimmunity serves not only to illustrate his understanding of language and its complexities but also to reveal a compelling structural similarity within and between general economic systems across the spectrum of human knowledge in relation to the processes of living beings in the context of their world.

Although the concepts of economy and game show similarities, the distinction between a restricted economy and a general economy locates, as already suggested, a significant difference between Wittgenstein and Derrida—not so much between the metaphors of game and economy but rather between different types of games and economies.

Wittgenstein employs the game metaphor in ways consistent with a restricted economy, but not in immediately obvious ways. Superficially, he appears to use the concept of game consistent with Derrida's understanding of a general economy—an economy whereby the boundary between a system and its "outside" is constantly renegotiated. This insight on the part of Wittgenstein is especially evident in PI#65 through PI#123. This sequence of comments includes overlapping discussion of the notions of game, boundary, rule following, and—with regard to the use and meaning of words—the substantial dissolution of doubt. Here the question of boundaries appears to be an issue as equally prominent for Wittgenstein as it is for Derrida. And Wittgenstein is no less aware than Derrida of the complexities presented by language in its raw usage as opposed to its ideal theorizations.

For example, in response to Wittgenstein's discussion of the notion of game and his pronouncement that a particular game may have no precise set of rules by which it is conducted, Wittgenstein's interlocutor protests, "But still, it isn't a game, if there is some vagueness *in the rules*." And Wittgenstein responds, "But *does* this prevent its being a game?" The interlocutor replies that it may be called a game but it most certainly is not a perfect game because, he adds, "it has impurities, and what I am interested in at present is the pure article." Whereupon Wittgenstein patiently continues, "[W]e misunderstand the role of the ideal in our language. That is to say: we too should call it a game, only we are dazzled by the ideal and therefore fail to see the actual use of the word 'game' clearly" (PI#100).

In this passage, the language game of the word "game" becomes itself an illustration of the limits of language games as well as an illustration of the unusual limitations imposed by the notion of the *ideal*. For Wittgenstein, language-users commonly and routinely think of the ideal as an "unshakeable" boundary: "You can never get outside it; you must always turn back. There is no outside; outside you cannot breathe" (PI#103). Wittgenstein wants to liberate language-users from the false and debilitating assumption that the ideal must rule through the imposition of an ironclad boundary—consistent with the "unshakeable" belief that "where there is sense there must be perfect order." But in response he insists: "...we are not *striving after* an ideal." "Ordinary vague sentences" work perfectly well for the ordinary purposes to which they are put (PI#98).

Wittgenstein's de-idealization of words, the acceptance of the permeable boundaries between the inside and the outside of the semantic structure of words, appears consistent with Derrida's proclamations. And indeed it is, recalling the discussion of "inside and outside" in Chapter 4, where both philosophers are shown to trample the boundary. But the difference between Wittgenstein and Derrida arises with respect to the nature of the boundary—how the boundary itself is understood to operate in the use of language.

For Wittgenstein, the use of a given word occurs in a given context and the combination of the word and the context constitutes the "ordinary vague sentences" that work perfectly well for ordinary purposes. For Derrida, this is fine as far as it goes. But it does not go far enough. Wittgenstein's insight stops short of giving adequate measure to what he confronts but nevertheless sidelines in his discussion of aspects in Part II of *Philosophical Investigations*: namely, that every instance of the use of words emerges with *more than one set of boundaries*. In their use, the meanings of words do not reside within one language game, one boundary, regardless of how careful or precise language-users may be in formulating sentences. More than one language game, more than one operation, may be read from utterances because the context remains *unsaturated*—open and incomplete. An unsaturated context imposes itself on every temporally moving utterance, thereby admitting and re-admitting the "outside" into the "inside" of what are thought to be univocal, discrete words and texts.

One of Derrida's favorite examples of this elusive boundary phenomenon occurs in his 1977 debate with John Searle where he repeatedly queries the reader: Am I serious? Whether, in a given utterance, one is serious or not cannot be definitively decided by the use of particular words in a particular context. The context of any given utterance cannot remove doubt about what language game, in this case serious or non-serious, may be in play. And, of course, this is only one of multiple binary tensions that may be read in and through any given utterance. The utterance boundaries cannot preclude the possible relevance of a layering of multiple language games—games such as: irony, exaggeration, comedy, drama, deception, entertainment, authenticity, bad faith, blame, guilt, anger, love, hate, victimization, despair, resentment, disinterest, acquiescence—among an endless variety of qualities of intention, mood, agency, and accident. Who can decisively locate or limit the effective inside and outside, the hue and the texture, of any given utterance and its context?

Wittgenstein knows the artificial limitation of context occurs routinely. But Derrida challenges the view that such limitations need also be accompanied by a routine assumption that the expedient drawings of contextual boundaries are routinely inconsequential. Communication exchanges negotiate and are negotiated by human actions but cannot be set and determined by any single language game presumed to be in play at the point of utterance.

The effectiveness of the game metaphor for Wittgenstein rests on a distinction crucial to his entire approach to language: namely, each word has, he claims, a language game "which is its original home." And it is after saying this that he famously adds: "What we do is to bring words back from their metaphysical to their everyday use" (PI#116). When words stray too far from the game that is their original home, they become unhinged, untethered to the life form from which functional meaning sprang. As a consequence, the unhinged language games into which words may stray succeed in evaporating meaning into what Wittgenstein regards as metaphysical hot air—the absence of proper grounding.

But this view meets Derrida's likely response: no use of language escapes the "ground," or absence of ground, of metaphysical air. There can be no escape from the metaphysics underlying the use of signs because there can be no escape from time and its division of being into the trace. This irreducible separation/relation is reflected in the binary tension of the irreducible divide between the signifier and the signified and the split in the identity of the sign resulting from the law of iterability, without which the sign could not function. This theme of the dual metaphysical identity of the sign is pursued further in Chapter 11 on metaphysics and Chapter 12 on time.

Wittgenstein believes the escape from metaphysics takes place by way of the escape from the false notion of ironclad boundaries imposed by the ideal. But the loosening of the boundaries of the ideal does not permit an escape from metaphysics. It only creates the necessity for deeper choices as a result of deeper doubts resulting from a deeper plunge *into* metaphysics.

Wittgenstein desires above all to bring doubt from the metaphysical level—where he views it to have led to near pathological confusion among philosophers—to the more manageable empirical level. He restricts doubt about the meaning of words to contingent empirical considerations alone, where doubt may be in play in particular unusual circumstances. In such cases a repair of the kind offered by Wittgenstein in numerous linguistic investigations or conducted by participants in a given language game will likely resolve the question because necessary clarification may be issued. But Derrida demonstrates that a doubt exceeding empirical considerations arises from the structural level of language.

The entropy of doubt at the structural level of sign operations gives rise to Derrida's distinction between ambiguity and undecidability, where ambiguity derives from misunderstandings that may be empirically resolved and undecidability derives from—to use Derrida's term—*aporias* that cannot be resolved, on the spot, by any empirical means whatever. Such aporias arise from the nature of signs the existence and function of which would not be possible without the universal and pervasive emergence of such possibilities. This circumstance regarding the nature of signs does not entirely escape Wittgenstein's notice but is nevertheless, as has been argued, sidelined and repressed in his investigations of language in the attempt to preserve the characterization of meaning in the use of words as routinely doubt-free.

In summary, Derrida emphasizes the necessity for viewing language in a way that includes features of the lower predictability and higher entropy of a general economy. Yet this emphasis remains in complementary relation with a restricted economy and its functionally discrete boundary features more readily associated with the game metaphor as Wittgenstein desires to use it. Wittgenstein insists his examples of simple or primitive language games illustrate the game structure of more complex examples. At every level of complexity the game metaphor appears adequate to Wittgenstein as descriptive of a system in itself complete and determinate in ways befitting particular instances of use. The notion of language game conveniently limits context by the imposition of an imaginary boundary assigning to an exchange a dominant game to the exclusion of other potentially relevant games that remain in play.

For Derrida, language games may seem complete in themselves but are accompanied in superposition by successive layering of language games compounded by the successive movement of context through space and time. This layering of meaning continually renews itself as it presents itself through the presencing/absencing of the trace. Contexts do indeed provide the illusion of a discrete boundary on the surface (the restricted economy), but Derrida's other "general theory" (implicit in the notion of a general economy), the other discourse existing alongside the classical discourse, reveals that the conserved economy remains layered with another economy admitting alternative viable readings through alternative discrete structurings of context. As Plotnitsky explains, "The dislocation created by a general economy is never a simple or uncritical dismissal of classical theories, but is instead their *rigorous suspension*—an analytical exposure of their limitations and a refiguring of classical concepts through a general economy.... Radical suspensions do appear to imply the introduction of complementary modes of description and analysis" [emphasis in original] (1994, 11). Such radical suspensions succeed in exposing the genuine suspense generated by aporias inherent to the complementarity of differing pairs, which for Derrida remain metaphysically irreducible.

PART III

Wittgenstein and Derrida on Central Philosophical Themes

10

Other Minds

In *The Blue Book* Wittgenstein says, "There is a temptation for me to say that only my own experience is real: 'I know that I see, hear, feel pains, etc., but not that anyone else does. I can't know this, because I am I and they are they'" (46). The grammar of thought, sensation, perception, experience, and similar terms facilitates the impression such processes are owned by particular bodies. I cannot have your experience, cannot have your toothache, in the sense I *can* have your gold tooth. This is the explanation for Wittgenstein's odd remark in *The Blue Book* about having toothache in another person's tooth: "I said that the man who contended that it was impossible to feel the other person's pain did not thereby wish to deny that one person could feel pain in another person's body. In fact, he would have said: 'I may have toothache in another man's tooth, but not *his* toothache'" (53).

The grammar of "have" in the sense of having a toothache and having a gold tooth induces an analogous relationship between these two expressions giving rise to philosophical troubles. Wittgenstein explains: "Now the case of his toothache, of which I say that I am not able to feel it because it is in his mouth, is not analogous to the case of the gold tooth. It is the apparent analogy, and again the lack of analogy, between these cases which causes our trouble. And it is this troublesome feature in our grammar which the realist does not notice" (49).

The grammar of use induces the notion there are two kinds of worlds, a mental world and a physical world, the former made of *aethe*-real, intangible substance and the latter of real, tangible substance. Wittgenstein calls attention to how the odd role of the aethereal arises in philosophy "when we perceive that a substantive is not used as what in general we should call the name of an object, and when therefore we can't help saying to ourselves that it is the name of an aethereal object" (47). But according to Wittgenstein, this philosophical tangle of two kinds of substance may be undone as easily as it is done: "I mean, we already know the idea of 'aethereal objects' as a subterfuge, when we are embarrassed about the grammar of certain words, and when all we know is that they are not used as names for material objects. This is a hint as to how the problem of the two materials, *mind* and *matter*, is going to dissolve" (47).

The "hint" for how the problem of mind and matter dissolves points toward retracing the steps back to how it was created. It was created through an accident of grammar and an analogy between one grammar for two referents in separate domains. The grammar for aethereal or metaphysical "objects" borrows the grammar of material objects. The expression, "I cannot have your toothache," does not follow from tests conducted to discover what is the case about toothache; it merely states the grammar of pain terminology. The surprise induced by the positive expression "I can have your toothache" records the violation of conventional ways of using pain terminology. Similarly, the expression "I cannot know whether you have toothache unless you open your mouth for me to see" makes as little sense. Seeing toothache itself is not possible and this is not simply a failure of human perception.

The grammar of sensation is such that it alludes to a substrate, a body, in possession of the sensations but the sensations are not like material objects. The private nature of sensation engenders the philosophical position of solipsism, which prompts the solipsist to make statements such as: I have no experience of anyone else's sensations and so I have no evidence of any experience other than mine. The grammatically induced construct of aethereal mind consciousness places into question the existence other minds.

But here Wittgenstein interrupts disbelief in the existence of other minds to ask, "How could I even have come by the idea of another's experience if there is no possibility of any evidence for it? But wasn't this a queer question to ask? *Can't* I believe that someone else has pains? Is it not quite easy to believe this?" (46). The question whether others' experiences are real rarely presents itself as a difficulty in ordinary life.

Wittgenstein's solution to the problem of other minds rests on the dissolution of the more general problem of knowledge. He explains, "When we look at everything that we know and can say about the world [to which may be added: everything that we know and can say about other minds] as resting upon personal experience, then what we know seems to lose a good deal of its value, reliability, and solidity. We are then inclined to say that an opinion is merely subjective, a matter of taste." Pushed to the extreme, the "merely subjective" reduces to solipsism. But Wittgenstein concludes, "Now, that this aspect should seem to shake the authority of experience and knowledge points to the fact that here our language is tempting us to draw some misleading analogy" (48).

The analogy induced through grammar is a false analogy, creating a superfluous, and ultimately superstitious, dualism of mind and matter through which the solipsist view appears to make sense. Dissolving confusions imposed by this false analogy requires understanding that the grammatical structure of talk about objects provides no sufficient reason for imputing object-like qualities in the case of every such locution. By disarming this analogy, the aethereal as a reality separate from, yet analogous to, the realm of material objects dissolves whereby it then makes as little sense to say, "I cannot have your pain," as it does to say, "I cannot have your death." This is not to say no sense whatever can be projected onto such statements but rather that their peculiarity provides the clue that they insert themselves into the wrong language game and thereby create unnecessary puzzles.

Wittgenstein's philosophy of language challenges the solipsistic view that "I can only know that my experiences are real because I cannot have another's experiences." But in pursuing this line of thinking, does not Wittgenstein propose to solve the ontological question of the existence of other minds with a mere semiological slight of hand?

The circumstance that no set of material facts in the world can rule out the solipsist's interpretation of the world presents a situation analogous to Wittgenstein's rule following paradox: Every action can be made out to accord with the rule, and, similarly, every material fact can be made out to accord with solipsism.

For example, the solipsist demands of experience that there be an experience self-evidently confirming the existence of persons and beings outside the solipsist's experience. But this is like asking to be paid in coin while insisting that all coin is counterfeit. Personal experience is insufficient to confirm the existence of a world beyond personal experience; yet all evidence that could be offered for what lies beyond personal experience necessarily qualifies as yet more experience filtered through the solipsist's sensory body. The world as experienced appears in every respect as it would if the solipsist were wrong and so nothing in experience prompts the solipsist's belief. Yet, similarly, no sensory evidence can refute his belief.

That the solipsist cannot be challenged in any way by evidence exposes the purely metaphysical nature of the belief. If taken seriously, this position must be viewed as acknowledgment of the unique status of the metaphysical "I"—the position from which all experience arises. Similar to the seeing of the optical "eye," the metaphysical "I" makes no appearance within the field of vision; instead, it frames the field of vision. This "I" cannot be found in experience but only derived from experience. In Wittgenstein's terms, it can be shown but not spoken of or articulated. As soon as any such attempt is made, the "I" recedes as it merely frames a new field. The "I" is always the subject and can never position itself as the object of experience. For this reason, solipsism pushed to its metaphysical limit can be challenged but cannot, it would seem, be thoroughly refuted by any form of evidence.

However, the solipsist falls prey to what ails metaphysics in general. As Gary Zabel notes, in Wittgenstein's later work "metaphysics survives, but at the price of relinquishing its claim to illuminate our situation within the world, of detaching its utterances from all contact with reality. The gears of metaphysical language continue to turn, but they no longer engage anything other than themselves" (1979, 20). Similarly, the net result of the metaphysical solipsist position qualifies at best as a superfluous addition to thought and speech. The solipsist may claim: Only my experiences are real; but this counts as nothing more than a peculiar way of speaking, as if one were to say: Only my experiences are blue (Compare PI#403). Acknowledging that for Wittgenstein the solipsist position cannot be refuted, Zabel concludes: "Wittgenstein's solipsism reaches its final and subtlest expression: not in the clear assertion of the uniqueness of his own subjectivity, but in the closure of metaphysical speech" (1979, 20–21). For Wittgenstein, the private sphere of the metaphysical "I," is separated from the public sphere of language by an insurmountable chasm. But the metaphysical "I" may be finally viewed as little more than an inconsequential shadow for purposes of communication.

As commentator Derek McDougall (2008) explains, it is not merely wrong to say something like, "I cannot have your toothache." This makes perfect sense in the context of its application. But when the philosopher abstracts from such usages of "have" and similar constructions to conclusions enabling the construction of notions such as "only my own experience is real," then the "picture" inherent in the grammar has been extended to the point where it exceeds any language game of practical use and now serves as the basis for a kind of ontology of sensations creating the illusion of a hermetically sealed subject or autonomous consciousness. Wittgenstein identifies this "picture" of mind as precisely the point where philosophers are misled. McDougall displays considerable philosophical honesty, however, when asking, "But what if it were to be complained that the idea of *consciousness* has an application of a special kind in a *philosophical* context that allows it to give rise to just those sorts of puzzles that have been considered [by philosophers]?" (56). And, interestingly enough, he replies, "There is no genuine answer to this question." If Wittgenstein's claim of illegitimacy for such applications of this so-called grammatically induced picture of mind remains unpersuasive, due to what McDougall—and Wittgenstein as well—acknowledge is a very "tempting" picture giving rise to a language game for which perhaps "there *is* a real point in playing" (44), then the reason for rejecting the picture lands with more muted significance.

Turning to Derrida, his view of language leads to a more persuasive sidelining of solipsism, centering not so much on the self-confirming and therefore self-defeating nature of the solipsistic bubble but rather on the metaphysical untenability of this bubble when placed alongside other compelling metaphysical assumptions. This untenability derives from what Derrida embraces as the ultratranscendental structure of being. For Derrida, the "I" of the personal subject is not interior to itself and neither is the metaphysical "I." Derrida's approach shifts the ground of argument from the evidential and empirical level to the solipsist's ultimate retreat— the metaphysical level.

The being of the trace on which Derrida's metaphysics rests precludes the possibility of an absolutely contained interiority. Every "I" is essentially contaminated by alterity, by "otherness," breaching any absolute wall of separation between inner and outer, self and other. The "I" is not an indivisible core but rather a trace moving and changing through time. Despite the fact the "I," similar to the "eye," remains always the register rather than the field of vision, it is no more singular and undivided than the sign. It does not constitute a closure but instead a rupture incapable of imposing an absolute boundary between a "self" and a "world" or a "self" and an "other." Self and world, self and other, leak into each other from the point of origin (assuming there need be an "origin"). From such point of origin, solipsism emerges dead on arrival. Philosophically, the question of other minds is turned on its head. The more pressing question becomes whether anything like an individual "I" as an indivisible entity—whether mind, self, ego—as unique separate, and undivided, remains possible.

The membrane between self and other presents no point of absolute impermeability. But, for Derrida, this does not mean either self or other remain fully accessible or fully transparent. The law of iterability applies not only to the being of signs but also to the being of all beings insofar as all existence falls within the stricture of time. Every self remains, at some level, mysterious not only to every other but also to itself. But mysteries always leave clues, which is to say traces, signs, texts. Texts may be *translucent* to the point of availing themselves to readings but never *transparent* to the point of guaranteeing a particular reading. The community of being-with-others remains simultaneously the privacy of not-being-with-others—not through *in*determinacy but rather *under*-determinacy of what is available to read. As time passes, new readings, new divisions in interpretation, continue to emerge through changing contexts.

Due to the structure of the self as a fold of self/other, the self must remain emergent and lacking in full transparency to itself. This configuring of the boundary and quality of subjectivity may be read in many of Derrida's texts, such as *Without Alibi*—published two years before Derrida's death in 2004 and including essays written between 1994 and 2000. In this text, Derrida explores the question of sovereignty, especially in the case of the subject, and the possible consequences of the deconstruction of the sovereignty of the subject.

In his commentary on Wittgenstein and Derrida, Ralph Shain, for example, remarks, "Many have thought that Derrida [like Wittgenstein] also leaves behind the Cartesian conception of subjectivity." But he then concludes that the essay "Typewriter Ribbon: Limited Ink (2)," included in the text *Without Alibi*, provides evidence that "the problem of other minds is retained within Derrida's aporetics." This conclusion, however, overlooks the subtlety of Derrida's critique of the subject. For example, Shain cites Derrida on the topic of lying: "No one will ever be able to demonstrate ... that someone has lied, that is, did not believe, in good faith, what he was saying. The liar can always allege, without any risk of being proved wrong, that he was in good faith when he spoke" (2002, 111). Shain then cites Derrida's continuation on the same page: "This necessity is nothing other than the solitude, the singularity, the inaccessibility of the 'as for me,' the impossibility of having an originary and internal intuition of the proper experience of the other ego, of the alter ego" (cited in Shain, 2007, 145; Derrida, 2002, 111). Shain understands this impossibility of an internal intuition of the other ego to be consistent with the closure of the Cartesian subject, the essence of consciousness that makes of it an ultimately impenetrable autonomous sovereignty. But this conclusion follows neither the force nor the substance of Derrida's deconstruction of the subject. In another context Derrida says of the subject:

> To deconstruct the subject does not mean ... that the subject is what it *says* it is. The subject is not some meta-linguistic substance or identity, some pure cogito of self-presence; it is always inscribed in language. My work does not, therefore, destroy the subject; it simply tries to resituate it [1984, 125].

This resituating of the subject involves situating it within a structurally open context—a claim Derrida defends with lines of argument, directly refuting the possibility of solipsism, in passages such as this: "[T]he other cannot be absolutely exterior to the same without ceasing to be other ... the same is not a totality closed in upon itself, an identity playing with itself, having only the appearance of alterity.... How could there be a 'play of the Same' if alterity itself was not already *in* the Same, with a meaning of inclusion ... ?" (1978, 126). The otherness of the other lies already within the self in self-division and this other submits to the limits of reading as would any other, as would any sign. The other as well as the self/other are "inscribed in language" and must be read, and perhaps misread, as might any sign. The dynamic of the self in the self/other relation, "interior" to each person, remains parallel to the dynamic of the self and the other in relations to those others "exterior" to each person. The subject as solipsist cannot shake the shadow of the other that remains essential to its own being. The subject does not and cannot live in a solipsistic bubble.

Nevertheless, there remains an "inaccessibility of the 'as for me.'" But this arises less from limits to *accessing* the "text" that is "me" and more from limits to *reading* the "text" that is "me." Even though the self may relate to itself in a way more direct than to another self, this access still requires *reading*. Both the other and the self/other remain—even in their structural openness—in some sense a "solitude," a "singularity," and a mystery. This mystery results from underdetermination, which, as in the case of the sign, is itself a result of the law of iterability set in motion by time. The self has access to itself that the other does not, but this access does not guarantee that the self is transparent to itself or necessarily accurate in its own knowledge and recollection of itself. Nevertheless, others are in no position to challenge claims made by the self in relation to inner experiences such as feelings, moods, sensations, dreams, intentions, etc.

This circumstance of nontransparency of the self to itself as well as to the other does not reintroduce the problem of other minds. The apparent reintroduction of the problem results from the necessity for reading, whereby the problem of reading *displaces* the problem of the Cartesian inaccessibility of the other. One person cannot transparently read another due to the limits of reading—not because the subject is in some sense entirely sealed off to the other and to the world.

Derrida's reasoning regarding this openness of the self/other subject may seem compelling until confronting an apparent consequence of this understanding of the subject. The self/other division of the self appears to provide the self with the perfect alibi, thereby explaining the title of Derrida's book. The subject, in its division, in its strangeness to itself, appears to have an alibi for absolving itself of responsibility for itself—including responsibility for actions. How, in the final analysis, can a self, lacking autonomy and sovereignty, lacking self-transparency, be held accountable? As Derrida asks, "How can one continue to say, 'Here I am'? How can one reaffirm the ineffaceable passivity of a heteronomy and a decision of the other in me? How can one do it without giving in to the alibi?" (2002, xxxiv-xxxv). His response is unequivocal:

You will never discharge, never acquit yourself, said I, somewhere between assertion and decision, between "you cannot" and "you must not, it is necessary that you not do that, especially not that." The impossibility of acquitting oneself, the duty not to want to acquit oneself; that is what I would have liked to attest to here, at the moment of signing, without "mercy" and without alibi [2002, xxxv].

Accountability for words and actions has never awaited full transparency. Accountability to others rests on due process—and how that may be defined in a community—not certainty. While the self may relate to itself in a way more direct than to another, this access, to repeat, still requires *reading*. Derrida understands the deconstruction of the subject need not and ought not give license to the irresponsibility of the subject any more than it need give license to any reading whatever of a text. The othering effects of *différance* in iteration and spatial/temporal repetition-with-a-difference complicate but do not destroy being and identity. The trace of the trace may lack a single thread running through the entire tracing but it cannot lack path and trajectory.

As will be argued in the chapter on time, Wittgenstein's texts offer no compelling evidence he shares Derrida's view of the pervasive and decisive role of time at the metaphysical level. For Wittgenstein, texts may be situated temporally, exposed to the movement of time, but only on a contingent level not a structural level. Wittgenstein assigns a role to time considerably short of the role Derrida assigns it. For Derrida, time is the *sine qua non* of signs and sign functioning. For Wittgenstein, time plays a role in the evolution of languages and the shifting of meanings but does not play an essential role in creating the possibility for meaning to arise.

However, Wittgenstein's view on the philosophical question of other minds, as sketched thus far herein, may be challenged as conceding too much to the solipsist position. Passages may be found in Wittgenstein's work suggesting a deeper and more ontological dismissal of the force of solipsism than the dismissal in Wittgenstein Zabel identifies. For example, Søren Overgaard (2006) argues that Wittgenstein attempts to defend a position between Cartesian subjectivity on the one hand and radical behaviorism on the other. This position abandons the view of mind as ontologically separate from objectified bodies while also rejecting the view of mind as simply an extension of the body. According to Overgaard, "Instead of contrasting inner and outer, mind (or soul) and body, Wittgenstein contrasts the whole living human being, and what is similar to it, with non-living things such as stones and bicycles (cf. Wittgenstein, 1963 [PI], Section 284)" (63). This view positions human beings as mind/bodies embedded within the world and community with others prior to any possible inference concerning the separation of mind and body—whether within the self or between self and others. Such inferred separation of mind and body, according to Overgaard's reading of Wittgenstein, derives from highly artificial philosophical parsings rather than lived experience. Overgaard's reading of Wittgenstein, however, remains partly consistent with Zabel's when considering that Overgaard's reading exposes Wittgenstein's rejection of the solipsist view as a view demonstrable by evidence from experience. But Overgaard does not consider, as Zabel does, Wittgenstein's additional analysis of solipsism, and acceptance of its position, as an irrefutable metaphysical position stemming from metaphysical closure and the closure of the metaphysical "I."

For both Wittgenstein and Derrida the *traditional* problem of other minds dissolves by way of a deeper understanding of the nature of language and the way in which an understanding of signs informs the nature of experience. But Derrida's understanding penetrates deeper, exposing how the public accessibility of signs remains structurally closed to being *fully* public. Consequently, all reading emerges as both public and private or neither public nor private and the world thereby presents an aporia of irreducible structural limits to knowledge and communication and to any discrete division between self and other. This aporia renders moot the claims of the solipsist. If consciousness may be said to be what the "I" has, it nevertheless escapes any full sense of what can be conclusively called "mine." The solipsist has no basis, other than the suggestiveness of the grammar of certain languages, to insist that personal experience includes and encloses the really real and that the existence of other minds is illusory. Nevertheless, in Wittgenstein's view, the irrelevance of evidence prevents opponents from disabusing the solipsist from speaking of personal experience as the really real. No reasoning can compel the solipsist to believe otherwise. From Derrida's angle, however, the solipsist is refuted at the metaphysical level—on the basis of the metaphysical groundless ground of *différance* and the trace, through which, in order to be at all, no being can be indivisible and self-contained. In other words, Derrida's ultratranscendental metaphysics, such as it is, offers a challenge to the basis of the solipsist position not found in Wittgenstein.

11

Metaphysics

Chapter 1 discussed how Wittgenstein raises the question "What is a sign?" only to defer answering the question. Instead, he offers a series of examples of the use of signs. In *Speech and Phenomena* (1967, 1973), Derrida examines Edmund Husserl's avoidance of this same question in his commentary on *Logical Investigations*. Derrida's commentary on Husserl's deferral of the question "What is a sign?" presents additional reasons for such a deferral, thereby adding further justification for Wittgenstein's similar deferral. However, as will become clear, points of comparison between Wittgenstein and Husserl emerge more as contrasts than similarities. In Wittgenstein's case the deferral derives more from his preferred method for confronting philosophy through appeal to particular cases of the uses of signs whereas Husserl's deferral results from his preferred phenomenological method, which aspires to transcend the sign altogether.

Logical Investigations, published in two volumes in 1900 and 1901, was Husserl's first major published work. His views in this work were later refined in *Ideas: General Introduction to Pure Phenomenology* (1913). The *Cartesian Meditations* (1950) and *Ideas II and III* (1952) followed in the 1930s but were published posthumously in the 1950s. While *Logical Investigations* does not represent Husserl's most developed views, this work does provide insight into basic elements of his phenomenological philosophy, especially concerning the status of signs. Derrida's analysis remains instructive not so much for his critique of Husserl's phenomenology as for the illustration of the opening moves in deconstruction, since *Speech and Phenomena* was among Derrida's earliest published works.

As Derrida notes, the "What is ...?" question serves as the inaugural question of traditional metaphysics by opening the question of being. Asking "What is a sign?" raises the inquiry to an "ontological plane" as it addresses the nature of the being of the sign and begins, as Derrida explains, "to assign a fundamental or regional place to signification in an ontology" (1973, 24). But raising this question also inaugurates—necessarily in Derrida's view—particular metaphysical assumptions. For example, when assuming, as Husserl did, that the sign presents the structure of an intentional movement, Derrida asks whether it remains possible to place the sign in the category of a being, of a thing in general, and therefore perhaps beyond the reach of the traditional "What is ...?" question. In other words, Derrida begins by suggesting that although Husserl rightly desires to avoid the metaphysical tradition of "What is ...?" questions, he nevertheless does not, and likely cannot, escape the gesture of generalizing the nature of the sign, as when, for example, he assigns to the sign the properties and structure of an intentional movement.

For example, refusing to answer the "What is ...?" question at the outset may signal an attempt to disconnect inquiry from classical presumptions in exchange for a new beginning. This disconnection leaves open the possibility the concept of the sign may not be one entity or process but perhaps a compounding of elements camouflaged under one name. And indeed, Husserl finds concealed behind the name of the sign two different but related signs; one he calls *expression* and the other *indication*. The *indicative sign* can be of two types. For example, certain markings visible on the surface of rocks signal the wear of glacial abrasion of rock against rock. This type of indicative sign is a *natural* sign. Anything produced through animal or human behavior, from cat scratches to typescript, may also serve to indicate; these *artificial* signs indicate the presence of intention. Like the natural sign, the artificial sign points to something beyond itself. However, the *expressive sign*, unlike the natural sign, extends beyond mere indication in its capacity to communicate meaning from one subject to another by means of a system of exchange. Expressive signs are organized through structure (grammar, syntax) and categories (meanings, concepts).

The distinction between indicative and expressive signs is not, as Derrida explains, the same as between nonlinguistic and linguistic signs. Linguistic signs, as any tool would, carry the trace of intention, but their use surpasses indication in the capacity to express particular intentions. They indicate but also exceed indication by having a function in a system of communicative exchange. When distinguishing indication from speech, Derrida remarks, "However interwoven with expression, the indicative sphere represents everything that cannot itself be brought into deliberate and meaningful speech" (1973, 36).

Moving to another level of abstraction, Derrida explains that for Husserl, "Ex-pression is exteriorization. It imparts to a certain outside a sense which is first found in a certain inside" (1973, 32). Derrida then notes that Husserl's understanding of expression extends, in his phenomenological methodology, to a departure from what might be expected when he further explains that in the case of this procedure, "...this 'outside' is 'neither nature, nor the world, nor a real exterior relative to conscious-ness'" (1973, 32). Oddly enough, the outside of which Husserl speaks remains *inside* as the meaning of this type of expression illuminates what he calls an "ideal ob-ject." This expression constitutes a form of speech with no need of being outwardly spoken. Derrida continues, "This outside is then ex-pressed and goes forth beyond itself into another outside, which is always 'in' consciousness."

Husserl at first conceived these expressions, these meaningful signs, to be a function of "solitary mental life." But after his discovery of the transcendental reduction, he describes this aspect of solitary mental life as "the noetic-neomatic sphere of consciousness," which is the sphere of con-sciousness within which expression performs an unusual going forth that nevertheless remains inside (1973, 32–33).

The *transcendental reduction*, mentioned above, comprises one of three reductions employed by Husserl constituting his brand of phenom-enological investigation. The transcendental reduction, isolates phenom-ena from the natural world, making it possible to examine them, not as existing objects in the world, but rather as objects existing in a sensible matrix, within the intentional constitution of human consciousness—of any human consciousness whatever (philosophically aligned with the notion of a *transcendental ego*). Insofar as the external world has been set aside, only experience remains—the realm of conscious life as conscious-ness itself experiences or structures a world.

The second reduction, Husserl's *eidetic reduction*, then mentally iso-lates an object from other objects for the purpose of identifying its essence by subtracting various features until only those features remain that, should anything more be removed, the object would no longer retain a sin-gular identifying essence. The object reduced need not be a physical object but may also be a product of the imagination, such as a unicorn.

The third reduction, the *phenomenological reduction*, also known as the *epoché*, entails setting aside all issues concerning what may belong to an "external world" versus what may belong to experience or conscious-ness. This reduction serves the purpose of permitting exclusive focus on the *description* of the experience of consciousness in action, whether this description be of an object in the natural world or an eidos, an object of the imagination. Thus, the phenomenological reduction refers to the eidetic reduction and transcendental reductions combined as these comprise, for Husserl, the philosophical method of phenomenology. In this sense, phe-nomenology is a life philosophy, an attempt to describe the experience of what it means to be conscious and to live in and through a world.

Returning to the discussion of signs, expression emerges from a sign charged with meaning. And meaning comes to a sign by means of speech. But the "speech" attracting Husserl's attention emerges prior to any expression in attempts at communication. This "speech" must not be confused with what might be called inner dialogue or conversation of the self with itself. This speech is the breath of the word heard at the instant it is spoken. Here the phenomenologist fixes on an ideal object, a meaning, residing only in a metaphysical space. Derrida notes, "In expression the intention is absolutely explicit because it animates a voice which may remain entirely internal and because the expressed is a meaning (*Bedeutung*), that is, an ideality 'existing' nowhere in the world" (1973, 33).

Concerning the analysis of Husserl's views thus far, it may well be asked how "speech," or even more generally language, becomes central in the phenomenological investigation of experience and the disclosures of transcendental reduction. Derrida even points out that Husserl "never wanted to assimilate experience in general (empirical or transcendental) with language" (1973, 31). The explanation for the intrusion of language lies in what may be conceived as another reduction—the reduction or isolation of the sign. And this reduction serves to transcend the sign insofar as the sign serves to *symbolize* what must be transcended in order for experience to be present and available to consciousness—to *any* consciousness—which is to say *transcendental* consciousness. This is why for Husserl and for the purposes of a phenomenological description and the attempt to exceed mere psychological description, expression must ultimately yield to an analysis beyond subjectivity.

Turning now to the question of transcendence and the ideal object, Derrida remarks, "A sign is never an event, if by event we mean an irreplaceable and irreversible empirical particular" (1973, 50). Unlike a sign, an event, is something that cannot be repeated. An event that seems to repeat only presents again with a *difference*, which is to say it can only be re-presented. Only when viewed as an *instance of repetition*, only as representation, can an event become a sign. Anything appearing as absolutely unique cannot represent and cannot, therefore, have meaning. Through the context of Husserl's views Derrida arrives at a noteworthy feature of the ideality of signs.

> A signifier (in general) must be formally recognizable in spite of, and through, the diversity of empirical characteristics which may modify it. It must remain the *same*, and be able to be repeated as such, despite and across deformations which the empirical event necessarily makes it undergo ... [the sign] can function as a sign, and in general as language, only if a formal identity enables it to be issued again and to be recognized. This identity is necessarily *ideal*. It thus necessarily implies representation [emphasis added] [1973, 50].

Returning to Husserl, as an investigation into and a revelation of ideal objects available to a transcendental consciousness—to objectivity construed as intersubjectivity—Husserl's phenomenology must proceed by way of a method free from any mediation or possibility of distortion. But if the ideal is that which is repeatable and repeatable only as representation, only as repetition-with-a-difference, then the ideal, like the sign and everything associated with it (such as language), becomes precisely what Husserl wants to exclude: namely, the *contamination of the ideal*. Derrida's analysis of the nature of the sign, as a necessarily temporal phenomenon, reveals there can be no pure idea, including no pure ideal.

As it turns out, Husserl is not blind to this contamination and so his phenomenology—in order to arrive at the destination of pure ideality he sees as necessary for objective, intersubjective, disclosure of phenomena—must posit a method free of representation. This disclosure must be one of *pure presentation*. Derrida's summary is worth citing at length:

> Does not the maintaining of this difference [between reality and representation, between simple presence and repetition]—in the history of metaphysics and for Husserl as well—answer to the obstinate desire to save presence and to reduce or derive the sign, and with it all powers of repetition? ... To assert, as we have been doing, that within the sign *the difference does not take place* between reality and representation, etc., amounts to saying that the gesture that confirms this difference is the very obliteration of the sign [1973, 51].

Thus, in Derrida's view, Husserl's phenomenology dissociates itself and the experience of reality from any and every form of representation in order to "save presence." The eidetic reduction aspires to achieve the unmediated pure presence of an ideal object residing in a transcendent metaphysical space. This is Husserl's view of *expression* as a form of "speech" *transcending all representation*. But, for Derrida, this form of "speech" remains foreign to anything resembling signification as it constitutes a retreat back into the heart of classical metaphysics, which he names the *metaphysics of presence*. This retreat brings with it a return, a repetition, of all the old antagonistic dualisms of traditional philosophy, including mind/body, essence/accident, appearance/reality, etc. And in this case, the repetition of the old traditional dualisms counts as merely a repetition of the same with little difference—a repetition of the quandary arising from previous attempts to go beyond signification, contrary to Husserl's ambitions.

Derrida traces Husserl's thinking along the tradition all the way back to Plato. He finds that, for Husserl, ideality defines being—ideality as repetition. However, this repetition, in the rarified metaphysical air of ideal objects, is postulated as a repetition of the identical and self-same. Derrida points out where this trail leads:

> For Husserl, historical progress always has as its essential form the constitution of idealities whose repetition, and thus tradition, would be assured *ad*

infinitum, where repetition and tradition are the transmission and reactivation of origins. And this determination of being as ideality is properly a *valuation,* an ethico-theoretical act that revives the decision that founded philosophy in its Platonic form. Husserl occasionally admits this; what he always opposed was a conventional Platonism. When he affirms the nonexistence or nonreality of ideality, it is always to acknowledge that ideality *is* a way of being that is irreducible to sensible existence or empirical reality and their fictional counterparts [1973, 52–53].

Since Husserl's phenomenological project requires direct apprehension—the immediacy of the self-presence of the self to itself—the model of meaning and being offered by the sign and signification as representation, must be replaced by another model—a parallel world in which the interval between names and objects and between signifiers and signifieds is in effect *displaced* by ideality. This displacement, however, imposes a difference between effective communication and the self as speaking subject. The self does not communicate with the representation of itself because communication *is not necessary.*

Derrida, however, disagrees and insists, "The primordial structure of repetition that we just evoked for signs must govern all acts of signification. The subject cannot speak without giving himself a representation of his speaking, and this is no accident.... Speech represents itself; it *is* its representation. Even better, speech is *the* representation of itself" (1973, 57).

For Husserl, even though from the point of view of the subject a kind of internal communication, an internal talking to the self, may seem to take place, nothing of the sort happens. The concept of communication, in Husserl's view, remains inappropriate to describe the immediacy and transparency of what he refers to as expression. Expression as self-presence, in Husserl's use, is pure presence, lacking any interval, and functions as an indivisible origin. For Derrida, this notion of pure presence, contradicts not only the nature of the sign but also the nature of being as anything capable of surviving beyond singular and unrepeatable events. This metaphysical orientation rests on the presumption that the being of the really real is, in fact, pure presence, along with the additional presumption that this pure presence remains self-evidently accessible to the appropriately attuned consciousness. These presumptions are, for Derrida, all too presumptuous and can be sustained only by insisting on an entirely unsustainable view of the sign.

Taking Husserl's views and Derrida's critique of Husserl's phenomenology of the sign in hand, it now remains to compare the metaphysical ground of this approach to the ground implicit in Wittgenstein's stance. With respect to contemporaries of his era, perhaps no one can be counted as providing a more paradigmatic instance of the view of language Wittgenstein opposes than Husserl. Husserl assigns the core meaning of signs to a transcendent realm of consciousness accessible by means of a transcendental reduction—bracketing and setting aside the natural world. Through the eidetic reduction, subjective mind transforms into transcendental mind, which offers the presentation rather than the re-presentation of meaning. This amounts to a breathtakingly complete capitulation to metaphysics and a metaphysical reification of the inducements of grammar and resurrects, once again, insoluble philosophical puzzles inherent in a variety of traditional philosophical dualisms.

Nevertheless, the objection may be raised that Wittgenstein is on record as having once claimed to be something of a phenomenologist himself, which may suggest more compatibility with Husserl than incompatibility. But any similarity derives only from superficial features, the most prominent of which must include Wittgenstein's assessment of the primary feature of his methodology and his way of doing philosophy.

While Wittgenstein's way of doing philosophy involves careful observation as opposed to speculative deduction, he nevertheless distinguishes his approach from that of hard science—with its focus on measurement, computation, and reduction to causal explanation. Instead, Wittgenstein focuses on behaviors—specifically the uses of words—and proposes to do nothing more than describe these behaviors, their purposes, and those cases in which these purposes go awry: "Philosophers constantly see the method of science before their eyes, and are irresistibly tempted to ask and answer questions in the way science does. This tendency is the real source of metaphysics, and leads the philosopher into complete darkness. I want to say here that it can never be our job to reduce anything to anything, or to explain anything. Philosophy really *is* 'purely descriptive'" (BB, 18).

Phenomenology also claims to be a descriptive method and it may be this similarity that prompted Wittgenstein to, on occasion, associate his approach with phenomenology. Like the phenomenologist, Wittgenstein wants to describe that which shows itself plainly to observation. Anything "hidden" becomes immediately suspect and essentially irrelevant: "Philosophy simply puts everything before us, and neither explains nor deduces anything.—Since everything lies open to view there is nothing to explain. For what is hidden, for example, is of no interest to us" (PI#126).

But the superficial similarity in favoring description only serves to hide the fundamental differences between Wittgenstein and Husserl. Husserl sets himself the task of describing what Wittgenstein would understand to be metaphysical objects—ideal objects embodying the essence of meaning and accessed through pure "mental activity" initiated through the eidetic reduction. Wittgenstein avoids this "path to darkness" and instead offers a way out by discovering and describing the frames, the language games, through which everyday words initially take on meaning and function in the role of communication.

Wittgenstein's distinction between "seeing" and "seeing as," between understanding and interpreting, might seem parallel to Husserl's distinction between expression and indication insofar as both provide the basis for a critique of the interval of interpretation as a step in grasping meaning. But, in Wittgenstein's distinction, the "seeing" in understanding develops as trained capacity whereas, in Husserl's distinction, the "seeing" in expression corresponds to an infallible process of regulated envisioning, a capacity any human consciousness possesses, through careful introspective probing, to directly access meaning. To state it simply, for Wittgenstein, the "seeing" corresponding to the grasp of meaning is culturally acquired whereas, for Husserl, this "seeing" is innately given, though it requires the eidetic reduction methodology to expose it.

Turning to another aspect of metaphysics and the metaphysical use of words, consider another symptom of when the use of words turns decidedly metaphysical, as Wittgenstein warns in the following passage from *The Blue Book*:

> ...in stating our puzzles about the *general vagueness* of sense experience, and about the flux of all phenomena, we are using the words "flux" and "vagueness" wrongly, in a typically metaphysical way, namely without antithesis; whereas in their correct and everyday use vagueness is opposed to clearness, flux to stability, inaccuracy to accuracy, and *problem* to *solution*. The very word "problem," one might say, is misapplied when used for our philosophical troubles. These difficulties, as long as they are seen as problems, are tantalizing, and appear insoluble [BB, 46].

Here Wittgenstein moves beyond general indictment of inappropriate grammatical frames as the source of philosophical and metaphysical confusions to the more specific claim that the use of certain words *in isolation from their antitheses* accounts for much in the creation of these troubles. On this point, it would appear Wittgenstein and Derrida are aligned. However, even though Derrida's deconstructions of oppositional relations do not dissolve oppositions and thereby do not support the use of terms without their antitheses, they nevertheless alter the structure of oppositions by way of a supplementation to the structure.

For Derrida, every opposition submits to a law of contamination. Every contrast remains exposed to deconstruction, which thoroughly alters the way in which "contrast" (opposition)—and therefore meaning— must be understood. This new understanding exceeds anything offered by Wittgenstein and his views of language and meaning and challenges metaphysics in a way exceeding his challenge.

Derrida's discussion of the opposition on which the sign itself depends presents a crucial illustrative example because it serves to model the structure of *every* opposition. This opposition is that between the signifier and the signified, which Derrida also expresses in this passage as the difference between the sensible and the intelligible:

> ...the concept of the sign cannot in itself surpass this opposition between the sensible and the intelligible. The concept of the sign, in each of its aspects, has been determined by this opposition throughout the totality of its history. It has lived only on this opposition and its system. But we cannot do without the concept of the sign, for we cannot give up this metaphysical complicity without also giving up the critique we are directing against this complicity [1978, 281].

Without the opposition between signifier and signified language would not be possible. So any critique of metaphysics and its fundamental dichotomies and oppositions, necessarily conducted through language, must continue to be founded on the indissoluble opposition in language itself— namely that between the signifier and the signified. Derrida then describes what occurs in the course of any presumptuous dissolution of this opposition of the signifier and the signified.

> For there are two heterogenous ways of erasing the difference between the signifier and the signified: one, the classic way, consists in reducing or deriving the signifier, that is to say, ultimately in *submitting* the sign to thought; the other, the one we are using here against the first one, consists in putting into question the system in which the preceding reduction functioned: first and foremost, the opposition between the sensible and the intelligible. For the *paradox* is that the metaphysical reduction of the sign needed the opposition it was reducing. The opposition is systematic with the reduction. And what we are saying here about the sign can be extended to all the concepts and all the sentences of metaphysics [1978, 281].

The metaphysical reduction of the sign needs the opposition it presumes to reduce because, without this opposition, *there is no sign*! And without the sign there can be no critical discourse or reflection on metaphysics or anything else. The nature of the particular oppositional structure between the signifier and the signified is, as might be anticipated, *complementary* such that the signifier and the signified form a system where one cannot exist without the other and each cannot be reduced to the other without effectively destroying the system, without destroying the sign and its functionality.

Returning to Wittgenstein, he insists on distinguishing between the metaphysical use of words (without antitheses) and ordinary use of words (with antitheses) whereas Derrida believes any use of words to be as metaphysical as any other. Derrida arrives at this conclusion by understanding the term "metaphysics" to be indissociable from oppositional relation—only now he understands the structure of oppositional relation and the structure of differences in a way exceeding the traditional structure, which characterizes Wittgenstein's view.

Wittgenstein's contrast between metaphysical and ordinary uses of words, non-antithetical and antithetical uses, may be deconstructed—which is to say, displaced and complemented (supplemented) by an additional logic of opposition. This logic posits no pure instance of either pole of the opposition—and no escape from metaphysics, which is to say, from Derrida's view, no escape from difference and division. Wittgenstein's notion of the non-antithetical use of words as the metaphysical use he wishes to sideline, dissolves under Derrida's deconstruction. The split identity of the sign, resulting from the law of iterability, ensures a tension of difference within every sign such that the non-antithetical has no foothold by which to raise itself to the point of emerging as a *pure* instance of the non-antithetical. It always remains contaminated by difference and the antithetical.

Derrida's deconstruction of opposition does not leave everything exactly where it was, metaphysically speaking. In the wake of deconstruction, all classical oppositional relations undergo the displacement exhibited in the deconstruction of the opposition between the signifier and the signified. Furthermore, no difference, no contrast, no separation remains immune to this deconstruction. This means that every presumed singular identity contains the seed of its other within its essence.

Derrida's famous statement, *il n'y a pas de hors-texte*, may be read as defining the limit of the absolute, the limit of the pure, the limit of transcendence. In this reckoning of the tradition, the opposition inside/outside offers no pure outside or inside. Since this level of abstraction may become confusing, a graphic simulation may prove helpful. The metaphysical limits of the absolute may be traced along an evolutionary path from premodern to modern to postmodern with correspondingly different oppositional structures.

Metaphysical dualism exemplified in the early works of Plato—offering a key instance of *premodern metaphysics*—may be diagrammed as below. X and Z represent the poles of the oppositional relation of Being and Non-being. X exists as pure, whole, absolute Being and Z as pure and absolute Non-Being, which may be more readily understood as Time. In the confrontation of Being and Non-Being, a hybrid emerges, Y, as a contamination of X by Z. Where X is the really real of true being and Z the contamination of X by the Non-Being of Time, then Y is the apparent world, the phenomenal world of Becoming. This metaphysical structure is hierarchical because X, as Being, represents the preferred ideal state and Z, as Non-being, represents the origin of the "fallen" hybrid realm of Y, the merging of Being and Time, that must be transcended in order to return to the ideal world of X. The steps of this hierarchical arrangement are depicted as follows:

X (Being, Ideality as reality)		
	Y (Appearance, becoming)	
		Z (Non-being, time)

Derrida describes this type of oppositional economy as *the* metaphysical exigency, a hierarchical structure of two pure extremes yielding a middle mixture of these extremes—a structure governing all the crucial metaphysical oppositions in premodern metaphysics.

Modern metaphysics, exemplified in Cartesian metaphysics, introduces a new configuration within the category of Being by dividing Being into two separate orders: *res cogitans* or mental substance and *res extensa* or physical substance. These categories were later reimagined more extensively in Immanuel Kant's Subject/Object dualism. In this dualism, both sides of the opposition are separate and pure but the Subject dominates the Object because, for the Subject, the being of the Object manifests only *through* the Subject. Subject/Object dualism replaces the strict antagonism between Being and Time with the less extreme tension of the subordination of Object to Subject. In the same stroke, however, this subordination introduces the question of solipsism as a philosophical problem, whereby the Subject in the Subject/Object split need not be imagined to include any other genuine subjects or objects beyond self and self-consciousness. Nothing is experienced apart from the "I," creating the dualism of the pure essences of Subject/Object whereby the Object can never be apprehended as it is in itself apart from consciousness. This modern configuration may be pictured as follows:

X (Subject, consciousness, mind)		
	Y (Phenomenon, Object as experienced)	
		Z (Noumenon, Object as is)

By contrast, *postmodern metaphysics* changes the structure of the dualism from opposing *essences* of unequal quality to parallel *forces* of equal quality such that every case becomes an instance of both X *and* Z—the superposition of X and Z in such a way that both do not necessarily manifest to appearance in particular contexts. X and Z form a complementary relation, whereby the oppositional boundary between cases of pure X and pure Z disappears and X and Z exist in tandem in *every* instance, just as when a coin toss lands on one side and the other side remains but disappears from view. The two sides are inseparable but not always equally manifested in a single view. X and Z forces always work in tandem and only in certain contexts do they appear to undercut or oppose each other. This postmodern structure of opposition applies to all the traditional oppositional relations, reconfiguring them from opposing essences to different, though not canceling, parallel forces. Nevertheless, in most instances a hierarchy emerges as one side dominates particular manifestations while the other side recedes, but this hierarchy is not structural in the sense that neither side is more original, dominant, or lasting in its essence. "Being" becomes the "Trace"—an essential entanglement of becoming in what was, in the modern structure, the field of confrontation between pure opposites.

X, Z → Trace (subject/object, presence/absence, space/time, self/other, etc.)

In conclusion, the metaphysical dualism consistent with Wittgenstein's philosophy corresponds to the modern oppositional economy, which is also consistent with the inability of his approach to rule out metaphysical solipsism. The tripartite structure of modern dualism appears in every part of Wittgenstein's thinking. For example, in his understanding of the opposition between grasping and interpreting a rule, X represents the grasping response, Z the endless regress of interpretation, and Y the range of hybrid instances or special cases requiring interpretation. The structure is similar with other key oppositions in Wittgenstein's philosophy such as the literal and the metaphorical, rule and application, and description and explanation. Both Wittgenstein and Derrida belong to metaphysical positions presenting forms of dualism, but Wittgenstein, despite his opposition to Cartesian mind/body dualism, still belongs more in the Cartesian modern tradition of oppositional structure whereas Derrida offers a genuinely different metaphysical alternative.

And yet the suspicion may still lurk as to whether one form or another of dualism must comprise the entire realm of available metaphysical options. What, then, of the mystical metaphysical position urging the view that everything is ultimately one? Commentators have read versions of such oneness along with claims of apophatic mysticism in the philosophies of both Wittgenstein (e.g., Mark, 1989; Moringiello, 2003) and Derrida. Such readings became so common in Derrida's case he felt obliged to directly respond. (e.g., Derrida, 1992d). Cannot a cosmic oneness transcend all possible contaminations, especially contaminations deriving apparent justification from the suspect realm of theory built up from the suspect realm of language? But this hope fails to confront the challenge that any presumed unity in the form of ultimate transcendental oneness must elide the essential role of time. As will be seen in the next chapter, this kind of oneness can be achieved only in the absence of time.

12

Time

As mentioned previously, when Wittgenstein confronts the metaphysical question "What is a sign?" he responds by offering examples. He notes this is not how Socrates proceeds. Socrates did not want examples of justice. He wanted a proper definition that would identify what all judgments rightly called just have in common. But in the course of the Socratic inquiry, definitions submitted by his interlocutors appear full of confusion as Socrates challenges the proposed definitions at every turn. Speaking through Socrates, Plato reasons that the use of words through different times and places must be poor reflections of an essential meaning transcending the temporal and everyday distortions of human applications. This transcendent spirit of words places them in a timeless realm where meanings are constant, true, and reliable but ultimately beyond human reach. It seems the best humans can hope for consists of true opinion rather than certain knowledge. By rejecting this approach, Wittgenstein appears to avoid the traditional philosophical trap leading to the conclusion: We do not really know what a sign is or what justice is or what anything else is. This conclusion strikes Wittgenstein as not merely counter-intuitive but self-defeating.

Any model of the workings of language necessarily rests on one or another conception of the being, the essential nature, of words. The Platonic model rests on a conception of the essential being of the word/concept as outside time. Since Wittgenstein abandons models of language aligned with metaphysical idealism/realism (the ideal as the really real), he offers an alternative conception of the being of the word and the sign. Insofar as he directs his efforts away from the task of looking for essences by turning toward the examination of particular instances, he thereby also turns the investigation toward examination of context. Granting significance to context in assessing the uses of words leads to acknowledging the importance of time, since specific location in time—temporal context—remains an inescapable feature of every particular instance of use.

Wittgenstein's thinking on the problem of identity presents an especially useful point at which to begin assessing the role of time in his view of language. In both his early and late work, he believes it nonsensical to say of a thing that it is identical with itself. For example, in the *Tractatus* he says, "That identity is not a relation between objects is obvious" (5.5301). Further on he adds: "Roughly speaking: to say of two things that they are identical is nonsense, and to say of one thing that it is identical with itself is to say nothing." (5.5303). And in *Philosophical Investigations* he proclaims, "'A thing is identical with itself.'—There is no finer example of a useless proposition, which yet is connected with a certain play of the imagination. It is as if in imagination we put a thing into its own shape and saw that it fitted." (PI#216). The notion of identity exhibits a useless redundancy.

Wittgenstein's understanding of identity is strongly influenced by the tendency to see it through the lens of mathematical logic and its imaginary timeless space. To assert something is identical with itself seems tautological, and therefore useless, when considering only presence in space. But this identity assertion acquires significance within the context of time. This may be better understood by turning the statement into its opposite assertion: "A thing is *not* identical with itself." For Wittgenstein, this negative statement would likely count as even more nonsensical than the positive version. But for Derrida the negative statement makes very good sense. For Derrida, the notion that a thing is identical with itself resembles more an empirical claim than a tautology. And, rather than being a "useless proposition" as Wittgenstein asserts, the proposition of identity counts instead, for Derrida, as demonstrably false. On the other hand, the notion that a thing is not identical with itself counts as demonstrably true.

The passage of time introduces change from one moment to the next, whereby it becomes not only possible but *inevitable* that a thing not be identical with itself from one moment to the next. From one moment to the next, nothing remains the same. This is as true of signs and words as it is of things (and everything also counts as a sign). Derrida considers identity temporally whereas Wittgenstein considers it in a logical space outside time. Indeed, from his remarks about identity in *Philosophical Investigations* it becomes clear Wittgenstein theorizes identity within a timeless frame. Were he to have included time in his logic, he would have been able to see genuine significance, rather than mere uselessness, in the statement: "A thing does *not* fit into itself."

Nevertheless, Wittgenstein's careful attention to examples and to context in the use of language gives decisive evidence he assigns time a crucial role in his view of language. He makes this explicitly clear: "We are talking about the spatial and temporal phenomenon of language, not about some non-spatial, non-temporal phantasm." Language and its uses exist in time and yet also appear to transcend time. This transcendence, however, can lead to confusion. He continues by making reference to the game of chess: "But we talk about it [language] as we do about the pieces in chess when we are stating the rules of the game, not describing their physical properties. The question 'What is a word really?' is analogous to 'What is a piece in chess?'" (PI#108). And the underlying question becomes: What is the function, the use, of the word or the piece?

The game of chess functions in time, but the functions of the pieces do not change over time. But Wittgenstein does not deny the functions or uses of the pieces *could* change over time if those who play the game of chess were to choose to alter the functions of the pieces. And with regard to language and language-games, he acknowledges the same: "When language-games change, then there is a change in concepts, and with the concepts the meanings of words change" (1969, #65). Clearly, however, in these passages Wittgenstein sees the role of time as contingent. The phrase "When language-games change" indicates change occurs at particular times and for reasons arising from changing human purposes and circumstances. Speaking of the implicit propositions that might compose what Wittgenstein calls "a picture of the world," he remarks, "The propositions describing this world-picture might be part of a kind of mythology. And their role is like that of rules of a game." But although this "mythology" may serve as the seemingly permanent background against which change may be understood and experienced, it also submits to transformation, as Wittgenstein explains: "The mythology may change back into a state of flux, the river-bed of thought may shift. But I distinguish between the movement of waters on the river-bed and the shift of the bed itself; though there is not a sharp division of the one from the other" (1969, #97).

In his early work, Wittgenstein may have thought logic to be exempt from time, but in his later work this view changes sufficiently that he poses himself the question (through his imaginary interlocutor): "So logic too is an empirical science?" Although he replies that this assumption would be wrong, he immediately offers the following hedge: "Yet this is right: the same proposition may get treated at one time as something to test by experience, at another as a rule of testing." Turning again to the metaphor of the river and its bed, he summarizes: "And the bank of the river consists partly of hard rock, subject to no alteration or only to an imperceptible one, partly of sand, which now in one place now in another gets washed away, or deposited." (1969, #94–99). Time, like a river, encounters rock that resists its flow more so than sand, thus distinguishing between the bed—and its variations in resistance—and the river, with its constant movement. His suggestion that the river and the bed are in some way wrapped together such that "there is not a sharp division of the one from the other" must be clarified to note that he draws the distinction between the "movement of waters on the river-bed" and "the shift of the bed itself." Wherever the waters go, there shall the bed lie. Time, like water, is an agency acting on material of varying resistance. Similarly, for Wittgenstein, language remains exposed to the agency of time. Parts of language, such as its grammar, offer more resistance than do other parts, such as its words.

This view of time in relation to language differs importantly from Derrida's view. In Derrida's view, time plays a *structural* role in language such that without it language and sign-using in general would not be possible. Derrida's understanding of the logic of identity extends beyond Wittgenstein's spatial logic to include both space and time as irreducible components of language *at the structural level*. Since Yale philosopher Martin Hägglund has fashioned a career in highlighting, explaining, and expanding on the theme of time in Derrida's thought, his account of its importance is worth exploring at length.

Derrida's account of the role of time, Hägglund explains, centers on a confrontation with the logic of identity. This logic of identity emerges from Derrida's understanding of time and governs his work from beginning to end and from top to bottom. Traditional metaphysics grounds itself in a notion of time in which time is conceived in relation to "the present." This notion of "the present" provides the basis for the logic of identity—the logic that a thing is identical with itself. The traditional notion of "the present" as the immediate and self-evident gives a logic to the notion of identity as the presence of the present, as pure present self-sameness. This rock of presence then serves as the basis for grasping the modifications of time as past and future. What has been present becomes past and what will be present approaches as the future.

Nevertheless, Hägglund explains that this traditional notion of time contains within it the means for undermining itself. The present moment never simply *is*. It *moves* and consequently cannot be adequately theorized as an "it." Presence manifests a continuous division of itself, sliding along in a sequencing of what has just been and what is yet to come. Presence must more accurately be understood as *presencing*, as *succession* rather than a discrete "now" or "moment." On the basis of this succession Derrida argues that it becomes necessary to see time as *différance*. The moment, the "now" of presence, remains always divided. As that which simultaneously passes away and comes to be, the moment *differs*. Derrida does not offer an alternative concept of time. Instead, he uncovers what the traditional concept has implied all along. And this traditional concept then, in Hägglund's words, "provides the resources to deconstruct the logic of identity" (2008, 15–16).

The temporal can never be in itself. This notion delivers the key to unraveling the traditional and exclusively spatial logic of identity. Nothing simply exists *in* time. Time is part of the internal structure of what is and, therefore, a metaphysics adequate to the task must include time as essential to the being of beings. As previously discussed, Derrida makes use of the term "trace" to refer to the spatial/temporal structure of the sign as well as the being of beings.

The temporal deconstruction of the internal structure of being creates a problem in the logic of identity: If nothing is identical to itself, how is any form of identity possible? How may it be possible for any thing to be experienced as the "same" thing from one moment to the next? In response, Derrida explains the trace of time. The trace is the "becoming-space of time" and the "becoming-time of space"—a phenomenon Derrida also refers to with the term *spacing* (1982, 13–14).

Concerning spacing as the becoming-space of time, Hägglund clarifies, "The trace is necessarily spatial, since spatiality is characterized by the ability to remain in spite of temporal succession. Spatiality is thus the condition for synthesis, since it enables the tracing of relations between past and future. Spatiality, however, can never be in itself; it can never be pure simultaneity" (2008, 18). Simultaneity could never emerge as an experience if space were not haunted by time. Consequently, concerning spacing as the becoming-time of space, Hägglund continues, "Simultaneity is unthinkable without a temporalization that relates one spatial juncture to another. The *becoming-time of space* is necessary not only for the trace to be related to other traces, but also for it to be a trace in the first place. A trace can only be read after its inscription and is thus marked by a relation to the future that temporalizes space" (2008, 18).

This understanding of time as succession is crucial for Derrida's deconstruction of the logic of identity as well as the synthesis of the trace. Hägglund concludes, "If the spatialization of time makes the synthesis *possible*, the temporalization of space makes it *impossible* for the synthesis to be grounded in an indivisible presence. The synthesis is always a trace of the past that is left *for the future*. Thus, it can never be in itself but is essentially exposed to that which may erase it" (2008, 18).

In other words, "spacing" according to Derrida, consists of the complementarity of space and time such that the trace *remains* by way of location in space and yet it *changes* by way of the succession of time. Hägglund continues by explaining the structural pervasiveness and comprehensive inclusiveness of this spacing and the consequences of the constitution of time as it extends beyond signs and human activities.

What I want to emphasize here is that Derrida describes the trace and *dif-férance* as conditions for life in general. They should not be understood as "transcendental" conditions of possibility in Kant's or Husserl's sense, because such conditions only apply to the experience of a finite consciousness. For Derrida, the spacing of time is an "ultratranscendental" condition from which *nothing* [emphasis added] can be exempt…. On the one hand, the spacing of time has an ultratranscendental status because it is the condition for everything *all the way up* to and including the ideal itself. The spacing of time is the condition not only for everything that can be cognized and experienced, but also for everything that can be thought and desired. On the other hand, the spacing of time has an ultratranscendental status because it is the condition of everything *all the way down* to the minimal forms of life. As Derrida maintains, there is no limit to the generality of *différance* and the structure of the trace applies to all fields of the living [2008, 18–19].

When Hägglund says, following Derrida, the structure of the trace "applies to all fields of the living," he means here to emphasize applicability to all life. But as he says previously to this, the spacing of time is a condition from which "nothing can be exempt." Not only all life forms but everything that exists owes its existence to the "spacing of time." Without succession and the complementarity of space and time implicit in it, existence would be frozen; nothing could happen. As already mentioned, with space, motion becomes possible and time emerges with motion such that space and time, by way of motion, are inseparable and irreducible one to the other.

The being of the trace belongs to the structure of everything that is. This ultratranscendental condition from which "nothing is exempt" provides further explanation for why Derrida says, "There is nothing outside the text." Everything that is, is a trace; and since the trace also belongs to the structure of all writing, everything that is may be seen as writing. All reading of writing amounts to interpretation because the divided identity of the trace presents superimposed writings from one context to another. For Derrida, no absolute boundary exists between writing and world. The "text" of signs extends into and is of a piece with the conditioning and transformation brought about through the "con-text" of the world.

Where Wittgenstein explores rules of use in a shifting spatial/temporal landscape of rules in language, Derrida exposes the space-time logic of succession, which then reveals laws governing every possible use of language, now or in the future. These differing stances concerning the role of time in language accord with different metaphysical assumptions about the being of signs and yield different orientations toward how meaning functions in the daily practice of using language.

By way of completing the metaphysical landscape drawn in the previous chapter, an analogy my be offered to help illustrate the differences between Wittgenstein and Derrida and why these differences count as important when considering the role of language in human community. The previous chapter described the general evolution of metaphysics by suggesting this evolution be understood as the progression from premodern to modern to postmodern alternatives. Key figures associated with this progression include, respectively, Plato, Descartes, and Derrida. Diagrams were presented to graphically indicate the shifts occurring in the different dualistic structuring of oppositional relations. As central in this development, time may be understood as presenting to philosophers the primary problem in the metaphysical landscape. Philosophers seek a foundation on which to firmly ground knowledge only to continue discovering that the ground still moves under the footings of their philosophical constructions. Every attempt to find immovable ground fails. A river flows, but the search for the riverbed ultimately comes up empty.

The history of metaphysics may be understood as the history of improvements in the direction of greater anticipation of the inevitable movement and change generated by the passage of time. Postmodern metaphysics, exemplified in deconstruction, offers considerable improvement over modern and premodern metaphysics. This improvement becomes especially important in the sphere of language because postmodern metaphysics introduces a structure of oppositional relation maximally anticipating the shifting ground of meaning under the influence of temporal succession and changing contextual boundaries. The more rigid structuring of oppositional relation in premodern and modern traditions results in greater vulnerability to events that are part of the nature of the temporal world within which human communities exist. Those responsible for using words to construct and implement laws and rules and who do not approach these activities from an orientation to language benefiting from an adequate anticipation of the limits of language invite blindsiding. While nothing may guarantee against loss, error, and miscommunication, a failure in adequate anticipation of the ways in which these failings arise counts as an unnecessary failure in disposition toward mitigation, especially in the wake of the postmodern era and its aftermath.

Wittgenstein and Derrida both include a crucial role for time in their understanding of language, but their considerations align with different metaphysical dispositions toward time. Although Wittgenstein's later work presents a critique of Descartes and mind/body, subject/object dualism, it nevertheless retains the classic dualistic metaphysical structure of Cartesian philosophy at the deeper level of being and time.

For Wittgenstein, time affects everything, including language, but does so from the *outside*; time *wears* on language as a river wears against the banks along which it flows. For Derrida, time affects language, and everything else, from the *inside*; without time there is no thing, no event, no position, no being—nothing. Time and space, time and matter, time and being—these oppositions name a complementarity such that each does not exist without the other. Time does not operate on being but instead entangles itself in the constitution of being. This complementary dualism of being and time exceeds the structure of dualism and oppositional relations in modern Cartesian metaphysics in what Hägglund, following Derrida, refers to as an ultratranscendental approach. Thus, the ways in which Wittgenstein and Derrida challenge Cartesian dualism are remarkably different, representing different views of time and metaphysical options between modern and postmodern philosophical traditions. As might be expected, changes in the metaphysical role of time require changes throughout the gallery of traditional philosophical categories, among which the notion of truth, addressed in the next chapter, has drawn wide attention and deep controversy.

13

Truth

Taking a cue from Wittgenstein, it might be helpful to begin the discussion of a concept as fundamental and provocative as truth with an example. In his Derrida biography, Benoît Peeters, describes an event occurring at a University of Alabama conference held in Tuscaloosa in 1987. This event marked the beginning of a controversy that was to have deep repercussions for Derrida personally, for the reputation of deconstruction generally, and for the question of truth broadly in the wake of postmodern cultural developments. According to Peeters, "[Derrida] mournfully handed out copies of a certain number of articles ... [Then] the participants held a 'discussion that lasted more than three hours and touched on both the substance of things and the decisions to be made.' Many were shocked and did not know how to react. But Derrida was categorical: the material should be published in full, and they ... were the ones who should publish it" (2013, 391).

The articles in question, totaling 170 and of which Derrida handed out only a sample, were written and published by Paul de Man during the war years of 1941–42 in *Le Soir*—a Belgian newspaper operating under Nazi control. Derrida and de Man had become friends and colleagues in the early 1970s when de Man arranged for Derrida to lecture at Yale. With de Man's support, Derrida's work became increasingly popular at Yale and de Man's own writings furthered the renown and influence of deconstruction throughout North American universities.

Among the articles Derrida distributed at the Tuscaloosa conference, the most disturbing was dated March 4, 1941—titled "The Jews in Contemporary Culture." It contained these statements: "[O]ne sees that a solution of the Jewish problem that would aim at the creation of a Jewish colony isolated from Europe would not entail, for the literary life of the west, deplorable consequences. The latter would lose, in all, a few personalities of mediocre value and would continue, as in the past, to develop according to its great evolutive laws" (cited in McQuillan, 2001, 129). The articles had been brought to Derrida's attention after their discovery by Ortwin de

Graef, a Flemish graduate student doing research for a thesis on the work of Paul de Man. Understanding there were many reasons Derrida ought to be made aware of the articles, not least of which because Derrida was Jewish, de Graef alerted friends of Derrida who then contacted him. Consequently, Derrida took a leading role in responding to de Graef's discovery and making the news public in his academic circle. However, before the *Le Soir* articles could be published by Derrida and his colleagues, word spread.

On December 1, 1987, the *New York Times* issued a front-page story with the headline: "Yale scholar's articles found in pro–Nazi paper." According to Peeters, "The unsigned article was full of mistakes and half-truths about Paul de Man and the political situation in Belgium during the Occupation." Predictably, the *Times* story launched a controversy of "considerable proportions" inside and outside academic circles across the United States and Europe. Paul de Man, the American champion of deconstruction, acquired the label: "The Waldheim of postmodernism." Overnight, it seemed, de Man was on trial in the court of public opinion throughout two continents.

Following the full public revelation of de Man's *Le Soir* writings, Derrida published "Like the Sound of the Sea Deep Within a Shell: Paul de Man's War" (1988a) in which he discussed the articles and his reaction to them and weighed the implications. This response drew forth a volley of disparaging commentaries—aimed at Derrida in particular and deconstruction in general. Many of these commentaries concluded Derrida shamelessly deployed a deconstructive defense of de Man—a defense illustrating not only the weaknesses and excesses of deconstruction in relation to questions of truth but also the questionable ends to which such weaknesses and excesses could be brought to bear. For these accusers, the truth of de Man's guilt concerning collaboration and the anti–Semitic statements he made in *Le Soir* remained obvious and attempts to suggest otherwise served only to discredit oneself as well as any method used to arrive at such hesitations.

Statements made by Derrida, drawn from "Paul de Man's War," were cited as exemplary of the cavalier approach to truth inherent in deconstruction: "...de Man's discourse is constantly split, disjointed, engaged in incessant conflicts ... all the propositions carry within themselves a counterproposition: sometimes virtual, sometimes very explicit, always readable, this counterproposition signals what I will call, in a regular and contradictory manner, a *double edge* and a *double bind*, the singular artefact of a blade and a knot" (1988a, 607).

Opponents of deconstruction were not surprised Derrida should find such "artefacts" in de Man's discourse. The "blades" and "knots" rendered

Derrida vulnerable to the charge of using his notorious "double edge" deconstructive maneuver in ways amounting to, as his detractors might say, shading the truth in an effort to cloud the facts and make excuses for his friend. Through 1988 and the early 1990s, the controversy that had erupted into a highly public trial of Paul de Man broadened into increasing indictments of Derrida and deconstruction.

Deconstructive textual analysis and it notorious "double-edge" reading strategies had already convinced many of Derrida's detractors that deconstruction not only introduced questionable fact-reading strategies but also fueled a theory of reading that could only be viewed as aiding and abetting the corruption of truth-seeking practices. At the same time, it so happened that one of the most egregious and often mentioned examples of the current wave of corruption in truth-seeking was gaining steady momentum—Holocaust denial. This brand of historical revisionism aroused extreme emotions and the phrase "Holocaust denier" became an epithet of scorn. In short order, Derrida found himself positioned by his critics at the head of this revisionist wave—accused of being the master of a method delivering a handy tool to Holocaust deniers. In the eyes of many, this tool left truth as collateral damage in the wake of a deconstruction tsunami sweeping across the North American continent.

For example, Heather Macdonald (1991) writes: "Deconstruction is in effect, though certainly not in intention, the highbrow version of Holocaust revisionism" (171). Furthermore, in view of the deconstruction of the subject conducted by Derrida and the moral nihilism resulting from the supposed loss of responsibility for actions on the part of this deconstructed agent, Macdonald claims, "Deconstruction cannot oppose fascism on moral grounds without invoking the very concept of the 'individual' that it seeks to undermine" (172).

Two years later, in an opinion piece for the *New York Times*, Michiko Kakutani continues in a similar vein: "Mr. Derrida offered deconstructive readings of de Man's pro–Nazi articles, which purported to show that the texts subverted their own declared intentions, a tactic not dissimilar to those employed by Holocaust deniers, who routinely take factual evidence of the Holocaust and deconstruct it to support their own assertions." Moving from this particular accusation to a more general indictment, Kakutani continues, "The point is that deconstruction purveys a stylishly nihilistic view of the world, which insists that all meaning is relative, that all truth is elusive, and therefore futile." Having defined deconstruction as a form of nihilism and as truth-corrupting, Kakutani then describes the ultimate consequences stemming from this questionable approach to texts and to life: "Such critical approaches irreparably divorce intellectual discourse from morality and ethics, and posit an ahis-torical world in which actions have no consequences and language has no real meaning" (1993).

Derrida's attempt to protect a friend against the worst—namely, a hasty judgment following serious accusations—became itself, for many critics, an instance of the worst. He was held to be in collaboration with a collaborator who ought to be brought to account—even if deceased (de Man died in 1983). Combined with human tendencies to search out and exploit openings, the deconstructionist's "play of *différance*," the play of the double-edge, might itself present the opening for the creation of something worse—the failure to appropriately respond to what calls out for response. This failure of appropriate response, it was argued, creates openings for other responses that could contribute in various ways to weakening the role of truth in human community, thereby weakening the social fabric. Who is to say, for example, that Derrida's dictum, "Iterability ... leaves us no choice but to mean (to say) something that is (already, always, also) other than what we mean (to say)" (1988b, 62) cannot be read to mean there is no use in speaking the truth because the truth cannot be spoken?

Long before these events, Wittgenstein anticipated such skepticism toward meaning along with its potential radical consequences for speaking truth. Returning to the discussion in Chapter 4, recall Wittgenstein's rule following paradox: "Every course of action can be made out to accord with the rule." Recall also that this claim occurs in the context of a discussion of interpretation such that the paradox may also be read as: "Every course of action can be *interpreted* to accord with the rule." The crisis this paradox creates with respect to rule following and which Kripke identified as the "most radical and original sceptical problem that philosophy has seen to date" (1982, 60) also reveals an analogous crisis with respect to truth. Just as every response may be interpreted to accord with the rule, so also every explanation may be interpreted to accord with the facts. The rule following paradox exposes a *structural* obstacle to truth. No given facts need be denied or discounted. Any given set of facts may be interpreted in such a way as to be made consistent with any particular claim or theory, thereby elevating it to the status of a contender for truth. It is not hard to see why this view presents itself as a crisis not only for meaning but also for truth. How may Derrida and Wittgenstein respond to such a crisis, given their respective frameworks?

Returning to Paul de Man, consider a literary example. He held Herman Melville in high regard and *Billy Budd* was a favorite text. Recall that the titular character strikes and kills the Master-at-Arms. However, the ship's commander, Captain Vere, reads conflicting meanings in Billy's action. He sees the sense in which Billy is both guilty and innocent of the killing. Yet despite this insight, he reluctantly puts Billy's neck in the hangman's noose. This story, with its portrayal of the double edge in an action, re-creates something like the world of Greek tragic drama where the actors cross boundaries and yet do so in ways pressing the reading of actions to undecidability—the point of difficulty necessitating decision.

Similarly, the question of de Man's guilt must, Derrida argues, extend beyond the texts of *Le Soir* to the broader context of life, to include not merely the question, "What do the words say?" but also the question, "What do the words *mean* in the context in which they were written?" Similarly, the question "What are the facts?" solicits the question "What do the facts mean?" Derrida always fastens on the formidable complexity of attempts to read—not merely what words may be read to *say* but what the words may otherwise *mean*, which must open the context to all that may have prompted the words.

Does the fact of writing for the Nazi controlled newspaper *Le Soir* make de Man a collaborationist? And does the article he wrote in *Le Soir* of March 4, 1941, make him an anti-Semite? He would not likely have denied his authorship. Looking at the broader text of the immediate historical situation of the war years as well as what was then known in 1988 of de Man's life before and after the war, Derrida finds the facts insufficient to warrant a conclusive guilty verdict on either the indictment of collaboration or anti–Semitism. The accused may be shown to have made contributions to *Le Soir* and to have written particular anti–Semitic statements but Derrida claims not enough of the whole text/context is known, that it is too quick and too early to declare a verdict. In "Paul de Man's War," Derrida presses readers following the de Man case to pause at a point of undecidability and take a breath instead of rushing to judgment. The text of an article does not end at the edge of the page. The question of de Man's guilt must extend, Derrida argues, beyond the texts of *Le Soir* to the broader context of life. The words may be thought of as the facts, but, in Derrida's view, an adequate context for these facts remained yet to be determined. More overlays of information were needed if particular undecidable junctures were to be overcome.

Had he lived longer, Derrida's view of de Man may have altered beyond what he could have anticipated with ensuing overlays of recontextualization of de Man's life and work. Following Derrida's death in 2004, the context of de Man's words in *Le Soir* broadened considerably as a result of investigative work by Evelyn Barish (2014). The strength of the indictments against de Man grew accordingly. Further revelations concerning his double life as the husband of two women simultaneously and his numerous lies about his credentials and past deeds cast a shadow over his entire life and work. But as such revelations build over time, they add layers of context to the image, decreasing undecidability in one layer while also simultaneously opening undecidability at another layer, a deeper layer of meaning. The question "Who was Paul de Man?" acquires new answers in response to new overlays while this same question nevertheless persists at another level. And no matter how much context may be added, no matter how many previously unknown details may be recovered or uncovered, the question "Who was Paul de Man?" will extend forward, expanded and modified, and awaiting potential further layers of information.

Such is the case with every person and every event. No matter how much context may be added to the image of the Holocaust, it will always make sense to ask "What was the Holocaust?" The ongoing meaning of the Holocaust remains contingent on questions always open to further answers. Beyond the names and identities, beyond every empirical measure and record, it may still be asked of the perpetrators: "Who were they?" Beyond every piece of material evidence documenting the camps and the chambers it may rightly still be asked: What is the meaning of these chamber ruins? But the work of many agents and agencies over many years makes the answers to these questions very different from that proposed by those who have been placed in the category of Holocaust deniers. The layers of evidence and context added through the work of historians, scientists, and courts include not only all the available relevant factual evidence but also the most salient, inclusive, and compelling explanations of the evidence. All historically prominent events, all past events of any kind, present themselves as signs because signs are all that remain of a past that is essentially absent. Such signs, as in the case of all signs, require, according to Derrida, more than calculation to read. The end result of such reading emerges as decision, not calculation. But such decisions, in order to be persuasive, require effort, training, and skill in their formation. In the case of deconstructive readings, Derrida's specific alignment of decision with his notion of undecidability must be carefully understood.

In Derrida's use, undecidability remains misunderstood if viewed as creating an impasse sufficient to assign interpretations equal status. Undecidability signals the point at which decision becomes necessary and where genuine decision beyond the model of mere calculation becomes *possible*. This is the context through which to reconcile Derrida's views concerning undecidability with his affirmation of the irreducible relevance of truth.

This juncture of undecidability and its relevance to questions of truth continues to mark the point at which Derrida's advocacy of deconstruction is most commonly misunderstood. For example, legal scholar Mark Bevir (2000) believes Derrida "rejects our philosophical tradition as ... centred on a misplaced faith in stable meanings and objective truth." He then assembles arguments to show that Derrida "cannot sustain his complete rejection of meaning and truth" (412). But Bevir's arguments make no reference to this key passage from Derrida's *Limited Inc*: "[T]he value of truth ... is never contested or destroyed in my writings, but only reinscribed in more powerful, larger, more stratified contexts. And ... within interpretive contexts ... that are relatively stable, sometimes apparently almost unshakeable, it should be possible to invoke rules of competence, criteria of discussion and of consensus, good faith, lucidity, rigor, criticism, and pedagogy" (1988b, 146). In this text Derrida demonstrates how his view of truth not only allows for "stable" meanings but in fact aligns in many respects with the position Bevir affirms, which embraces rather than rejects truth.

But setting aside such confusions, does not undecidability expose junctures at which it becomes necessary to *decide* what is true rather than *submit* to what is true? Within layers of text where undecidability reigns, is truth then, at bottom, a *mere* decision? Unlike Wittgenstein's "solution" to the problem of the application of rules, Derrida's "solution" to the identity crisis of the sign when confronting the question of truth appears to amount to a negotiation more than a solution.

Based on the accumulated discussion in this and the previous chapters, it would appear that the operative difference between Wittgenstein and Derrida resides in Derrida's more thorough separation of sign and meaning by characterizing signs as always manifesting structurally equivocal layers rather than reducing, ultimately, to functionally univocal determinations. In situations presenting competing claims for truth, however, Lee Braver cites a provocative question raised by Wittgenstein: "Is it wrong for me to be guided in my actions by the propositions of physics? [...] Supposing we met people who did not regard that as a telling reason.... Instead of the physicist, they consult an oracle.... Is it wrong for them to consult an oracle and be guided by it?—If we call this 'wrong' aren't we using our language-game as a base from which to *combat* theirs?" (Braver, 206; Wittgenstein, 1969, #608–609).

Wittgenstein also acknowledges the potential obdurate nature of this "combat": "Where two principles really do meet which cannot be reconciled with one another, then each man declares the other a fool or a heretic." Pondering whether a resolution remains possible in such stand-offs, he adds: "I said I would 'combat' the other man,—but wouldn't I give him *reasons* [*Gründe*]? Certainly; but how far do they go? At the end of reasons comes *persuasion* [*Überredung*]. (Think what happens when missionaries convert natives)" (Braver, 206; Wittgenstein, 1969, #611–612). But how is such persuasion achieved—even if only in the attempt to persuade oneself?

For Derrida, every such persuasion—the embracing of what will count as truth—may rightly be called a *decision*. Decision involves a leap and this leap constitutes a new start, as it must always confront what is new in a situation even where the situation bears strong resemblance to past situations. Whatever rules may be in place to guide such a decision they do not apply themselves with the ease of a mere calculation. Wittgenstein appears to agree when he says, "If I am given a general (variable) rule, I must recognize each time afresh that this rule may be applied here too (that it holds for this case too). No act of foresight can absolve me from this act of insight. Since the form in which the rule is applied is in fact a new one at every step. But it is not a matter of an act of insight, but of an act of *decision*" (Braver, 182; Wittgenstein, *Philosophical Grammar*, 1974, 301).

But Wittgenstein seems not quite decided. In the *Brown Book*, composed after *Philosophical Grammar*, he says something a little different: "It is no act of insight, intuition, which makes us use the rule as we do at the particular stage point of the series. It would be less confusing to call it an act of decision, though this too is misleading, for nothing like an act of decision must take place, but possibly just an act of writing or speaking" (BB, 143). This last remark aligns with Wittgenstein's distinction between response and thinking, seeing and seeing-as. Though it would seem Wittgenstein makes a concession here to interpretation with the mention of decision, he clearly shows reluctance using that label because he knows this word implies too much in the way of interpretation. For the Wittgenstein of *The Blue and Brown Books*, any decision in applying the rules is, in the vast majority of cases, a decision that has effectively *already been made* and is inherent in the customary practices of a linguistic community.

Derrida, however, has likened decision to a strategic wager. For example, he says, "Thus, a strategic wager always consists in making a decision, or rather in giving ourselves over to decision—paradoxically, in making decisions we cannot justify from start to finish.... There is a strategic wager because the context is not absolutely determinable: there is a context, but one cannot analyse it exhaustively.... We have to accept the concept of a non-saturable context, and take into account both the context itself and its open structure, non-closure, if we are to make decisions and engage in a wager" (Derrida and Ferraris, 2001, 13).

As Derrida describes it, the decision is a wager because it resembles a leap—a leap beyond a justification complete from "start to finish." But the decision is more than a *blind* leap because it is strategic, which is to say it involves assessing the odds, so to speak. It involves measures of testing the boundary of relevant context, weighing evidence, and assessing possible consequences of the decision. Such a decision qualifies as neither a calculation nor a blind leap and it must remain tentative due to its continued exposure to the "yet-to-come."

This view of decision, however, may seem out of alignment with the Kierkegaardian view Derrida appears to defend in *The Gift of Death* (1995b, 65) where he claims, "the instant of decision is madness." But while decision may indeed contain an element of madness as it exceeds full reason and control, the strategic wager never entirely forsakes reason in arriving at the door of "madness" that is decision. This deference to reasons remains consistent with Derrida's claim that, "As soon as I speak to the other, I submit to the law of giving reason(s)" (*Rogues*, p. 101), recalling that this "other" also includes the "other" that is part of the self.

But again, Wittgenstein may seem in agreement when he suggests, "But doesn't it come out here that knowledge is related to a decision [*Entscheidung*]?" (1969, #362). And here the word "knowledge" may also be replaced with the word "truth." Wittgenstein's answer, however, is revealing: "And here it is difficult to find the transition from the exclamation one would like to make, to its consequences in what one does." The sense of it being a decision is, for Wittgenstein, not reflected in the action. This becomes clearer a few passages later when, referring to the sentence, "I know that that's a hand," Wittgenstein comments:

> The fact that I use the word "hand" and all the other words in my sentence without a second thought, indeed that I should stand before the abyss if I wanted so much as to try doubting their meanings—shews that absence of doubt belongs to the essence of the language-game, that the question "How do I know …" drags out the language-game, or else does away with it [1969, 370].

What looks like decision rests, for Wittgenstein, on the precedent of "This is what we do." The difference between being guided by physics or by an oracle resides in different language games and reliance on language games in turn derives substantially from previous training. With Derrida, naming necessarily remains more complex. Even when appearing to follow collective practice, assessing what may be true remains responsive to an undecidedly public/private specter (ideal) of truth always out of reach and yet sufficiently discernable as to continue offering direction or inspiration for each singular decision-maker. This is why Derrida's philosophical position, contrary to the claims of critics such as Macdonald, does not entail the loss of reason or personal responsibility for decision. Decisions may (and usually do) bear collective influence and yield collective consequences, but they are always stamped with personal signatures and have their roots in personal responsibility. In short, truth, like the meanings of words and signs, is always layered and the operative layers remain tied to context, which itself is never static.

Speaking more directly, Derrida says, "I tried to suggest that the question of truth is not outmoded. Truth is not a value one can renounce.

The deconstruction of philosophy does not renounce truth—any more, for that matter, than literature does. It is a question of thinking this other relation to truth" (Derrida and Ferraris, 2001, 10). This "other relation" to truth takes into account the "other general logic," the complementarity in layered meaning, the doubling of the sign, discussed in previous chapters.

Placing these considerations back into the frame of the *Billy Budd* narrative, when necessity for decision arises, every decision-maker is then condemned to the dilemma of Captain Vere. When forced to decide, "What did Billy Budd do?" the question necessarily evokes, "Who is Billy Budd?" Similarly, "What did Paul de Man do?" evokes, "Who is Paul de Man?" And, "What were the gas chambers used for?" evokes, "What is the meaning of the events called the Holocaust?" Even if *what* has occurred may be granted beyond contention, the *meaning* of what has occurred still requires interpretation. Answers are provisional negotiations turning on one or another edge of undecidability, requiring decision, and remaining always answerable to the further "coming of the other."

This remarkable situation regarding the pursuit of truth reflects the economy of every ideal, whereby the immanent conditions the transcendent and the transcendent conditions the immanent. The determination of truth at a particular point in time may present itself as *universal* for all readers only from within the current temporal context. Maxime Doyon's remarks when discussing transcendence (in the context of deconstruction) are especially helpful in illuminating this issue.

> [H]istorically determined and conditioned, ideal objects—or universal truths—are in an immanent sense *vulnerable* and *precarious*. They are vulnerable and precarious, not because they are not truly universal, but because the very opening of the universal sphere can only be accomplished in history through specific contingent practices like writing [139].

The "opening of the universal" transpires as the necessary temporal conditioning of the transcendent without which the transcendent, the universal, could have no being, no manifestation, whatsoever. The transcendent emerges only through the immanent while the immanent inevitably exposes the impossibility of the transcendent and conditions it towards forgetfulness. This circumstance regarding the transcendent must not be understood as an existential disappointment but rather as the opportunity or chance through which and by which all experience emerges. As Doyon concludes, "It is a chance, for without this possibility, we would be outside history as such ... [and] no such knowledge [regarding the universal, the true] would ever be possible" (139). Truth—the transcendent, the universal—comes to life only through the immanent, the particular, the temporal—the situated of the *decision*. Similarly, decision—the immanent, the particular—gains life as truth, as transcendence, only by exceeding the moment while remaining nevertheless historically contingent. This is why, for Derrida, transcendence becomes "quasi"-transcendence. The transcendent never fully surpasses the immanent while the immanent never fully surpasses the transcendent; otherwise nothing like the sign would be possible and, similarly, nothing like truth would be possible.

Collectively, then, the question of truth becomes: In the pursuit of healthy society, *to what extent* can its members—given limitations of time and resources—pursue truth when, in many situations, the path to truth may require the care, time, and attention demanded by decision? Accepting the challenge of seeking truth requires the patience and discernment necessary to understand the structural limitations imposed by the nature of signs. These structural limitations expose signs to potential unintentional as well as intentional distortion and corruption. Understanding these structural limitations makes it possible to develop greater discernment concerning the *task* of predicating truth. This means truth must never be presumed to be entirely in hand—always yet beyond reach, always open to further pursuit, always contingent, provisional, awaiting the next overlay of information and the next decision. The extent to which a society confronts the complexity of significant questions of truth in action and symbolic action may well constitute a measure of the extent of its civilization.

With an understanding of the limits to the determination of truth, the stakes collectively rise for the quality of perception, judgment, and work required in confronting the tension between insight and blindness, truth and lies. As the pursuit of truth confronts layers of undecidability, truth requires corresponding decisions. Between truth and its determination stand human beings—judges, juries, experts, panels, committees, legislatures, and other key decision-making persons and bodies. This irreducible element of the human in decision argues for taking great care in filling these decision-making roles with persons of demonstrated capacity for rising to the challenge. Both Wittgenstein and Derrida have, on occasion, been aligned with those who disparage or renounce the value of truth. But despite its irreducible and frustrating lack of closure, "Truth," to repeat Derrida's remark, "is not a value one can renounce." On this point, Wittgenstein and Derrida surely agree.

14

Violence

Turning to the theme of violence following a chapter on truth may seem odd. But within the context of inquiry into language there could be no more relevant continuation. Although Wittgenstein does not feature the link between language and violence as does Derrida, the contrast between them regarding the act of interpretation proves to be of central importance in understanding the emergence and role of violence. Wittgenstein grasped the pitfalls of theorizing interpretation as a necessary feature of all communication and warned that this path would lead to interpretation running amok in an aporia of endless regress. But for Derrida, pulling back from the aporetic precipice of interpretation is not an option. Communities remaining blind to the necessarily aporetic effects of language do not avoid the consequences of these effects.

Before language, the world already appears as a world of signs for living things. But with language it becomes possible to impose a system of signs that in a very real sense re-writes the world. Language introduces a new technology, a new manipulation, a new *violence* into the world. This form of violence becomes more clearly apparent when understanding that a sentence such as "This is a tree" reads functionally as "See this object *as* a tree." Any animal in the forest may encounter an object and properly read it as a familiar object. But when humans *name* that object a "tree," it enters into a system of meaning much larger and more complex than can be achieved by animals lacking language.

Speaking of the technology of language, renown media theorist Marshall McLuhan once remarked, "The word 'to read' means 'to guess.'" Here McLuhan refers to its etymological derivation from the Germanic influenced Old English word "rædan," meaning "to guess." McLuhan continues, "Reading is actually the activity of rapid guessing, because any word has so many meanings, including the word 'reading,' that to select one in a context of other words requires very rapid guessing.... The very nature of reading calls for quick decisions and guessing" (1977). "Quick decisions and guessing" describes "interpretation"—from the Latin root meaning "translation." In this sense, applied words are at best useful guesses and function as metaphors translating the phenomenal world through the action of "seeing-as." To write or read the world is to act upon it.

In his discussion of the theme of violence in Derrida's early work, Rick Elmore (2012) emphasizes the necessarily selective basis of language as naming when he identifies the paradox Derrida finds at the heart of signification: "[I]n order to represent anything at all, every representational system, mode of inscription, and system of writing must leave something unrepresented, eliminating the possibility of a 'complete' or 'pure' representation.... It is ... in this claim about the paradoxical structure of language and writing that Derrida will locate the problem of 'violence'" (35–36).

Assuming it were possible for a representation to be an exact reproduction of what it represented, such a representation would fail in its function as would a map constructed on a one-to-one scale with the territory being mapped. Not only does a representation need to be *other* than what it represents, it must necessarily be a *selection* of what it represents. This necessary highlighting of certain features at the expense of other features generates difference, which, despite every intention to prevent it, violates what it seeks to represent.

It may be argued that this use of the word "violence" counts as "violence on violence," stretching the term, as Wittgenstein might suggest, too far beyond its home language game, kidnapping the word from its domestic residence where perhaps a less "violent" means of expression may be found. But, as will be seen, the violence metaphor is perhaps more appropriate than may at first be apparent.

As becomes apparent in the chapter on truth, truth itself is a form of violence. The imposition of truth tethers the action of reading in such a way as to expose the reader to a violation of expectations. Speaking of truth and politics, Hannah Arendt gives memorable expression to this view when saying, "Conceptually, we may call truth what we cannot change; metaphorically, it is the ground on which we stand and the sky that stretches above us" (Arendt, 264 as cited in La Caze, 204).

The reader of signs must be prepared to suffer a kind of violence, must open up to what may be read, if reading is to remain informative and deliver readings beyond mere self-reproduction. This requires becoming vulnerable to the influence of the text, vulnerable to what may be read as "other." Speaking of this violence of the text, Ruth Sonderegger remarks, "Just as we, in our external readings, must expose and criticize the blind spots of the text, so must we submit to the 'violent' initiation into a new language, in order to get to know the blind spots of our own language, and all this in the name of truth" (1997, 203).

Extending her reading metaphor, Sonderegger explains that interpreters speak one language while they also learn another and without this trading of vulnerability between text and reader, this openness of violating and being violated, nothing new can happen. This exchange (of violence) creates change. In summary, Sonderegger, following Derrida, notes the displacement of a traditional opposition: "Instead of differentiating between violent and non-violent readings it would be better to think of the whole process of understanding as a violent *conflict*, an irresolvable conflict between two moments constitutive of the process of understanding. Such an understanding of understanding would not imply or require that there are readings and understandings that are exempt from this general violent conflict" (204).

No part of the exchange remains exempt from conflict. This "general violent conflict," however, remains grounded in the paradox of representation, which, in Elmore's words, inaugurates "the structural necessity of violence in all modes of signification and meaning" (36). This structural necessity in representation, which Derrida refers to as an originary *arche-writing*, grounds originary violence, which Elmore, following Derrida, refers to as *arche-violence*. Arche-violence "marks this structural violence as the origin of all other violence."

At this point in Elmore's commentary, however, he slips into a misleading choice of expression concerning Derrida's account of arche-writing and violence when he says, "The violence of *arche*-writing is originary insofar as it introduces the possibility and opens the space for all other violence, since the irreducible fact of difference, the possibility of contamination, corruption, and misrepresentation, must be *anterior* [emphasis added] to any particular instance of such contamination and corruption" (37). But contrary to Elmore's claim, the *possibility* of contamination, corruption, and misrepresentation is not *anterior*, either logically or temporally, to particular instances of contamination. The "irreducible fact of difference" does not translate into possibility but rather *necessity*—the necessity of contamination, corruption, and misrepresentation *in every instance*. The difference here is important for understanding the significance of Derrida's account of writing and violence.

There need be no talk of possibility because necessity reigns with regard to violence and necessity is the trace of the transcendent *in the contingent*. The transcendent does not exist or come into being apart from the immanent and the contingent. The transcendent and the immanent, the structural and the empirical, are co-originary and inseparable and yet not reducible one to the other.

Nevertheless, Elmore seeks to draw a distinction between contingent or *empirical violence* and necessary or *structural violence*. Derrida allows for this distinction but does not draw the distinction in the way Elmore describes. Elmore cites Derrida referring to three measures of violence, among which the first two are arche-violence and reparatory violence. Reparatory violence emerges in reaction to arche-violence. In Derrida's words, it is "protective, instituting the 'moral,' and functions as a barrier to exclude, deny, and repress originary violence." A third level of violence refers to what is more commonly called violence, the violence of an agent or agency intending to do physical or psychological harm. Following his citation of Derrida, Elmore concludes, "[O]riginary violence [arche-violence] cannot in itself have content or appear, as it is nothing more than an open space of possibility" (39).

Elmore's explanation of Derrida's three categories of violence obscures the effects Derrida attempts to understand. For Derrida, arche-writing and arche-violence are co-originary. The moment of origin is itself an empirical instance and from this moment forward every inscription, every sign, becomes an instance of contingent violence, an instance of a particular unique expression or manifestation of violence. Derrida's reference to the "third" violence ought not to be understood as forming a contrast between an "open space of possibility" (arche-violence) and "possible or not" violence (empirical violence). All violence counts as contingency within necessity, or necessity within contingency, in the particularity of instances of violence in a temporal world constrained to create one form or another of violence.

Every decision and choice of action is based on a reading of signs and since the reading of signs necessarily involves misrepresentation, then every action—whether verbal or nonverbal—inevitably enacts violence in the community of others as well as in the natural world. Humans do inadvertent and unintentional harm to each other every day as every *vision* necessarily creates a measure of *division*. Every reading of a situation has unforeseen consequences affecting an indeterminate range of other persons. Also, measures of violence in the form of restrictions and controls extend necessarily from the structure of life in human community, inextricably tied to the structure of arche-writing and its co-originary arche-violence.

While a measure of violence through *exclusion* cannot be avoided when functioning in the world, choice exists concerning violent behaviors. The action of exclusion must be carefully understood in Derrida's tripartite division of violence into originary, reparatory, and coercive violence. On this point, Valeria Campos-Salvaterra offers a reading of Derrida on violence differing from Elmore's reading and more consistent with the wider context of Derrida's account of violence. Campos-Salvaterra explains, "That the first level of violence is called originary does not mean that it has to be acknowledged as foundational in relation to secondary levels [such as reparatory and coercive violence]. 'Secondary' forms of violence are not derived from the transcendental violence, since they are nothing but variations—iterations—of the differantial [the adjectival form of *différance*] nature of violence itself" (159). In an insightful passage worth quoting at length Campos-Salvaterra continues:

> If violence cannot by definition be formalized because of its differential nature, the notion of an economy of violence must also reflect this continuous inner adjustment. If economy is an economy of violence, then economy itself should be understood as being constitutively out-of-joint.... Ultimately, the non-static, historic, and dynamic way of understanding violence makes it impossible to engage in a classic critique. Instead, violence has to be economized: for Derrida, the least violence must always be *chosen*—without a repeatable formula and regarding every different context as unique [emphasis added] [159].

When saying that the least violence must be "chosen," Campos-Salvaterra means, following Derrida, that the least violence, as well as the worst violence, has no accompanying formula or calculation by and through which the least violence may be guaranteed or the worst violence necessarily prevented. This is the consequence of the strategic wager that is decision: nothing is guaranteed.

The traditional dialectic of exclusion and inclusion characterizing violence becomes, in Campos-Salvaterra's word, "economized," which is to say that what is contingently excluded remains fundamentally included; and what is contingently included remains, also, contingently excluded. Similarly, no static hierarchy of included and excluded actors exists in this dynamic economy of exchange.

In this more dynamic economy of violence, exclusion must be carefully understood to include even as it excludes. Only an inadequately conceived economy initiates a variety of the dialectic of opposites creating the possibility for imposing an exclusion that *absolutely* excludes as it excludes. Absolute exclusion denies fundamental inclusion within the economy itself. Where an economy corresponding to a *general* economy (as described in Chapter 9) gives rise to contingent evaluation, taxonomy, and hierarchy, a restricted economy absolutizes or idealizes these effects into rigid judgments, labels, and classes. This restricted economy gives rise to highly polarized exclusionary divisions that may all too easily extend into a logic providing the rationale for operationalizing conflicts into cleansings, pogroms, and exterminations.

The choice, the decision, to engage in campaigns of absolute exclusion, as in genocide, becomes possible within groups in which the identities of its members follow the exclusionary polarities modeled in the restricted economy. This polarization and rigidity in identity formation may then lead to violence in response to extreme change or disruption in the structure of the broader community. For example, media theorist Marshall McLuhan, mentioned previously, discusses extreme social change and disruption initiated by the introduction and pervasive spread of new technology within a community or culture (see, for example, Benedetti and DeHart, 1997). The electronic age introduced first radio and then television, both of which in different ways dramatically changed the speed and breadth of communication. Radio magnified the power of voice while television magnified the power of sight—extending at the speed of light the frontiers of human communication beyond local communities and into the larger world. The expanded flow and pace of information overwhelmed human capacities for adaptation—capacities rendered all the more vulnerable by the features of a restricted economy, thereby changing both the circumference and the quality of community.

The arche-violence of which Derrida speaks, accompanying the technological extension of arche-writing, introduces motivations for violence unknown in the animal kingdom. The progression of new technologies from printing press, telephone, and radio to television, computer, and internet added extreme factors of complexity and disruption to community. Where the sword magnified the power of the human hand, these new technologies magnified the violent potential of language and sign systems in general. Continuing technological developments, while increasing the capabilities of human action, also further increase the power of the means of destruction as well as disrupting identity formation, which increases the triggers for conflict. This combination of increased speed and volume of communication and expanded weaponry technologies may have devastating consequences, as already evident in the extreme instances of war and genocide in the 20th and early 21st centuries.

Since personal identity necessarily develops through community, these radical technological changes, affecting the entire environment of communities and their boundaries, succeed in disrupting the customary processes for identity formation—processes historically conducted primarily through language communication. As McLuhan explains, "Violence, whether spiritual or physical, is a quest for identity and the meaningful. The less identity, the more violence" (as cited in Benedetti and DeHart, 1997). Derrida would have likely concurred. Identity issues may intensify into extreme violence when people sense a loss of identity or must struggle to gain or preserve identity. Violence serves identity formation through radical exclusion of other persons or groups—persons or groups found to be sufficiently different in identity to reinforce, by contrast, the loss of identity experienced among those perpetrating the violence. This clash of identities then results in conflict that easily escalates from campaigns for domination to those of extermination. The agon gives way to aporia and the aporia gives way to the abyss. The combatants plunge into a groundless free fall of violence, which then precludes no atrocity.

These are the dangers wrought by naming, writing, and language from which no person or community remains immune, especially when the economy of violence suffers from the distortions arising at the extremities of the dialectic of opposition in a restricted economy. Although the progression to extreme violence may be a natural progression in the sense that it derives from natural conditions and escalates through disruptions also of natural origin in the evolution of human adaptation, the recourse to exclusionary violence as a response to such disruptions is not inevitable and, in fact, highly dysfunctional. Through gaining an understanding of the forces at work, the progression can be managed in ways sufficient to minimize what Derrida calls "the worst."

Preventing the worst requires all sides in conflict understand the looming abyss and the consequences of falling into it. These consequences are stark and simple: there are no winners. Awareness of what lies ahead reaffirms commitment to the general economy within which all sides necessarily belong. But, unfortunately, this mutual awareness can in many cases be achieved only after having learned the hard way that the abyss holds no rewards for any party in a deadly conflict. In such hard cases, only the survivors are left to gain mutual awareness and begin the daunting task of finding a way out of the abyss.

In Derrida's view, words are already and always swords. They cut, divide, and separate as they categorize and include. Surprisingly, even while arche-writing with its co-originary arche-violence, may foster conflict, this writing, this use of language, nevertheless remains essential for and unavoidable in building human community. Language makes the world a place where humans may rise above the blood violence of the animal kingdom into a place where the violence of the world may be managed and negotiated to prevent the worst. Through the economization of violence, the violence of words turns upon and overcomes the violence of swords—creating the possibilities for civilization through the word of law.

This civilization, this negotiated accord, requires understanding language at the deepest level—the level of metaphysics, where all oppositions and conflicts, real and imaginary, are seen to stand on the paradoxical ground of complementarity inherent in a general economy. Here, the other, even as the "opposition" or "enemy" never ceases to operate as a reflection of the self and its irreducible yet generative division—the layer of difference of the self from itself that cannot be absolved without thereby also terminating the possibility of any "self" whatever. Difference and division are irreducible and yet essential for self, other, and community.

Only when these are accommodated in light of a general economy may highly functional, least-violence, human community be achieved.

Turning to Wittgenstein, his placement of interpretation in the category of a special case rather than a necessary part of reading/writing counts, from Derrida's view, as a form of violence—not *through* language but *on* language. It constitutes an attempt to constrain what cannot be constrained in the effort to attain greater clarity in the use of language. Certainty and the grounds for certainty preoccupied Wittgenstein throughout his life. Language appeared to him, throughout human history, to have functioned more as an obstacle than an asset in realizing and accepting the kind of certainty he associated with attaining "peace" both in philosophy and in life.

Contrary to Derrida, Wittgenstein sees human failing in the use and management of language games—rather than the structural constitution of language itself—as the likely contributor to the confusion and conflict abetting violence in the world. Yet both philosophers are aligned in believing a decisive human response will be required to confront the limits of language and address the ways in which, through inadequate grasp of its limits, its use may promote violence.

Regarding any such decisive intervention, however, Derrida's emphasis on the inevitability of interpretation rather than Wittgenstein's emphasis on established agreement in use emerges as more conducive to what will diminish violence rather than promote it. The primary reason for this assessment can be summarized as the power of *doubt*. Doubt prompts hesitation in assigning labels and drawing conclusions. Such hesitation may often prove sufficient to arrest progression into active and reactive forms of violent action. Holding labels and conclusions in provisional status makes it far more difficult to burn bridges between individuals and groups. Such operationalizing of doubt need not be confused with paralysis in the face of immanent threats. Doubt induces caution, multi-perspectival vision, and broad anticipation in response to differences, especially differences appearing to pose a threat. In uncertain situations, doubt fosters defense rather than aggression and measured action rather than rash reaction.

However, this rationale for supporting doubt as a strategic attitude in human orientations encounters a significant challenge in the recent work of R. Krishnaswamy (2021) in his book *Wittgenstein and the Nature of Violence*. Krishnaswamy understands language as becoming detrimental and conducive to coercive violence when its power of abstraction serves as a wedge to create an artificial gap between the transcendent and the immanent while removing the gap between knowledge and power, between institutional law and law enforcement.

Wittgenstein enters Krishnaswamy's line of thought by way of his identification of the failure of mental activity and intention to provide appropriate ground for meaning in language and communication. Criteria for meaning are not found, following Wittgenstein, in cognitions or mental content behind words but are instead discovered as "embodied" in pre-existing social and cultural practices within groups and communities. Krishnaswamy further notes, "A central element of a Wittgensteinian understanding of criteria is that criteria are not universal" (2012, 176). Drawing together themes of transcendence, law, power, criteria, and violence, he concludes:

> [W]e can say the violence of power is manifested only when the criteria of embodied lives are considered to be absolute. Any absolutist claims to correctness go against the grammar of our social existence. The formal institution of statist law, for example, has come to be the largest and most pervasive currency. Law becomes violent when the normative calculus of its imposition is taken to be universal and transcendental to the condition of life itself. When we look for justification of moral behavior outside our everyday engagement[—]in absolute notions of humanity, dignity, etc.[—]the violence of law becomes explicit [2021, 177–178].

At this point, Krishnaswamy's conclusions are not directly inconsistent with conclusions concerning doubt and conclusions concerning violence argued herein.

Oddly enough, however, Krishnaswamy's reading of Wittgenstein on the role of skepticism is difficult to align with these conclusions. It becomes hard to square his view of the absolutizing power of cognitive constructs with his abhorrence of skepticism. For example, he says, "[W]hat Wittgenstein has successfully shown is that scepticism is a by-product of the game of finding foundational reasons. Scepticism is not an attack from without but an immanent attack from the inside, which can never be won, and that is partly why it is an insidiously violent poison in our modern conscience" (2021, 174–175).

But skepticism is not adequately viewed as the by-product of the search for foundational reasons. Skepticism is more rightly seen as a crucial form of resistance to the seductive tendency toward absolutizing, which Krishnaswamy identifies as one of the primary culprits prompting violence. In arriving at this view of skepticism, he claims to follow Wittgenstein in understanding meaning as embodied in practices such that meaning may simply be read from embodied practices in the manner of self-evident description. Krishnaswamy says, for example, "[W]hen we look for questions of justice, the criteria of justice cannot come from outside the practices in which people engage. The nature of what is it to be just, fair, generous, etc. can come only from a *mutual recognition* of these concepts [emphasis added]" (2021, 179).

But at this point it must be asked: What happens when "mutual recognition of these concepts" does not materialize and disagreement concerning "shared" concepts arises instead? In response, Krishnaswamy backs himself into a corner: "The reason for acting and the pragmatic concerns that we have in our life are both expressions of our life form to which [we] are tied. Criteria can't be questioned, because they, like life, lie at the limit of all questioning" (2021, 177).

The dictate that "criteria can't be questioned" marks the point of slipping back again into the trap Krishnaswamy seeks to avoid, namely the trap of absolutizing. Criteria suddenly become self-evident and self-applying. This much is confirmed when he claims, "[W]e know that the reasons for adopting a particular standard can't go on forever. Our daily use of words shows that the criteria and their application of that criteria hang together" (2021, 176–177). But it may now be asked: How does "our" daily use of words show the criteria in ways that are operationally unambiguous such that their application appears to be one with the criteria themselves?

Krishnaswamy anticipates the trouble his position creates when he rightly asks, "[H]ow does one morally evaluate the cannibal or the murderer if we adopt this Wittgensteinian approach?" His answer is not reassuring: "I am not saying that these real moral questions will necessarily be quickly resolved through my approach" (2021, 179). Not only may these moral questions fail to be quickly resolved through his approach, they may instead be bypassed altogether in the recourse provided by his approach: "The criteria and their application … hang together."

Krishnaswamy fails to understand, and perhaps Wittgenstein as well, that resistance to absolutizing must necessarily include resistance to the notion of criteria that apply themselves. Questioning criteria that apply themselves counts as an indispensable routine in resistance to the absolutizing of concepts and stands as a cornerstone in the foundation of any program of skepticism and doubt.

It must, however, be acknowledged that exposing applications and criteria to questioning may lead to what Derrida and Wittgenstein both agree constitutes an aporia of endless regress into interpretation, explanation, and giving reasons. For Wittgenstein, this aporia emerges as an abyss plunging into darkness—or if not darkness, then pure futility. For Derrida, on the contrary, this aporia emerges as *sine qua non*, and not merely for language. Like a fractal formula, the endless regress is precisely the endless opening—the opening for the movement, change, diversity, and adaptation that makes life possible. Consequently, this aporia, another effect of arche-writing and arche-violence, must be embraced and negotiated through provisional decision-making led by doubt. It ought not to be shunned and sidelined—because such aporia and its enigmas are of the essence not only of life and language but also of everything that is.

Conclusion:
The Signs of Life

That is not what I meant at all;
That is not it, at all.
  —*T. S. Eliot, The Love Song*
    of J. Alfred Prufrock

By way of differing yet defensible ways of viewing language, Wittgenstein and Derrida present an image of language that may seem like the Jastrow image—both a duck and a rabbit. And if that were the case, the choice between them might seem no more consequential than duck or rabbit for dinner or chocolate or vanilla for dessert. But Derrida denies the difference between every difference resolves to a matter of taste. And, given the choice between his view of language and Derrida's view, would Wittgenstein, in this case, want to say: Oh, I don't know. It's as you please?

The two traditions of Analytical and Continental philosophy are sometimes portrayed as being irreconcilable. But philosophers such as Frege, Russell, Wittgenstein, Popper, and those of the Vienna Circle bridge the gap between the continent and Britain and provide impetus for asking whether the two traditions are really so different from each other. These traditions speak different languages, literally and figuratively, but the difference might not be so much one of language as idiom. Both traditions represent remarkable efforts in pursuit of absolute certainty. Descartes often draws blame for initiating the philosophical bewitchment with certainty in his proclamation *cogito ergo sum*. From this moment forward the question "What can I know?" preoccupies philosophers on both sides of the channel through the period up to and including the first half of the 20th century.

The first prominent philosopher to anticipate the eventual break with tradition, Friedrich Nietzsche, gains fame for having announced the discovery that "God is dead." The death of God thesis functioned as metaphor for the death of the transcendental signifier and the birth of perspectivism

161

accompanied by the loss of certainty in the realization that certainty is a ghost. Coming to terms with the loss of certainty and thereby also the loss of any definitive meaning for life engages existentialist philosophers from Kierkegaard to Heidegger and from Sartre to Camus.

Across the channel, analytic philosophers—joined by those from the continent such as Frege, Wittgenstein, and the participants in the Vienna Circle—wrestled with questions of certainty through various attempts to press the world and language into the molds of mathematics and logic. These analytical endeavors met with rejection—matching Nietzsche's rejection of tradition on the continental side—in Richard Rorty's *Philosophy and the Mirror of Nature* (1979). The plain truth of certainty lies buried alongside God and nothing short of a miracle, which is to say epidemic cultural memory loss, may resurrect these specters again in their former glory. Postmodernism emerges, like a revenant, out of the ash of modernism, leaving many in a renewed state of doubt, as if the end of the philosophy of mirrors were the beginning of a philosophy of smoke and mirrors.

But a philosophically acquired sense of doubt, loss, and confusion may be mitigated when recognizing two important moments in the postmodern turn: (1) the possibility of certainty of the kind desired by philosophers was an illusion all along and (2) if certainty of the kind desired had been possible then life itself would not have been possible.

Derrida's ruminations have given good cause to believe any system or general economy enabling the possibility for certainty would thereby also disable the potential for life itself by excluding temporality and its consequences. Either nothing at all could happen in a world of certainty or what could happen would be entirely predictable and foreseeable from beginning to end, leaving life with no reason to be lived. So, rather than languishing in the pain of loss of certainty, Derrida, in the robes of a postmodern messiah, brings the Panglossian good news that this world may be the best of all possible worlds—even though it may present, along with the life it offers, the ever-present potential for what he calls a "return of the worst."

Although Derrida belongs in the era of postmodernity, "postmodernist" or "postmodernism" were not terms with which he wanted to be associated because of the many faulty views lumped into these postmodern categories. His philosophy, like Heidegger's, reaches back across time to the era of Greek philosophy. But whereas Heidegger prefers association with the pre–Socratic philosophers, Derrida forms a rather unexpected association with Plato. Hardly a single tenet of Plato's philosophy survives Derrida's scorched-earth scrutiny and yet something like a phoenix of Plato's metaphysics emerges from the ashes and looks for all the world surprisingly like Platonism. But similarities between Plato's Theory of Forms and other approaches to the word/meaning relation are not surprising given the endlessly challenging knot of persistent issues surrounding this relational nexus that continue to defy solutions eliciting broad consensus.

Parallels between deconstruction and the tradition of standard Platonic interpretation labeled as Platonism and its corresponding Theory of Forms, emerged from a conference led by Drucilla Cornell in 1989 intended to address the topic of "deconstruction and the possibility of justice." This conference arose in the wake of the media publicity storm swirling around the scandal that had recently emerged from revelations about Paul de Man's wartime collaborationist writings in the Belgian newspaper *Le Soir* (discussed in Chapter 13). Claims had surfaced from every direction accusing the practice of deconstruction of being little more than a means of twisting words to mean whatever may be convenient for the moment, while thereby laying waste to concerns for truth and justice. The topic of the conference did not conceal the implication that deconstruction might possibly be one of the most recent and most threatening obstacles to truth and justice. In this context, Derrida's assertion that "deconstruction *is* justice" in his presentation titled "The Force of Law: The Mystical Foundation of Authority" counted as stunning, especially considering his previous reluctance to define deconstruction in any simple formulaic phrasing. Moreover, given Derrida's broad application of his deconstructive practices to a wide variety of texts, many were of the opinion at the time that nothing was beyond the reach of deconstructive unraveling. So, the shock of his revelation to the audience at the conference doubled when he added the further revelation: "justice is undeconstructible."

The claim that justice is undeconstructible would appear to be consistent with features of a Platonic ideal essence—a form perfect in all respects and from which humanity fashions its crude copies due to human imperfection in the capacity to recollect the ideal form. The notion of perfection possibly implicit in the word "undeconstructible" seemingly re-creates yet another instance of the metaphysics of presence Derrida had, up to that point in time, spent his career dismantling.

If, however, there was a kind of repetition of Platonism in Derrida's claims about justice it was yet another instance of his often repeated phrase: repetition-with-a-difference. And this difference is far more than ornamentation. John D. Caputo counts as among those who have adequately understood the implications of repetition-with-a-difference when he explains: "Deconstruction does not set its sights on justice as the goal or *telos* within a positive horizon of foreseeability—like a Platonic *eidos* or a Kantian regulative idea—which for Derrida is what constitutes the horizon of 'possibility,' or a possibility as a 'horizon,' a positive vision of justice" (1997, 133). The undeconstructible is not a positive vision or ideal with identifiable form. Instead, the ideal serves as something like the proverbial carrot tied to a stick dangling in front of the donkey. The ideal is *intended* always to be out of reach, beckoning forward, serving as a light, which, in its absence, would result in darkness on the path ahead where the path ahead is not straightforward like a rail but continually presenting new twists and turns for which light is needed. The horizon of the undeconstructible is the horizon that remains always the horizon.

The law, however, remains *always* deconstructible. Justice, as the undeconstructible ideal, lies beyond the reach of institutionalized laws, providing instead the impetus for writing the law and revising the law. Through constant revision, laws may better accord with changing circumstances and the evolving capacities of communities to realize and carry out current demands for justice. Caputo continues, "Justice does not exist, is nothing present, no thing, is not found somewhere either here, in present actuality, nor up ahead as a foreseeable ideal, a future-present. Rather, 'there is (*il y a*) justice, which means: justice solicits us from afar, from the future, from and as a future always structurally to come, calls 'come' to us, preventing the walls of the present from enclosing us in the possible" (1997, 135). Justice is the impossible that gives rise to what becomes possible while never relinquishing its role as the impossible, always out in front, not as a fixed vision but rather as a moving, evolving, and haunting nonpresence.

Current laws do not count as inferior recollections of a transcendent ideal but instead as current instances of inspiration made possible by the light of a lamp continually receding into the distance ahead. For Derrida, this process arises from the nature of being and what life must be if life is to be possible. The attaining of an ideal would be the same as death—the end of all movement and potential for movement. Thus, Derrida's Platonism arrives as Platonism-with-a-difference by breaking with the traditional understanding of Plato and the Theory of Forms. In a dramatic reversal of traditional Platonism, the ideal serves the real and remains inadequate to it rather than the real being but a copy of and inadequate to the ideal.

However, as Caputo continues his analysis of Derrida and Plato, he announces the possibility, based on Plato's discussion of *khôra* in the *Timaeus*, that Plato himself may eventually have entertained views with considerable similarity to those evident in Derrida's use of the term *différance*. *Khôra* is the unnamable no-thing that is neither one nor two, both one and two, neither one nor many, both one and many, neither present nor absent, both present and absent, neither here nor there, both here and there—the no-thing beyond difference that accounts for all difference, movement, being, and life. Plato's reference to *khôra* hints at a metaphysical shift—a shift initiating the deconstruction of the Theory of Forms.

The shift from the metaphysics of *eidos* to that of the trace, from pure presence to the presence/absence of presencing, may be understood with regard to the life of the sign as a shift from the grammar of *is* to that of *as*. In its escape from the notional stasis of the true object, the sign does not declare: This particular object *is* an apple. Instead, the sign exhorts: See this particular object *as* an apple. The grammar of *as* also thereby induces a shift from the literal *is* to the metaphorical and analogical *as*, in which case the term "literal" becomes itself a metaphor. Derrida argues in his essay "White Mythology" (1982) that, due to the nature of the sign, philosophy is no more exempt from the use of metaphor than literature and poetry and, by extension, science. Or, phrased in a slightly different way, all language using, all sign using, is in its essence in every instance neither literal nor metaphoric, both literal and metaphoric.

The force of this shift from *is* to *as* may be seen in the shift from the classical "What is X?" question to the "What may X justifiably be seen as?" question. This difference underscores a change from philosophical emphasis on the ontological, the question of *is* and the question of *being*, to include an axiological complement in the question of the *similarity and difference* of judgments. Classical determinations of truth and falsity cannot preclude judgments concerning sameness and difference. In this transition all understanding of facts remains inextricable from determinations of context. Here facts and judgments can no more be entirely separated than can text and context or facts and values. However, it is important to understand that this is not the same as to say facts are "as you please" anymore than contexts are "as you please."

Moreover, this shift in emphasis with regard to the function and functioning of the sign means that all issues requiring decision that communities must confront become *political* in nature. This does not mean that questions of truth may be thrown to the wind. Far from it. As discussed in Chapter 13, assessments of truth become provisional as they turn on contingent judgments of the reading of facts based on negotiated and articulated boundaries of context. And insofar as particular judgments of truth carry the day, these judgments will have derived from the relevance and persuasiveness of the boundaries of context contingently circumscribed and operationalized.

Wittgenstein's relationship with Plato's work is also nuanced and complicated. His anti-essentialism, anti-foundationalism, anti–Cartesianism, and explicit renunciation of the Theory of Forms, combined with his reliance on a methodology of citing examples and adopting a broad anti-metaphysical stance, would seem to preclude alignment with the

Plato/Socrates nexus of philosophical insights. Yet Continental scholars such as Begoña Ramón Cámara (2013) find connections between Wittgenstein's philosophical outlook, described as "the world seen *sub specie aeternitatis*," and classical Platonism. She argues Wittgenstein's thinking connects to Plato's "by many links, especially by his ethics, his aesthetics, and by some essential features of his religious temperament" which remain consistent among elements of Wittgenstein's worldview extending from the *Tractatus* forward (2013, 160). However, since the view of Wittgenstein argued herein centers on his later work on language, pairing of Wittgenstein and Platonism must be seen to present considerable contrast rather than similarity.

Placed in contrast to classical Platonism, Wittgenstein may then be thought to occupy a position closer to Derrida. But Wittgenstein's understanding of the force and function of the ideal separates him from, rather than aligns him with, Derrida. Writing in the same text as Cámara, co-authors Silvana Borutti and Fulvia de Luise explain that for Wittgenstein "the 'ideal' is not—platonically—tension and utopia, a 'model' to attain, but … that which holds us firm within our horizon, it is the model that gives us eyes with which to see" (2013, 145). Rather than beckoning toward an impossible possibility, as in Derrida's account of the ideal of justice as the always "yet to come," Wittgenstein assumes an orientation toward the ideal as that which reorients—as a well-chosen example or analogy might—back toward what is *already* known and evident in practice.

Differing from the Plato/Socrates account of knowledge as recollection, Wittgenstein advances a view of conceptual orientation as a recollection that does not recall transcendent ideal forms but instead the practices and forms of life from which the language game associated with a given word and concept initially emerges. Recall again Lee Braver, as cited in Part I, as he explains in his discussion of parallels between Wittgenstein and Heidegger, in Wittgenstein's account of rule following, "We are habituated to react to orders or pictures or pointing in certain ways through a process much closer to Pavlovian conditioning than to discoursing in the Platonic Academy" (2012, p. 157).

Returning to Wittgenstein's Beetle Box Analogy, it is as he suggests. The contents of the box can be anything or nothing or constantly changing. But Derrida parts company with Wittgenstein when showing the same circumstance holds for the word associated with the box. The word, as a signifier having a use in the language, cannot be made transparent any more than the contents of the box. Simply because the word has a use in the language does not entail that its use is fully transparent. As Kripke has illustrated in his discussion of rule following, coordinated activity does not necessarily indicate coordinated understanding.

Nothing illustrates this circumstance more repeatedly and reliably than the machinations of law and politics, where words among actors may appear aligned and actions may appear coordinated—until events expose these words and actions to be anything but aligned and coordinated. The French Revolution provides an iconic, as well as ironic, illustration. People rallied around the words Liberty, Fraternity, Equality—until they did not, whereupon it became obvious through the behaviors of particular persons and their agendas that these words concealed very different understandings regarding the perfection of their meanings.

But the enigma, the contents of the Beetle Box, extends beyond the text of language and into the text of nature. Consider that no less an enquirer than Einstein, pondering the difficulties facing scientists trying to understand physical processes, offers an analogy resembling Wittgenstein's Beetle Box.

> In our endeavor to understand reality we are somewhat like a man trying to understand the mechanism of a closed watch. He sees the face and the moving hands, even hears it ticking, but he has no way of opening the case. If he is ingenious he may form some picture of the mechanism which could be responsible for all the things he observes, but he may never be quite sure his picture is *the only one* which could explain his observations. He will never be able to compare his picture with the real mechanism and he cannot even imagine the possibility of the meaning of such a comparison [emphasis added] [Einstein and Infeld, 1938, 31].

More than one theory accounting for the currently evident workings of the natural world is always possible. And due to the temporal nature of the world, its "story" is never finished. More events always stream into the story. So long as observations are incomplete so also must be any theory used to account for observations. These two consequences constitute features of radical nonclosure of the world as a system. Events may always transpire prompting revision of any current theory and any current theory may suddenly, through a shift of perspective, cast light on evidence that seemed to contradict it.

Although Einstein's Watch Analogy is similar in form to the Beetle Box Analogy, Einstein takes a different lesson from the unknown content, the inner workings of the watch. He does not suggest what may be inside the watch counts as irrelevant. His sights are set on something more than predictability. No theory completely satisfies him because his attitude toward theory-building prevents him from being lulled into complacency, even by significant measures of success in predictability. Wittgenstein, on the other hand, advises canceling out what remains in the Beetle Box. Predictability suffices. If the word associated with the box serves a purpose in the community and appears to facilitate action and coordinate predictable behavior, then little remains that need concern the philosopher regarding language and its uses.

Einstein acknowledges the picture of the inner workings of the watch may be only a crude image or even a completely different image from what is actually inside. Similarly, Wittgenstein understands the Beetle Box may contain different things, may be constantly changing, or need contain nothing at all. But for Einstein, the difference between the picture and the inside of the watch remains relevant to future experience. The model presented by the picture may fail to adequately account for every detail of what is currently observed or may fail to account for a detail emerging in the future. For Wittgenstein, infelicitous details accompanying the use of language may be largely ignored insofar as these eccentricities of detail do not create sufficient discrepancy between utterance and response to introduce dysfunction into the order—or appearance of order—in social functions.

Extending the analogy in this way reveals the extent to which the communication game Wittgenstein outlines may be the equivalent of settling for a thin broth served between communicators instead of a hearty soup. And the reply that language-users may not *know* what they are missing meets the response that the potential to *see* more is greatly contingent on communicators' attitudes concerning the promise of communication for furthering the possibilities for seeing more. Since individual boxes present a soup of ingredients the values of which cannot be adequately determined, Wittgenstein's "'dividing through' by the thing in the box" may amount to throwing out some of the vegetables. And this discounting and discarding of the vegetables would be done solely for the comfort of asserting that when language-users use language they do indeed communicate. But, as has been argued, more is at stake in communication than Wittgenstein's lines of argument concerning language adequately emphasize.

In contrast, Derrida's views of language and its operations necessitate a disposition toward use discouraging the presumption of communication in favor of the presumption of *doubt* about communication. In the course of demonstrating the necessity for this disposition, Derrida exposes several features of language that may be explicitly stated as laws. These laws constitute a science or, to use Derrida's word, a *grammatology* of language insofar as identifying *laws* may be understood as indicative of and constitutive of a science. Unlike in the case of natural science, however, these laws of language do not so much increase predictability in the use of language as establish the basis for understanding why predictability in use need not always or necessarily coincide with predictability of meaning. This entropy, this uncertainty in the predictability of meaning, explains why Derrida refuses to claim that the use of language and signs can be reduced to what is more commonly understood as a science.

The laws of language that may be extracted from Derrida's early writings may be summarized as follows: (1) The sign sustains meaning across different spatial and temporal contexts through its capacity for repeatable use (The Law of Non-Singularity); (2) The sign divides its identity according to what *remains* from one context of use to another and also what *enters* from one context of use to another, preserving over time no essential core of unchanging traits (The Law of Non-Identity); (3) The sign operates within an economy or system having no closure, no absolute outside (*il n'y a pas de hors-texte*) (The Law of Non-Transcendence). These laws together mark the limits of language and signs in such a way that any "science" of semiotics can only predict that predictions of meaning necessarily fall short of presumption and measures of strict reliability.

For Derrida, the sign is a manifestation of the being of the *trace*. In this regard it is worth noting that for Derrida every trace, which is to say every being and every sign, constitutes an event. Every event remains singular and unrepresentable until it is witnessed, whereupon it gains identity by placement into a recognition register. As a witnessed trace, it also becomes, through memory and the artificial memory of media archiving, a re-markable trace, iterating across intervals in time, in the complementarity of identification and singularity, same and other, all the way through to its core.

The horizon for language Derrida presents exceeds Wittgenstein's horizon and in doing so generates a substantially different politics of the sign by way of establishing substantially different metaphysical grounding. This difference turns primarily on a difference in the way in which the being of the sign is understood. For Wittgenstein, the sign has the being of the *tool* and revolves around human activities within the contexts of temporally changing periods or cultural eras. In Derrida's metaphysics, time plays a more radical role, and serves as part of the essence (or non-essence) of everything that is. Therefore, it remains insufficient from Derrida's view to factor time in relation to context in the way Wittgenstein does. Choosing Derrida's metaphysical path grants time a role more consistent with evidence from the physical sciences and the logic of succession indicated in the complementarity of space and time. This metaphysics also aligns with the evidence of temporally bound sign operations—as Derrida's laws of the sign attempt to articulate, laws that reflect the inescapable *as-structure* of the sign.

The choice, then, between Derrida's and Wittgenstein's accounts of language may be seen as a choice between the metaphors of the tool and the trace. But this choice refuses to reduce to either/or as it continually slips into both/and. In doing so, however, language acquires a structure and a being requiring a crucial shift in attitude toward its tool-like aspect. The addition of the feature of the trace carries consequences, and between the tool and the trace lies a sea of consequences difficult to adequately address in a concluding chapter. But the most significant consequences and the values associated with them can be briefly identified.

Language understood as a tool prompts a fixation on its refinement for human purposes and a sense of its instrumentality as potentially in need of repair or adjustment when it appears to fail to meet expectations. This fixation emerges as central in Wittgenstein's *Tractatus* and concludes with a subtle admonition regarding this fixation. In the case of his later work, the emphasis shifts; rather than the instrument requiring adjustment, the *user* of the instrument requires adjustment in an ongoing effort to prevent attempts to use it in a manner for which it is ill suited.

By contrast, words and signs assigned the being of the trace prompt more modest expectations, consistent with structures whose mode of being exceeds that of the instrument as a result of the more radical indexing of time in the being of the trace. The shape-shifting being of the trace, like fire, wind, and wave, prompts a measure of caution toward its potential for service in human purposes alongside its potential for exceeding human control.

Though remaining, like Descartes, in the modern metaphysical fold, Wittgenstein's metaphysical orientation nevertheless attempts to correct the Cartesian mind/body, mind/matter, privileging of *res cogitans* over *res extensa*. The body-centered, action-centered philosophy presented by Wittgenstein reconnects humanity with the natural world, from which Cartesian metaphysics had alienated it. The metaphysics implicit in Wittgenstein's philosophical approach shifts human instrumentality from a position *beyond* and *above* the physical world to an instrumentality taking cues from nature rather than controlling nature. As Lee Braver remarks, both Wittgenstein and Heidegger share metaphysical ground in returning status to nature and to a natural attitude toward the world, which may account in part for Wittgenstein's attraction to rural communities and Heidegger's retreats to the Black Forest (2012, 37–40).

Derrida, on the other hand, challenges Cartesian dualism with the metaphysics of the trace. The being of the trace displaces the philosophical tradition's hallmark emphasis on essence with an emphasis on the complementarity of contradiction, as in the presence/absence of the trace—a contradiction implicit in the manifestations of the flame and the wave, as phenomena both "there" and "not there." But this uprooting of Cartesian dualism does not surpass duality. The duality remaining in Derrida's philosophy emerges as one in which each side of the binary has equal status, though not necessarily equal visibility in every unfolding event. As is the case in particle/wave duality in physics, the context through which a given phenomenon becomes circumscribed determines which aspects stand out in observation. And, as already suggested, this context emerges as neither singularly chosen nor entirely given, yet both chosen and given, as evident in the labor of decision.

The Derridean critique of metaphysics exceeds mere critique by introducing complementarity into the structure of oppositions, contrasts, and contradictions. Complementarity factors as a crucial transformative supplement to the mind/body model of oppositional relation but also, when applied more broadly, to all manner of conflicts between persons and factions in human communities. The irreducible structure of complementarity, applied throughout metaphysical dualities, generates a politics of complementarity. Concerning political implications, inclusion and negotiation define the logic for management of conflict because the feature of entanglement models the opposing sides such that the elimination of one side threatens not only the ground but also the existence of the other side. This necessity for inclusion and negotiation contrasts with that of division and categorical exclusions—the latter being the logic of resolution consistent with the extreme dialectical and hierarchical polarization promoted by traditional metaphysical binaries as in mind/body, original/copy, good/evil.

On the issue of the practical implications of the politics of complementarity, it remains crucial, in this conclusion, to fend off a popular misunderstanding associated with the complementarity implied in deconstruction. This misunderstanding receives exemplary statement in a law journal article by Jack Balkin (1994), which includes extensive discussion of Derrida's 1989 essay "Force of Law: The Mystical Foundations of Authority." In Balkin's view, Derrida desires to present his deconstruction of oppositional relation as thoroughly consistent with egalitarian social and political policies. Derrida's exceptional claim that "deconstruction is justice" derives from the deconstruction of oppositional boundaries. But the deconstructive challenge to boundaries, argues Balkin, weakens the basis for evaluating between the poles of any given opposition by eliminating the essential difference characterizing traditional dichotomies. This effacement of boundaries appears to render deconstruction impotent to promote one faction against another.

Balkin believes, "Derrida has not shown a necessary connection between deconstruction and justice" because he has instead "shown that one can only deconstruct these oppositions in a way that produces increasingly egalitarian results" (1994, 17). Deconstruction may appear to accomplish a reversal of the hierarchy of opposites such that the less dominant pole may assume the position of equal status, but it does so by sacrificing any leverage for justifying a choice between one side and another. Deconstruction's egalitarianism appears to lead to a variety of nihilism, where one choice cannot be shown to be better than another.

According to Balkin, "Derrida might have chosen to deconstruct or problematize the distinction between justice and injustice, between liberty and slavery, or between tolerance and bigotry" such that it may be used equally well to justify injustice, slavery, and bigotry. He concludes, "Deconstructive argument does not cease to operate when the conclusions one might draw from it are inegalitarian."

However, Balkin misjudges the effect of understanding oppositional relation as complementary. Each side of the opposition remains *always already* contaminated by the other, thereby obviating the argument that one side can be cleanly separated from the other. But this does not lead to homogenization. Neither side exists without the other, yet *difference* remains. This requires a new understanding of how difference is structured. The difference of each pole of an opposition becomes an essential element rather than a contaminating intrusion for its opposite. In this relation of opposites, the poles necessarily work together in an ongoing negotiation *because there is no other option* due to their essential entanglement. Therefore, complementarity precludes justification of natural dominance or essential exclusion based on *constitutional* qualities inherent in one or the other side of the difference.

Granting the complementarity and entanglement of opposites, no metaphysical rationale remains for promoting the injustice of institutionalized enslavement, intolerance, or exclusion. Social injustice, slavery, and bigotry result from excluding particular persons or factions from legitimate participation in a given economy of exchange based on distinguishing such persons and factions as constitutionally unequal in that economy. Such exclusions are based on assumed essential inequalities of role and value not warranted by the structure of opposites informed by the metaphysics of complementarity.

Any duality containing a pole judged to be inferior in essence to its opposite pole cannot count as a genuine duality in deconstructive metaphysics. Such models exist only as inventions in human society, as human cultural constructions open to deconstruction. The paucity of correlates in the natural world testifies to the inapplicability of exclusionary dichotomies and leaves little basis on which to appeal as justification for exclusionary oppositional structures in human societies. Such unjustifiable orientations derive from the tendency, fueled by runaway emotions or delusional fantasies of purity, to abstract and absolutize the oppositional poles to absurd nihilistic extremes. When institutionalized or codified in religious or political beliefs and rituals, such nihilistic extremes provide a rationale for the radical exclusionary practices of sacrificial scapegoating, racial and ethnic cleansing, and genocide.

The quality of community consistent with deconstructive complementarity must necessarily be tied to the rejection of the promotion and endorsement of policies based on essential exclusions. And since policies promoting injustice, slavery, and bigotry gain traction on the basis of mistakenly imposed essential exclusions, enlistment on the side of such policies is made groundless by the deconstruction of traditional oppositional relations. Exposing such positions as groundless renders them impotent—not by any corresponding acts of exclusion, elimination, or subtraction but by demonstrating the ground on which such structures and policies stand to have insubstantial analytic, empirical, or metaphysical basis.

The inclusiveness of complementarity dictates constant human negotiation *against* misguided policies of exclusion evident in slavery, racism, bigotry, and similar categorical exclusions while recognizing that such destructive agendas may continually stem from extreme factions that may remain influential in world and community affairs. Radical exclusionary motives are not rendered by deconstruction as policies on the same footing as inclusionary policies and must be confronted and negotiated as obstacles in communities where they continue to find adherents.

By way of further clarification, consider statements by Gregory Fried (2000), who has also criticized the capacity for a deconstructive philosophical orientation to advance a cooperative agenda in the political realm. Concerning political theory, Fried believes Derrida has succeeded in making only faint gestures or gestural feints. He asks, "What kind of political guidance does Derrida offer us, then?" and answers, "Perhaps no guidance at all ... if by guidance we mean some kind of foundation for the calculation of correct, or even prudent, action." In support of this assessment he cites a remark from Derrida he views as exemplary of this deficiency: "I would say that deconstruction loses nothing by admitting that it [that is, deconstruction itself] is impossible.... For a deconstructive operation possibility would rather be the danger, the danger of becoming an available set of rule-governed procedures, methods, accessible approaches" (Fried, 2000, 242; Derrida, 1992a, 328).

But here Derrida remains consistent in his approach. As in the case of justice, truth, freedom, etc., deconstruction is itself, in its "impossibility," undeconstructible while its procedures in particular cases remain deconstructible, similar to existing laws and their applications. The impossibility of the ideal and its endless pursuit does not entail the loss of concrete guidance; instead, as Fried indeed acknowledges, endless pursuit preserves the attitude of perfectibility. But Fried argues that if the ideal of justice is undeconstructible, then so, too, must be the ideal of injustice. Justice and injustice, then, appear to operate as ideals of equal status. Similarly, it will be possible to proceed down the list of oppositions, finding every dark side of the opposition to have equal status with the so-called light side. Consequently, the basis for moral preference disappears, leaving in its wake moral and juridical chaos.

Fried's argument, however, repeats Balkin's error and misunderstands and thereby underestimates the logic of complementarity. The complementarity of justice and injustice means that each term operates indissociably from the other. The ideal of justice is better understood as the entangled pair justice/injustice; to speak of one is to also speak of the other.

But where a conflict exists regarding two opposing views of the justice/injustice nexus, this conflict does not turn on a question regarding the ideal (because the ideal is undeconstructible, beyond the reach of deconstruction). It turns on opposing real-world articulations. No one goes to war against justice/injustice; wars may only materialize over particular articulations of what counts as justice/injustice. And these articulations, like particular laws, always remain deconstructible.

In complementarity, ideals operate as indissociable pairs. The ideal of justice, for example, becomes instead the ideal of justice/injustice. As such, they cannot be fundamentally opposed in the sense of cancelling. Every form of applied justice entails injustice just as every injustice carries with it a layer of justice. And, still, this is not the same as to say that justice and injustice amount to the same or that communities ought to forsake the pursuit of justice. Justice in human community cannot be realized without the trade-off of collateral injustices. The challenge becomes one of discovering negotiations in which what come to be viewed as injustices are accepted along with a greater justice achieved (compare, for example, Nick Vaughan-Williams' helpful discussion [2007], 118–119; see also Moore [2017, 2020]).

In human violent conflicts, complementarity means that deadly warfare operates as a collective version of suicide, as self-immolation—not because self and other are one but because self and other are inseparably entangled. The substitution of warfare for negotiation reflects as much a failure in adequate grasp of the entangled nature of real world oppositions as it does a moral failure. Fried is wrong to suggest deconstruction leads to loss of the means for moral judgment; instead it leads to perhaps the only viable foundation for moral judgment—the entanglement of every opposition, of every person, which then requires inclusionary negotiation as the only viable path forward.

Derrida refers to the process of perfectibility of an ideal as requiring *vigilance*—vigilance toward existing laws, rules, institutions, and authority figures. In place of "vigilance," Fried uses the term "suspicion" to characterize this attitude (2000, 244). But the two terms are not equivalent. "Suspicion" primarily conveys distrust whereas "vigilance" conveys watchfulness consistent with overcoming difficulties, obstacles, risks, unforeseen consequences, and the like. The vigilance of embracing endless perfectibility certainly does not preclude endorsement of particular practices, rulings, decisions, laws, and institutions; nor does it preclude criticism. Instead, vigilance requires constant reassessments while nevertheless taking a stand at particular junctures of conflict and submitting reasons for that stand.

Examples of such endorsements and guidance, in the political sphere, may be found in many places in Derrida's writings, nowhere better exemplified than in his remarks about what he refers to as the "bin Laden effect" in the wake of the attack on the World Trade Center. After remarking on how important it is to have "faith in the perfectibility of public space and of the world juridical-political scene," Derrida clearly does not hesitate to make a choice as he says: "[I]f I had to take one of the two sides and choose in a binary situation, well, I would." He denounces this "bin Laden effect" for its "cruelty, the disregard for human life, the disregard for law, for women, the use of what is worst in technocapitalist modernity for the purposes of religious fanaticism." He further clarifies his reasons for this choice:

> Despite my very strong reservations about the American, indeed European, political posture, about the "international antiterrorist" coalition, despite all the de facto betrayals, all the failures to live up to democracy, international law, and the very international institutions that the states of this "coalition" themselves founded and supported up to a certain point, I would take the side of the camp that, in principle, by right of law, leaves a perspective open to perfectibility in the name of the "political," democracy, international law, international institutions, and so on [2003, 113–114].

Balkin, Fried, and those with similar criticisms misunderstand metaphysical complementarity and thereby misjudge the depth of deconstructive reach in its structuring of differences. This reach supports the claim that deconstruction is indeed *justice* insofar as it undermines the ground for radical exclusions and fixed hierarchies while exposing the deeper ground for universal inclusion. The basis of deconstruction in essential inclusion supports only *contingent* exclusions for purposes of coordinating cooperative community through judgment of behavior rather than person. Essential inclusion of persons in the economy of human community does not entail an inclusive tolerance toward all behavior. In fact, such essential inclusiveness entails the necessity for constant negotiation within communities regarding the laws, rules, and regulations required for insuring that restrictions on behavior create the best environment for sustaining complementary living of each and all. This is by no means an easy negotiation but it may be made easier through recognition of the complementary structure of oppositions where individual and cultural differences must be negotiated and regulated in ways sufficient to maximize social cooperation and breadth of prosperity. Nevertheless, cooperative human society, even when guided by the structure of complementarity, cannot be achieved without considerable wisdom in community judgment and decision-making, for which reason educational, legislative, and judicial institutions must always be held to high standards.

The deconstructive orientation may not end violent resolution of differences but it will erode ground for the justification of exclusion necessary for enacting the most destructive violence. This most destructive violence—the favorite choice of autocrats—consists of the programmatic elimination of opposition as a routine recourse for responding to conflict and regulating partisan politics. Beyond this undercutting of radical exclusion and the worst violence, the recognition of metaphysical complementarity carries other advantages for collective and interpersonal life, such as the previously discussed elevation of the role of doubt in communication, where the question "Have I understood?" becomes routine. Contrary to the common assumption, it is doubt and not certainty that enables. It does so by promoting consciousness-raising circumspective vigilance. The complementarity package—universal inclusion and vigilant doubt—may prove to be of lasting benefit for the future of human community by maximizing coordination between individuals and groups, as well as between humans and the natural world, while minimizing rationales for deadly violence and environmental destruction.

Drawing to a close, this discursion on the enigma of meaning hopefully leaves readers with a new, or perhaps renewed, attitude toward words and signs. Language, through its naming, is a short cut, mapping a terrain that is not the whole terrain. And yet this terrain can never be approached or understood apart from these short cuts. Derrida has demonstrated the short cut of difference between map and mapped to be quite natural, not to be confused with a shortcoming. Nevertheless, as has been argued, signifiers, as short cuts, can be dangerous, as can any tool, when used without informed care and caution adequate to shifting multi-use potential.

The nature of language as a tool changes when supplemented with the being of the trace. The trace changes the essence of the tool by placing it within a temporal, moving context, a context within which the tool's identity becomes mobile and divided as it acquires aspects from every new context through which it is used. This entanglement between tool and trace may also characterize the difference: Wittgenstein/Derrida. To side with

Wittgenstein alone remains inadequate. Wittgenstein without Derrida can make language appear misleadingly whole. And yet Derrida without Wittgenstein can make language appear misleadingly broken. Wittgenstein calls forth Derrida, not as opponent but as supplement, drawing out the both-and/neither-nor complementarity of difference.

Wittgenstein's genius and his contributions to understanding the complexities of language must continue to be appreciated, but Derrida's contribution emerges with a metaphysical depth beyond the positions Wittgenstein occupies. Derrida's contribution counts as a significant gain in what many have long argued to be beyond what philosophy can offer—genuine *progress* for the quality of human community. Progress results from the ongoing perfection of communication and cooperation as crucially dependent on improved understanding of the structural temporal aspects of signs and languages and the limits imposed by such structures. Such understanding highlights the benefits of circumspection regarding the potential for misreading in the reading of signs as well as the benefits of vigilant attention to the endlessly shifting, persistently unpredictable, but thoroughly engaging "yet to come" of the other future and the future of the other.

Commentary on Interpretation and "Internal Relation" in Response to Gordon Baker and Peter Hacker (1985); Baker (2004), Hacker (2007)

While reading Wittgenstein's unpublished works (*Nachlass*) in an effort to better understand his comments on rule following, especially his comments in *Philosophical Investigations*, Oxford professors Gordon Baker and Peter Hacker became concerned with Kripke's reading of Wittgenstein on rule following. In 1983, they collaborated to write the essay "On Misunderstanding Wittgenstein: Kripke's Private Language Argument." Their readings in the *Nachlass* gave them clarity concerning the purpose of Wittgenstein's comments on rule following and this clarity led them to conclude, "It was evident that Kripke's interpretation flew flagrantly against Wittgenstein's manifest intentions in these important passages [in *Philosophical Investigations*], misconstruing their meaning, misidentifying their target, and misrepresenting their thrust" (vii).

What Kripke identifies as a significant form of skepticism in *Philosophical Investigations*, referred to as *rule-skepticism*, struck Baker and Hacker as a "bizarre" interpretation of Wittgenstein. They claim to have shown "Wittgenstein's arguments were antithetical both to the rule-scepticism that he was supposed to have invented and also to the sceptical solution which he allegedly proposed to meet this new form of scepticism" (viii). However, after a public presentation of their essay to the Oxford Philosophical Society, they learned that many among those attending claimed that, although Kripke may have been wrong in attributing his interpretation of rule-skepticism to Wittgenstein, rule-skepticism nevertheless presents a profound problem with important philosophical implications.

This response came as a surprise to Baker and Hacker since, in their view, the entire rule-skepticism issue, rather than being a profound problem, instead gives evidence of a profoundly mistaken and confused line of thinking. In light of this confusion, Baker and Hacker concluded it was necessary to write another essay, titled "The Illusions of Rule-Scepticism," debunking the claims of rule-skepticism apart from the question of any origin the notion might be perceived to have in the work of Wittgenstein.

After composing these two essays, Baker and Hacker realized that it might not be self-evident to readers what Wittgenstein's purpose may have been in addressing rule following issues so extensively in *Philosophical Investigations*. So they felt obliged to compose a third essay concerning this topic, titled, "Rule-Scepticism and the Harmony Between Language and Reality." This essay features the notion of the "internal relation between rules and their applications," to which they believe Wittgenstein appeals in *Philosophical Investigations* as the reason why the use of language precludes rule-skepticism as well as the need for any process of interpretation as a means for generating the relation between rules and applications. In the following year, 1984, Baker and Hacker combined these three essays into the book *Scepticism, Rules, and Language* (published 1985).

However, as will be argued, the critique of rule-skepticism offered in Baker and Hacker's three essays fails to close the case, thereby leaving rule-skepticism largely intact and philosophically significant. In addition to the defense of rule-skepticism, this chapter concludes with a brief discussion of Baker's later work wherein he retracts much of his earlier work with Hacker on Wittgenstein. Before his death, Baker advanced the thesis that Wittgenstein must *not* be understood to identify philosophy's purpose as one of dissolving *general* philosophical enigmas emerging from the quest for meaning. Instead, according to Baker, Wittgenstein proposes a therapeutic intervention by means of dissection of particular misunderstandings and misconceptions propagated through the use of words and concepts by *individual* philosophers who have, unwittingly, tied themselves into exasperating and confounding philosophical knots. Thus, Baker's later work views Wittgenstein's philosophy as a text offering examples illustrating how individual philosophers may proceed to untie the particular unnecessary philosophical knots they have created for themselves.

Beginning now with Baker and Hacker, they suggest Kripke's illustration supporting rule-skepticism—the plus/quus example—imagines a situation that will not arise. It will not arise because rules and their applications are too intimately connected. They ground their argument in a mysterious notion used sparingly by Wittgenstein (only once in *Philosophical Investigations*): the previously mentioned *internal relation*. Making reference to Wittgenstein's mathematical example in PI#185, they say, "Whether acting thus-and-so (writing '... 1002, 1004, 1006 ...') is a correct application of a given rule has nothing to do with my past intentions or with what I meant in the past, but only with the rule. That acting thus is correct is an aspect of the internal relation between the rule and its extension. Writing '... 1002, 1004, ...' in compliance with the order 'Expand the series +2' [rather than 1000, 1004, 1008 ...] is a *criterion* for following this instruction" (89).

In Wittgenstein's example, the actual rule followed or not followed does not become obvious until 1000 is reached. Baker and Hacker object that following the rule by writing 1000, 1004, 1008 ... has not been prompted in any way by the command to "expand the series +2" nor by any other instruction or example. At this point in their argument, Baker and Hacker ignore Wittgenstein's further remarks: "In such a case we might say, perhaps: It comes natural to this person to understand our order with our explanations as we should understand the order: 'Add 2 up to 1000, 4 up to 2000, 6 up to 3000 and so on'" (PI#185). Baker and Hacker do not mention this part of PI#185 and seemingly do not give it any weight.

Teaching the rule by instructing what to do cannot include a list of everything *not* to do. It is possible some may understand the rule described to them as being more complicated than it actually is. Countless ways to misunderstand cannot be explicitly ruled out by the explanation of the rule or the observation of finite instances of its performance. Wittgenstein squarely confronts this quandary whereas Baker and Hacker seek to work their way around it by appeal to the notion of internal relation. But in doing so, they require the notion of internal relation to shoulder more weight than it can carry and more weight than it would appear even Wittgenstein thought it could carry.

Referring back to Kripke's illustration and summarizing the situation he claims it creates, they surprisingly acknowledge the following: "[W]e must determine precisely how he [the rule follower] does interpret the rule (since it is always open to various interpretations), i.e., *which* rule he is following. All the evidence we have to go on as to his interpretation of the rule ... is the applications made of it hithereto. That the sign '+,' for example, expresses the addition function, is an hypothesis, resting on the data of his past applications of '+.' But like all scientific hypotheses, it is underdetermined by the data" (62).

Here Baker and Hacker correctly characterize the nature of Kripke's challenge to rule following by noting that hypotheses about rules—including intentions, purposes, or understandings—may indeed be made based on the evidence, the external data. But they acknowledge these data are *underdetermined*. With this acknowledgment, they create an opening for interpretation—both in relation to attempts to grasp the rule and attempts to confirm if the rule is being followed. Their acknowledgment of underdetermination in hypotheses may be thought as sufficient in itself to undermine their claims about the inapplicability of rule-skepticism. Nevertheless, believing they follow Wittgenstein, they find underdetermination in hypotheses to be irrelevant to the issue of rule following. In explanation they claim rule following and its confirmation are not of the order of hypotheses!

Baker and Hacker believe Wittgenstein debunks the paradox of rule following he identifies in PI#201 as nothing more than a muddle induced by the unfortunate crossing of the grammar of language games. For Baker and Hacker, the rule always rules. This is evident when they say, "Correctness and incorrectness are determined by the internal relation between the rule and what counts as accord with it. It is not a *discovery* that '1002' follows '1000' in the sequence of even integers. Rather, getting this result is a *criterion* for following the rule of this series" (77).

Baker and Hacker promote confusion by essentially making an application of a rule into a criterion of the rule while assuming this labeling somehow immunizes applications from the troubles of rule-skepticism. But underdetermination precludes that rule criteria can guarantee an application. No particular application can thereby function as reliable criteria for rule following. As one of few commentators on Baker and Hacker to notice this problem, Patricia Werhane (1992) notes, "...one should also want to be careful not to ... conflate rules themselves with their applications." Doing so "blurs the idea of a rule with its applications so as to invite an identity of these two." This creates the problem of being unable to "evaluate rule-following and suggests that rule-following is dictated by conventions which themselves cannot be brought into question" (1992, 158–159; see also Williams, 2010, 178–180). In such circumstances not only the rules (conventions) but the following, the applications, also cannot be brought into question. Then the rule, the guide for action, becomes lost and ceases to matter and narrow patterns of rigid behavior assume the rank of rules.

Given underdetermination, no rule following behavior transparently reveals *which* rule is followed. Instead of submitting to this limitation, Baker and Hacker weakly respond: "What these premises of rule-scepticism share is a failure to acknowledge that acting in certain ways (what is called 'acting in conformity with the rule') are *criteria* for understanding a rule, and that acting otherwise is a criterion for failing to understand it." In other words, in response to the rule-skeptic who asserts behavior *cannot* provide conclusive criteria for demonstrating a particular person follows a particular rule, Baker and Hacker assert behavior can and does provide such criteria while offering no compelling evidence in support of this claim other than the mysterious notion of internal relation. This type of reply corresponds to what is commonly called begging the question and they are not shy about doing so.

For Baker and Hacker, the rule-skeptic, "...presupposes the possibility of separating the grasp of a rule from knowledge of how to apply it." Such separation, they claim, overlooks the intimate connection between the grasp of a rule and being able to apply it. They claim, "The principle that to understand a rule is to know what would count as acting in accord with it allows of no general exceptions" (101).

Baker and Hacker hold to their criticism of rule-skepticism despite admitting that no rule can be formulated by words or ostensive definition or in any other manner such as to indicate in every possible future instance how it is to be followed. In other words, they admit that the connection between a rule and its applications is not a *causal* connection while nevertheless realizing that in order to prop up their argument against the rule-skeptic they must appeal to a type of connection between a rule and its applications that very nearly approximates a causal connection. They are fully aware of how vulnerable this assumption is when they claim, "The crucial problem is to explain how an internal relation can be defeasible. Defeasibility amounts to the absence of any entailment, while an internal relation must be a necessary connection. Can there be necessary connections that fall short of entailment?" (111).

Wittgenstein, in Baker and Hacker's view, answers "yes." They explain, "...evidence is typically held to render a proposition certain if and only if it confers upon it the degree of probability of 1. But philosophers have commonly thought that only entailment confers the probability of 1 upon an hypothesis. Yet Wittgenstein suggests that undefeated criterial support renders the proposition supported certain. How can this be?" (111). Indeed, how can this be?

Impressed by the possibility that a rule follower's observed actions in conformity with a rule might actually be "mere coincidence" and that apparently correct conclusions might be derived from systematic misunderstandings of the rule which would become apparent only in future instances, the rule-skeptic, according to Baker and Hacker, mistakenly jumps to the conclusion that the defeasibility of such inferences provides all the evidence needed to show that doubt is warranted, "that there is no such thing as certainty that a person understands a rule correctly or no such thing as certainty that he knows how to apply it over a full range of its applicability ..." (113). Baker and Hacker then make what is perhaps their most shocking claim: "There is no cogent argument proving that the mere fact of defeasibility (the *possibility* of defeat) justifies doubt or the denial of certainty. The *presence* of defeating conditions justifies doubt, but the *intelligibility* (imaginability) of defeating conditions does not" (114).

This conclusion is obviously wrong. To take a more extreme example as illustration, their argument is analogous to asserting this: the presence of defeating conditions concerning my life, such as an imminent threat of death, justifies anxiety, but the intelligibility (imaginability) of defeating conditions, such as my death at some unknown future time, does not justify anxiety. While the two forms of doubt and anxiety are not the same, existential philosophers through the 19th and 20th centuries have had much to say about the potent role in life of defeasibility in the latter case.

The presence of *possible* defeating conditions does not merely justify doubt. It takes doubt to the level of *necessity*. To ignore the necessity for doubt is to ignore reality. And this is done only at a cost. Rule-skepticism doubt is warranted in all cases and must be negotiated by exercising a measure of doubt appropriate to the exigencies of a given situation. Those who constantly negotiate doubt with regard to human communication and behavior are prepared for the unexpected. And the unexpected may be the most confounding occurrence when entirely unanticipated.

But Baker and Hacker persist again: "The supposition that defeasibility justifies doubt is tantamount to the absurd proposal that possible doubt is a kind of doubt, that imaginable reasons for doubt in *other* circumstances are, in *these* circumstances here and now, actual reasons for doubting" (114).

But the rule-skeptic asserts that in these circumstances *here and now*, whatever they may be, as well as in every other circumstance, doubt remains not only possible but must be *embraced*. This necessity for doubt is made evident in Kripke's example (along with Wittgenstein's example in PI#185) showing that even apparent rule following behavior may mask behavior following a different rule. All rule following and its confirmation are, contrary to Baker and Hacker, of the nature of hypotheses.

In the physical sciences, where causal relations are sought, accepted theories regarding these relations are nevertheless still treated as working hypotheses, always open to doubt and to further information and review. This doubt—call it structural doubt—is even more relevant in the non-causal realm of human rule following where the connections between rules and applications are bound by mere "internal relations." If someone appears to be in pain, there may be good reason to act quickly, but this need not and ought not to obscure the structural doubt accompanying every instance of perceived pain behavior. Embracing structural doubt heightens awareness toward unfolding cues in situations, priming the senses for ongoing revisions of initial assumptions.

But again, Baker and Hacker are having none of it. They believe this line of thinking undermines altogether the ability to read behavior: "Furthermore, doubt is only intelligible within an established framework of concepts, for *what it is* that is being doubted must stand firm. But the very concept of an ability is partly determined by the grammatical fact that such-and-such conditions (e.g., behaviour in certain circumstances) justify attributing that ability to a person. If this justificative nexus were served, then it would be wholly unclear what it is that is held to be doubtful. For that this internal relation obtains is an aspect of the concept of this ability. To call it into doubt is not to deny the apparent facts, but to disrupt the concept" (114).

If the internal relation were half as connected as they claim, then it would make no sense to suppose it would be "wholly unclear what it is that is held to be doubtful."

The so-called "internal relation" or quasi-entailment of the connection between a behavior and a rule would not in the least be disrupted by placing this connection in the sphere of structural doubt. Instead, granting the place of doubt in these circumstances only clarifies the nature of the relation and assigns to it a role more proper to its nature, which is: doubt plays a crucial role in maintaining continued attunement to other persons and to the world. To doubt that a particular behavior *necessarily* displays a particular meaning need not entail a denial that the behavior is part of the nexus of criteria routinely associated with that meaning or concept.

If the study of language demonstrates anything, it certainly demonstrates the underdetermination of word meanings, that words point in more than one direction at a time and that reading their use across varied contexts requires quick assumptions—assumptions that, in Derrida's view, *always* miss the mark in some way. Embracing structural doubt creates an attunement aiding in this process of reading by holding presumptions to a more tentative status.

The stress Baker and Hacker place on the notion of internal relation and the quality of connection this entails between rule and application collapses the distinction between performance and instructions for performance such that a performance of the rule, which is judged by others to follow the rule, counts as criterion for the rule. This is as much as to claim that a rule applies itself. But this notion fails to acknowledge that behavior appearing to follow the rule may be guided by a different rule, which may only become apparent at some future point in time. The stress Baker and Hacker place on the notion of internal relation appears to exceed anything Wittgenstein places on it. Its near absence in the key works of *Philosophical Investigations* and *The Blue and Brown Books* is telling.

Nevertheless, the view of signs advocated by Wittgenstein concerning the lack of interpretation in routine sign use, traffics in a similar area of dubious conjecture about the operative relation between rules and their applications. It remains doubtful Wittgenstein understood and endorsed this connection in quite the extreme to which Baker and Hacker describe. But his position on the role of interpretation appears closer to theirs than to

Derrida's, which assigns a much more crucial role for interpretation. Wittgenstein stresses the conformity achievable through training, but he acknowledges the limits of training in ways that preclude the kind of reliability Baker and Hacker assign to the internal relation between rules and applications.

By way of conclusion, Baker and Hacker compose a paragraph summarizing the key points in their commentary on Wittgenstein and rule-skepticism. Here is a division of this summary into four points with attached critical responses consistent with the preceding critical commentary:

1. "A correct understanding of the internal relations between rules and their applications, and between understanding a rule and applying it correctly, robs rule-scepticism of its charms." On the contrary, this "correct understanding" is an overestimation of the strength of the connection between rules and their applications.

2. "Wittgenstein laboured to make clear the nature of these internal relations." Wittgenstein devoted obsessive attention to the relation between rules and applications because he knew the complexities of this relation threatened the basis of understanding and communication. However, his solution, while not as extreme as Baker and Hacker's, falls short of adequate recognition of the limits of language and signs.

3. "He emphasized that behaviour is a *criterion* for possession of an ability, and, in the specific case of understanding rules, that how one applies a rule is a criterion for how one understands it." Certainly specific behaviors may be viewed as necessary evidence for possession of certain abilities but it cannot be emphasized enough that such evidence is not *sufficient* for determining *which* rule may be in operation in relation to these behaviors.

4. "And he stressed that internal relations are not cemented together by third entities (in this case, by interpretations)" (115). The notion that "internal relations" are "cemented together"—regardless by what means—is too strong a metaphor for the kind of relation obtaining between rules and applications. But among possible metaphors for identifying the nature of the relation between rules and applications the term "interpretation" is one of the most helpful.

Hacker vs. Baker (2007)

Following Gordon Baker's untimely death in 2002, Katherine J. Morris compiled writings Baker had been composing during the last decade of his life and edited them into a book published as *Wittgenstein's Method:*

Neglected Aspects (2004). These writings constitute a radical break with the views previously published by Baker and Hacker. Apparently, Baker came to view his work with Hacker as entirely too strident in style and misguided in substance in light of new insights he began to have concerning the thrust of Wittgenstein's writings. The special significance of these writings seemed now to center on methodology rather than dominant arguments, such as Baker and Hacker presumed to be the case with the so-called Private Language Argument.

In Baker's new line of interpretation he argues that *Philosophical Investigations* and the collection of Wittgenstein's later notes and writings give evidence of a consistent methodology. The nature of this methodology remains highly therapeutic but instead of being directed at resolving high profile *general* philosophical knots such as mind/body dualism, the problem of other minds, and the rigor of concepts, Wittgenstein is now understood to be emphasizing the many ways in which language may induce particular troubling confusions for *individual* philosophers. These troubles arise through the expanded use of particular terms beyond contexts for which they were initially appropriate and within which they were initially brought into use.

This is not to say Wittgenstein believed in facts of grammar to which language users must adhere, as if he were the grammar police, but rather that facts of grammar exist relevant for consideration when doing philosophy, when attempting to discern matters important to conducting a healthy relationship toward language and functioning in the world. For Wittgenstein, philosophers are all too easily led by the habit of generalizing from narrow linguistic contexts to broader life contexts without paying sufficient attention to the possible ways in which such generalizations mislead more than lead.

Baker's new insight into Wittgenstein, espoused and further advanced by Graham McFee in his book *How to Do Philosophy: A Wittgensteinian Reading of Wittgenstein* (2015), is not without merit. Like Henry Staten's view, this reading of Wittgenstein emerges with support in sections of textual evidence Baker cites. Nevertheless, as Baker's former co-author Peter Hacker argues, Baker's new interpretation lacks sufficient textual support to induce persuasion. Hacker's response to Baker's new understanding—entitled "Gordon Baker's Late Interpretation of Wittgenstein"—moves in the right direction when he says, "If Baker's interpretation were right, one of its consequences—whether intended by Baker or not—would be that Wittgenstein is a figure of very minor importance. For he is, Baker insists, relevant only for those who are suffering intellectual torment, and who need conceptual psychotherapy to ameliorate their condition. Baker's Wittgenstein is an 'intellectual

GP' much influenced by Freud, with a book of case histories of individual treatments of his tormented friends and acquaintances (pp. 68, 132, 173n, 12, 184)" (Hacker, 36).

Although the claim that Baker's view reduces Wittgenstein to a minor figure may count as an exaggeration, Hacker is correct to suggest Baker's Wittgenstein is made to play a role in which he appears largely out of character with regard to what is known about his ambitions concerning topics with which he became obsessed. According to Wittgenstein biographer Ray Monk, Wittgenstein saw his philosophical work as relevant not only to the entire history of philosophy but, more important, to the entire history of Western culture (when, for example, Wittgenstein speaks of the unjustifiable hegemony in his era of science and its methods). And while Freud is a significant figure in the history of this culture, Wittgenstein—as Hacker notes—did not and would not have been content to play the role of Freud's analogue in the sphere of philosophy. Wittgenstein went his own way, plowing up new ground on the way. Characterizing Wittgenstein's approach to philosophy as broadly analogous to the work of any other intellectual figure, contemporary or otherwise, counts perhaps as analogous to the kind of conceptual error Wittgenstein became famous for identifying and providing means for avoiding.

In his response to Baker, Hacker admirably summarizes Baker's departure from the core of their past mutual agreement in Wittgenstein interpretation while providing a comprehensive and, it would seem, damaging critique of it. Hacker's critique of Baker, however, does not move him in the direction of a critique of their former work together and the particular understanding of Wittgenstein it represents. In fact, near the end of his response to Baker, Hacker reaffirms this position and lists a summary of its features, whereby he claims Wittgenstein "resolved many of the deep problems that have dogged our subject for centuries." Problems about:

1. "the nature of linguistic representation"
2. "the relationship between thought and language"
3. "solipsism and idealism"
4. "self-knowledge and knowledge of other minds"
5. "the nature of necessary truth and of mathematical propositions"

In addition to these achievements, according to Hacker, Wittgenstein upended the status quo in the philosophy of logic and language and offered an "array of insights" into philosophy of psychology, mathematics, and foundationalist epistemology. Finally, he instigated a form of philosophy focused not on expanding the frontiers of human knowledge but instead on clarification in the use of concepts and forms of thought relevant to forms of life (Hacker, 37).

Hacker speaks rightly in noting Wittgenstein's attention to these problem areas and in believing that Wittgenstein had important and provocative points to make regarding all of them. But, as argued in Section I, Wittgenstein most certainly did not "resolve" these major problems in philosophy. Instead, he adopted engaging stances and presented worthwhile supportive arguments, but these arguments fall short of providing compelling resolutions to these problems. And in some cases these "resolutions" give rise to further problems—as has been argued, for example, concerning his insistence on the absence of interpretation in the use of language and the ways in which this insistence ushers in problems relating to justification and the application of words.

In conclusion, Hacker's critique of the late work of Baker on Wittgenstein must be acknowledged as insightful and accurate while, nevertheless, his continued affirmation of the substance of their previous work together must be understood as notably flawed, especially on the issue of "internal relation."

Clarification of Derrida's View of Oppositional Relation in Response to Ralph E. Shain (2007)

In "Derrida and Wittgenstein: Points of Opposition," Ralph E. Shain performs a commendable service in reviewing the existing literature comparing the philosophies of Wittgenstein and Derrida. In the summary section of his essay he rightly notes, "These analyses have shown that one of the factors which has vitiated much of the usefulness of these studies has been the urge of the writers to have Derrida and Wittgenstein hold the same view." Shain further divides this general urge into three particular pitfalls: "Sometimes this urge reduces Wittgenstein to Derrida (Staten and Mulhall) or Derrida to Wittgenstein (Rorty and Mulligan). Another is the appropriation of both Derrida and Wittgenstein for an antecedently conceived project, such as pragmatism (Margolis), transcendental philosophy (Garver and Lee) or the theory of communicative action (Sonderegger)" (2007, 144).

Shain ultimately asserts, "I think it is fair to draw the conclusion that a confrontation between Derrida and Wittgenstein has yet to take place." Agreement with Shain's conclusion counted as one source of inspiration for this book, along with his suggestions for points of possible difference needing further inquiry. Shain proposes four areas for future inquiry he believes "have a special significance and where it is easiest to see that Derrida and Wittgenstein come close to direct opposition" (2007, 144–145). These areas are: (1) the problem of word meanings highlighted in Wittgenstein's use of the term "family resemblance" and Derrida's use of "dissemination"; (2) the problem of interiority as featured in the problem of other minds; (3) the problem of contrasts as raised by Wittgenstein's claim that any word used without a contrast counts as a metaphysical use; and (4) the role of time in relation to the structure and complexity of language. The chapters in Parts II and III address these topics and are directly inspired by Shain's suggestions.

Shain also draws attention to the problem of contrasts and the metaphysical use of words—a use Wittgenstein understands as deriving from the loss of contrast between terms. Shain notes a possible similarity between Wittgenstein and Derrida on the importance of contrast but is hesitant in this assessment of similarity. As will be argued, it turns out he is right in this hesitation. Shain begins formulating the possible similarity between Wittgenstein and Derrida with this citation from Wittgenstein:

> ...in stating our puzzles about the *general vagueness* of sense experience, and about the flux of all phenomena, we are using the words "flux" and "vagueness" wrongly, in a typically metaphysical way, namely without antithesis; whereas in their correct and everyday use vagueness is opposed to clearness, flux to stability, inaccuracy to accuracy, and *problem* to *solution*. The very word "problem," one might say, is misapplied when used for our philosophical troubles. These difficulties, as long as they are seen as problems, are tantalizing, and appear insoluble [BB, 46].

In this passage, Wittgenstein moves beyond general indictment of inappropriate grammatical frames as the source of philosophical confusions to the more specific claim that the use of certain words *in isolation from their antitheses* accounts for much in the creation of these troubles. Shain then cites Derrida as appearing to draw a similar conclusion in his deconstruction of Lévi-Strauss' contrast of the *bricoleur* and the *engineer*. In Lévi-Strauss' use, the linguistic bricoleur *borrows* whatever language and instrumental words may be available at hand for a given task. The engineer, however, "*construct[s]* the totality of his language, syntax, and lexicon [emphasis added]" Shain then cites a passage from Derrida where he believes Derrida argues that Lévi-Strauss' contrast fails because the concept of the bricoleur "has no contrast": "...as soon as we admit that very [*sic*, this word should be 'every'] finite discourse is bound by a certain *bricolage* and that the engineer and the scientist are also species of *bricoleurs*, then the very idea of *bricolage* is menaced and the difference in which it took on its meaning breaks down" (Shain, 146; Derrida, 1978, 285).

If Derrida understands language, and thereby meaning, as a system of differences, a system of contrasts, as tracings of traces, then when difference breaks down, meaning also breaks down. Granting as much, cannot Wittgenstein be understood as saying substantially the same thing in his passage cited above and in his critique of non-antithetical uses of words? The similarity between Wittgenstein and Derrida concerning the importance of difference and contrast is, however, once again only superficial, as a more extensive examination of the context of Derrida's passage cited above discloses. Understanding the force of Derrida's remarks requires understanding further the concept of the bricoleur. Just previous to this passage Shain cites Derrida where he says:

> In this sense the engineer is a myth. A subject who supposedly would be the
> absolute origin of his own discourse and supposedly would construct it "out of
> nothing," "out of whole cloth," would be the creator of the verb, the verb itself.
> The notion of the engineer who supposedly breaks with all forms of *bricolage*
> is therefore a theological idea; and since Lévi-Strauss tells us elsewhere that
> *bricolage* is mythopoetic, the odds are that the engineer is a myth produced by
> the *bricoleur* [1978, 285].

Here Derrida points to the sense in which the engineer is myth and fiction
insofar as in practice the engineer cannot break from "all forms of bricolage." Thus begins a paradigmatic example of deconstruction in practice.
Derrida introduces a reversal into the oppositional tension of the engineer
and the bricoleur, whereby the bricoleur as discoverer and borrower displaces the primacy of the engineer as creator and inventor such that the
engineer becomes a species of bricoleur. This would seem to dissolve the
bricoleur/engineer opposition in favor of the bricoleur, along with the dis-
covery/invention opposition in favor of discovery.

While Shain initially merely hesitates in drawing a conclusion regarding possible similarity between Wittgenstein and Derrida on the issue of
contrasts, he ultimately rejects this conclusion when he says, "It might
appear that Derrida is accepting.... Wittgenstein's conclusions. However, I
believe that Derrida's view is different, in that for him meaning can 'break
down' but not be dissolved" (2007, 146).

This is the correct conclusion. Instead of a collapse of the contrast and
a loss of sense, a remaining antithesis, a difference, emerges between the
two terms exceeding the structure of the old opposition. The nature of the
interval between them shifts from one of difference to that of *différance*
such that Derrida might well say, "Who is not a linguistic bricoleur? Who
is not a linguistic engineer?" Both the engineer and the bricoleur are
effects of *différance*. The two terms refer to no instances that remain pure
and instead contaminate each other all the way to the core, and yet their
contrast does not dissolve. This is to say they move in superposition with
each other and yet cannot be collapsed one into the other. Every context of
use of one or the other term points to contamination and adequate inquiry
exposes this contamination. Words are not "given" from above but derive
from the creative behaviors of humans in community; and yet because
words also have no autonomous point of creation they amount to origin-
less discovery and borrowing from what already exists in the generation of
new additions to further meanings through use in new contexts.

In his essay *Différance*, Derrida expresses the situation this way:
"Differences are thus 'produced'—differed—by differance. But *what* differs, or *who* differs? In other words, *what is* differance? ... If we answered
these questions even before examining them as questions, even before

going back over them and questioning their form (even what seems to be most natural and necessary about them), we would fall below the level we have now reached" (1973, 145). This "level" that has been reached corresponds to a level of metaphysics wherein the nature of agency, the nature of the subject as agent, and the structure of the language through which these natures are routinely discussed, must all submit to examination and interrogation—due to what is assumed rather than demonstrated in these natures and structures. Such examination and interrogation, of course, count as hallmarks of deconstruction as these investigations expose complementarity as the necessary supplement existing within and alongside the classical structure of oppositional relation.

Another mode of understanding oppositional structure supplements the traditional structure. Every contrast submits to the law of contamination, which alters the way in which "contrast"—and therefore meaning—must be understood. This new understanding exceeds anything offered by Wittgenstein and his view of the ground of meaning and language and challenges metaphysics in a way exceeding his challenge.

Recalling the discussion in Chapter 11, Derrida understands the opposition on which the sign itself depends—the opposition between the signifier and the signified—as modeling the structure of every metaphysical opposition, which he also expresses as the difference between the sensible and the intelligible.

Shain is right to hesitate in finding full similarity in the views of Wittgenstein and Derrida regarding the role and nature of contrasts and his hesitation is helpful in opening the way to a deeper understanding of Derrida's philosophy. On one level, Derrida challenges the contrast between opposites (the classical contrast) while, on another level, he upholds the contrast (in the contrast of complementarity). Escape from the classical structure of contrasts does not signal an escape from metaphysics or from contrasts but rather an escape to another level of metaphysics whereby the classical structure acquires an additional feature. While this may seem a subtle shift, it inaugurates a shift in metaphysical orientation with significant consequences for language and life, as explained in the concluding chapter.

In sum, Derrida differs from Wittgenstein's claim concerning non-antithetical concepts. For Derrida, so-called non-antithetical concepts remain within the antithetical orbit and not only count as metaphysical but also expose another quality of metaphysics in the supplement of complementary structure.

Bibliography

Altieri, Charles. (1976). "Wittgenstein on Consciousness and Language: A Challenge to Derridean Literary Theory." *Modern Language Notes.* Vol. 91, 1397–1423.

Arendt, Hannah. (1993). *Between Past and Future.* London: Penguin.

Baggini, Julian. (2020). Think Jacques Derrida was a Charlatan? Look Again. *Prospect Magazine,* October 4. https://www.prospectmagazine.co.uk/magazine/-jacques-derrida-philosopher-not-overrated.

Baker, Gordon P. (2004). *Wittgenstein's Method: Neglected Aspects.* Katherine J. Morris, Ed. Oxford: Blackwell Publishing, Ltd.

Baker, Gordon P., and Peter M.S. Hacker. (1985). *Skepticism, Rules, and Language.* Oxford: Blackwell Publishing, Ltd.

Bala, Arun. (2017). *Complementarity Beyond Physics: Niels Bohr's Parallels.* London: Palgrave Macmillan.

Barad, Karen. (2007). *Meeting the Universe Halfway: Quantum Physics and the Entanglement of Matter and Meaning.* Durham, NC: Duke University Press.

Barish, Evelyn. (2014). *The Double Life of Paul de Man.* New York: Liveright Publishing Corporation.

Benedetti, Paul, and Nancy DeHart, Eds. (1997). *Forward Through the Rearview Mirror.* Cambridge, MA: MIT Press.

Bevir, Mark. (2000). Meaning, Truth, and Phenomenology. *Metaphilosophy,* Vol. 31, no. 4, 412–426. https://doi.org/10.1111/1467-9973.00158.

Borradori, Giovanna, Ed. (2003). *Philosophy in a Time of Terror: Dialogues with Jürgen Habermas and Jacques Derrida.* Chicago: University of Chicago Press.

Borutti, Silvana, and Fulvia de Luise. (2013). Writing and Communicating Philosophy: Consonances between Plato and Wittgenstein. In *Wittgenstein and Plato: Connections, Comparisons, and Contrasts.* Luigi Perissinotto and Begoña Ramón Cámara, Eds. New York: Palgrave Macmillan.

Braver, Lee. (2012). *Groundless Grounds: A Study of Wittgenstein and Heidegger.* Cambridge, MA: MIT Press.

Brockriede, Wayne. (1985). Constructs, Experience, and Argument. *Quarterly Journal of Speech.* Vol. 71, no. 2, 151–163. https://doi.org/10.1080/00335638509383725.

Burik, Steven. (2009). *The End of Comparative Philosophy and the Task of Comparative Thinking: Heidegger, Derrida, and Daoism.* Albany: State University of New York Press.

Burke, Kenneth. (1966). *Language as Symbolic Action.* Berkeley: University of California Press.

Burke, Kenneth. (1984). *Permanence and Change.* Berkeley: University of California Press. (First published 1935).

Cámara, Begoña Ramón. (2013). The World Seen Sub Specie Aeternitatus: Wittgenstein's Platonism. In *Wittgenstein and Plato: Connections, Comparisons, and Contrasts.* Luigi Perissinotto and Begoña Ramón Cámara, Eds. New York: Palgrave Macmillan.

Campos-Salvaterra, Valeria. (2018). "The Original Polemos: Phenomenology and Violence in Jacques Derrida." In *The Meanings of Violence: From Critical Theory to Biopolitics.* Gavin Rae and Emma Ingala, Eds. New York: Routledge.

Cantor, Georg. (1955). *Contributions to the Founding of the Theory of Transfinite Numbers*. Philip E.B. Jourdain, Trans. New York: Dover Publications, Inc. (First published 1915).

Caputo, John D. (1997). *Deconstruction in a Nutshell*. New York: Fordham University Press.

Crary, Alice, and Rupert Read, Eds. (2000). *The New Wittgenstein*. New York: Routledge.

Critchley, Simon. (1992). *The Ethics of Deconstruction: Derrida and Levinas*. Cambridge, MA: Blackwell Publishers.

Culler, Jonathan. (1982). *On Deconstruction: Theory and Criticism after Structuralism*. Ithaca, NY: Cornell University Press.

D'Amato, Anthony. (1990). Pragmatic Indeterminacy. *Northwestern University Law Review*, 148, Vol. 85, 1–43.

Derrida, Jacques. (1972). "Structure, Sign, and Play in the Discourse of the Human Sciences." Richard Macksey, Trans. In *The Structuralist Controversy: The Languages of Criticism and the Sciences of Man*. Richard Macksey and Eugenio Donato, Eds. Baltimore: Johns Hopkins University Press. (The symposium where Derrida presented this essay occurred in Baltimore, 1966).

Derrida, Jacques. (1973). *Speech and Phenomena and Other Essays on Husserl's Theory of Signs*. David B. Allison, Trans. Evanston: Northwestern University Press. (First published in France 1967).

Derrida, Jacques. (1976). *Of Grammatology*. Gayatri Chakravorty Spivak. Trans. Baltimore: Johns Hopkins University Press. (First published in France 1967).

Derrida, Jacques. (1977a). Signature Event Context. *Glyph 1: Johns Hopkins Textual Studies*. Samuel Weber, Trans. Baltimore: Johns Hopkins University Press. Vol. 1, 173–197.

Derrida, Jacques. (1977b). "Limited Inc." *Glyph 2: Johns Hopkins Textual Studies*. Samuel Weber, Trans. Baltimore: Johns Hopkins University Press. Vol. 2, 162–254.

Derrida, Jacques. (1978). *Writing and Difference*. Alan Bass, Trans. Chicago: University of Chicago Press.

Derrida, Jacques. (1979). *Spurs: Nietzsche's Styles*. Barbara Harlow, Trans. Chicago: University of Chicago Press.

Derrida, Jacques. (1981a). *Dissemination*. Barbara Johnson, Trans. Chicago: University of Chicago Press.

Derrida, Jacques. (1981b). *Positions*. Alan Bass, Trans. Chicago: University of Chicago Press.

Derrida, Jacques. (1982). *Margins of Philosophy*. Alan Bass, Trans. Chicago: University of Chicago Press.

Derrida, Jacques. (1985). *The Ear of the Other: Otobiography, Transference, Translation*. Peggy Kamuf, Trans. Christie McDonald, Ed. Lincoln: University of Nebraska Press.

Derrida, Jacques. (1987b). *The Post Card: From Socrates to Freud and Beyond*. Alan Bass, Trans. Chicago: University of Chicago Press. (First published in France 1980).

Derrida, Jacques. (1987c). *Truth in Painting*. Geoffrey Bennington and Ian McLeod, Trans. Chicago: University of Chicago Press.

Derrida, Jacques. (1988a). Like the Sound of the Sea Deep Within a Shell: Paul de Man's War. Peggy Kamuf, Trans. *Critical Inquiry*. Vol. 14, 590–652.

Derrida, Jacques. (1988b). *Limited Inc*. Evanston, IL: Northwestern University Press.

Derrida, Jacques. (1988c). *Memoirs for Paul de Man*. Cecile Lindsay, Jonathan Culler, Eduardo Cadava, and Peggy Kamuf, Trans. New York: Columbia University Press. (First published in France 1986).

Derrida, Jacques. (1989). *Of Spirit: Heidegger and the Question*. Geoff Bennington and Rachel Bowlby, Trans. Chicago: University of Chicago Press. (First published in France 1987).

Derrida, Jacques. (1990). Force of Law: The "Mystical Foundation of Authority." In *Deconstruction and the Possibility of Justice*. Mary Quaintance, Trans. Drucilla Cornell, Michael Rosenfeld, and David Gray Carlson, Eds. *The Cardozo Law Review*, Vol. 11, nos. 5–6.

Derrida, Jacques. (1992a). *Acts of Literature*. Derek Attridge, Ed. New York: Routledge.

Derrida, Jacques. (1992b). *The Other Heading: Reflections on Today's Europe*. Pascale-Anne Brault and Michael B. Naas, Trans. Bloomington: Indiana University Press. (First published in France 1991).

Derrida, Jacques. (1992c). *Points. .. Interviews, 1974-1994*. Peggy Kamuf and Others, Trans. Elisabeth Weber, Ed. Stanford: Stanford University Press.

Derrida, Jacques. (1992d). "How to Avoid Speaking: Denials." In *Derrida and Negative Theology*. Ken Frieden, Trans. Harold Coward and Toby Foshay, Eds. Albany: State University of New York Press.

Derrida, Jacques. (1993a). *Aporias*. Thomas Dutoit, Trans. Stanford: Stanford University Press.

Derrida, Jacques. (1994a). *Specters of Marx: The State of the Debt, the Work of Mourning, and the New International*. Peggy Kamuf, Trans. New York: Routledge.

Derrida, Jacques. (1994b). The Deconstruction of Actuality: An Interview with Jacques Derrida. *Radical Philosophy*. Vol. 68, 28-41.

Derrida, Jacques. (1994c). Nietzsche and the Machine. Richard Beardsworth, Interviewer. *Journal of Nietzsche Studies*. Vol. 7, 7-66.

Derrida, Jacques. (1995a). *Archive Fever: A Freudian Impression*. Eric Prenowitz, Trans. Chicago: University of Chicago Press.

Derrida, Jacques. (1995b). *The Gift of Death*. David Wills, Trans. Chicago: University of Chicago Press.

Derrida, Jacques. (1995c). *On the Name*. David Wood, John P. Leavey, Jr., and Ian McLeod, Trans. Thomas Dutoit, Ed. Stanford: Stanford University Press. (First published in France 1993).

Derrida, Jacques. (1997). *Politics of Friendship*. George Collins, Trans. New York: Verso.

Derrida, Jacques. (2002). *Acts of Religion*. Gil Anidjar, Ed. New York: Routledge.

Derrida, Jacques. (2002). "Faith and Knowledge: The Two Sources of 'Religion' and the Limits of Reason Alone." Samuel Weber, Trans. In *Acts of Religion*. New York: Routledge.

Derrida, Jacques. (2002). *Negotiations: Interventions and Interviews 1971-2001*. Elizabeth Rottenberg, Trans. and Ed. Stanford: Stanford University Press.

Derrida, Jacques. (2002). "Typewriter Ribbon: Limited Ink (2)." In *Without Alibi*. Peggy Kamuf, Trans. and Ed. Stanford: Stanford University Press.

Derrida, Jacques. (2003). "Autoimmunity: Real and Symbolic Suicides—A Dialogue with Jacques Derrida." In *Philosophy in a Time of Terror: Dialogues with Jürgen Habermas and Jacques Derrida*. Borradori, Giovanna, Ed. Chicago: University of Chicago Press.

Derrida, Jacques. (2005). *Rogues*. Pascale-Anne Brault and Michael Naas, Trans. Stanford: Stanford University Press.

Derrida, Jacques. (2007). *Learning to Live Finally: The Last Interview*. Pascale-Anne Brault and Michael Naas, Trans. Hoboken, NJ: Melville House Publishing.

Derrida, Jacques. (2017). Interview: Abraham's Melancholy. Michal Ben-Naftali, Interviewer. Ellie Anderson and Philippe Lynes, Trans. *The Oxford Literary Review*. Vol. 39, no. 2, 153–188. (Interview conducted March 2004).

Derrida, Jacques, and Elisabeth Roudinesco. (2004). *For What Tomorrow: A Dialogue*. Jeff Fort, Trans. Stanford: Stanford University Press.

Derrida, Jacques, and Geoffrey Bennington. (1993). *Jacques Derrida*. Geoffrey Bennington, Trans. Chicago: University of Chicago Press. (First published in France 1991).

Derrida, Jacques, and Maurizio Ferraris. (2001). *A Taste for the Secret*. Giacomo Donis, Trans. Giacomo Donis and David Webb, Eds. Malden, MA: Blackwell Publishers Inc.

Desilet, Gregory. (1989). "Nietzsche Contra Burke: The Melodrama in Dramatism." *Quarterly Journal of Speech*. Vol. 75, 65–83. https://doi.org/10.1080/00335638909383862.

Desilet, Gregory. (1991). "Heidegger and Derrida: The Conflict Between Hermeneutics and Deconstruction in the Context of Rhetorical and Communication Theory." *Quarterly Journal of Speech*. Vol. 77, 152–175. https://doi.org/10.1080/00335639109383950.

Desilet, Gregory. (1999). "Physics and Language—Science and Rhetoric: Reviewing the Parallel Evolution of Theory on Motion and Meaning in the Aftermath of the Sokal Hoax." *Quarterly Journal of Speech*. Vol. 85, 339–360. https://doi.org/10.1080/00335639909384268.

Desilet, Gregory. (2006). *Our Faith in Evil:*

Melodrama and the Effects of Entertainment Violence. Jefferson, NC: McFarland.

Desilet, Gregory. (2009). "Toward a Rhetorical Theory of Language: Parallels Between the Work of John Macksoud and Jacques Derrida." In *John Macksoud's Other Illusions: Inquiries Toward a Rhetorical Theory.* Craig R. Smith, Ed. West Lafayette, IN: Purdue University Press.

Desilet, Gregory, and Edward C. Appel. (2011). Choosing a Rhetoric of the Enemy: Kenneth Burke's Comic Frame, Warrantable Outrage, and the Problem of Scapegoating. *Rhetoric Society Quarterly.* Vol. 41, no. 4, 340–362. https://doi.org/10.1080/02773945.2011.596177.

Dewey, John. (1958). *Experience and Nature.* New York: Dover Publications, Inc. (First published 1925).

Diamond, Cora. (2001). "How Long Is the Standard Meter in Paris?" In *Wittgenstein in America.* Timothy McCarthy and Sean C. Stidd, Eds. New York: Oxford University Press.

Direk, Zeynep, and Leonard Lawlor, Eds. (2014). *A Companion to Derrida.* Malden, MA: John Wiley & Sons, Ltd.

Doussan, Jenny. (2013). "Time and Presence in Agamben's Critique of Deconstruction." *Cosmos and History: The Journal of Natural and Social Philosophy.* Vol. 9, no. 1, 183–202.

Doyon, Maxime. (2014). "The Transcendental Claim of Deconstruction." In *A Companion to Derrida.* Zeynep Direk and Len Lawlor, Eds. Malden, MA: John Wiley & Sons, Ltd.

Einstein, Albert, and Leopold Infeld. (1938). *The Evolution of Physics.* New York: Simon & Schuster, Inc.

Elmore, Rick. (2012). "Revisiting Violence and Life in the Early Work of Jacques Derrida." *Symplokē.* Vol. 20, nos.1–2, 33–49.

Evink, C.E. (2004). "Jacques Derrida and the Faith in Philosophy." *The Southern Journal of Philosophy.* Vol. 42, 313–331.

Frank, Manfred. (1997). *The Subject and the Text: Essays on Literary Theory and Philosophy.* Helen Atkins, Trans. Andrew Bowie, Ed. Cambridge: University of Cambridge Press. (First published 1989).

Frege, Gottlob. (1950). *The Foundations of Arithmetic: A Logico-Mathematical Enquiry into the Concept of Number.* J.L. Austin, Trans. Evanston: Northwestern University Press. (First published 1884).

Frege, Gottlob. (2013). *Basic Laws of Arithmetic Vols. 1 and 2.* Philip A. Ebert and Marcus Rossberg with Crispin Wright, Trans. and Eds. Oxford: Oxford University Press. (First published 1893 and 1903).

Fried, Gregory. (2000). *Heidegger's Polemos: From Being to Politics.* New Haven: Yale University Press.

Gaon, Stella. (2004). "Judging Justice: The Strange Responsibility of Deconstruction." *Philosophy and Social Criticism,* Vol. 30, no. 1, 97–114. https://doi.org/10.1177/0191453704039399.

Garver, Newton. (2009). "Derrida and Wittgenstein—Again." (This text is Garver's Preface to the second edition of the Korean publication of *Derrida and Wittgenstein*).

Garver, Newton, and Seung-Chong Lee. (1994). *Derrida and Wittgenstein.* Philadelphia: Temple University Press.

Gier, Nicholas F. (2007). "Wittgenstein and Deconstruction." *Review of Contemporary Philosophy.* Vol. 6.

Glendinning, Simon. (1998). *On Being With Others: Heidegger, Derrida, Wittgenstein.* New York: Routledge.

Glendinning, Simon, Ed. (2001). *Arguing with Derrida.* Malden, MA: Blackwell Publishers Inc.

Glock, Hans-Johann, and John Hyman, Eds. (2017). *A Companion to Wittgenstein.* Malden, MA: John Wiley & Sons, Ltd.

Goldberg, Daniel S. (2006). "I Do Not Think It Means What You Think It Means: How Kripke and Wittgenstein's Analysis On Rule Following Undermines Justice Scalia's Textualism and Originalism." *Cleveland State Law Review.* Vol. 54, no. 3, 273–307.

Golumbia, David. (1999). "Quine, Derrida, and the Question of Philosophy." *The Philosophical Forum.* Vol. 30, no. 3, 163–186.

Grene, Marjorie G. (1976) "Life, Death, and Language: Some Thoughts on Wittgenstein and Derrida." In *Philosophy In and Out of Europe.* Berkeley: University of California Press.

Hacker, P.M.S. (2007). "Gordon Baker's Late Interpretation of Wittgenstein." In *Wittgenstein and His Interpreters:*

Essays in Memory of Gordon Baker. Guy Kahane, Edward Kanterian, and Oskari Kuusela, Eds. Oxford: Blackwell Publishing, Ltd. 88–122.

Hägglund, Martin.(2008). *Radical Atheism: Derrida and the Time of Life.* Stanford: Stanford University Press.

Harris, Daniel W., and Elmar Unnsteinsson. (2018). "Wittgenstein's Influence on Austin's Philosophy of Language." *British Journal for the History of Philosophy.* Vol. 26, no. 2, 371–395. https://doi.org/10.1080/09608788.2017.1396958.

Heidegger, Martin. (1962). *Being and Time.* John Macquarrie and Edward Robinson, Trans. New York: Harper and Row, Publishers. (First published in Germany 1927).

Husserl, Edmund. (1970). *Logical Investigations, Vol. 1.* J.N. Findlay, Trans. New York: Routledge & Kegan Paul Ltd. (First published 1901).

Husserl, Edmund. (1970). *Logical Investigations, Vol. 2.* J.N. Findlay, Trans. New York: Routledge & Kegan Paul Ltd. (First published 1901).

Hyde, Michael. J., and D. Kevin Sargent. (1993). "The Performance of Play, the 'Great Poem,' and Ethics." *Text and Performance Quarterly.* Vol. 13, 122–138. https://doi.org/10.1080/10462939309366038.

Jamieson, Michelle. (2017). "Allergy and Autoimmunity: Rethinking the Normal and the Pathological." *Parallax,* Vol. 23, no. 1, 11–27, DOI: 10.1080/13534645.2016.1261659.

Kakoliris, Gerasimos. (2013). "The Undecidable *Pharmakon*: Derrida's Reading of Plato's *Phaedrus.*" In *The New Yearbook for Phenomenology and Phenomenological Philosophy, Vol. XIII.* Burt Hopkins and John Drummond, Eds. New York: Routledge.

Kakutani, Michiko. (1993). "Critic's Notebook: When History Is a Casualty." *New York Times,* April 30. Online access April, 2019.

Katsumori, Makoto. (2011). *Niels Bohr's Complementarity: Its Structure, History, and Intersections with Hermeneutics and Deconstruction.* New York: Springer.

Kripke, Saul. (1982). *Wittgenstein on Rules and Private Language.* Cambridge, MA: Harvard University Press.

Kuusela, Oskari, and Marie McGinn, Eds. (2011). *The Oxford Handbook of Wittgenstein.* New York: Oxford University Press.

La Caze, Marguerite. (2017). "It's Easier to Lie If You Believe It Yourself: Derrida, Arendt, and the Modern Lie." *Law, Culture and the Humanities.* Vol. 13, no. 2, 193–210. https://doi.org/10.1177/1743872113485032.

Law, Jules David. (1989). "Reading with Wittgenstein and Derrida." In *Redrawing the Lines: Analytic Philosophy, Deconstruction, and Literary Theory.* Reed Dasenbrock, Ed. Minneapolis: University of Minnesota Press. 140–168.

Lipstadt, Deborah E. (2005). *Denial: Holocaust History on Trial.* New York: HarperCollins Publishers.

Lipstadt, Deborah E. (2012). *Denying the Holocaust: The Growing Assault on Truth and Memory.* New York: The Free Press. (First published 1993).

Livingston, Paul. (2008). *Philosophy and the Vision of Language.* New York: Routledge.

Livingston, Paul. (2012). *The Politics of Logic.* New York: Routledge.

Macdonald, Heather. (1991). "The Holocaust as Text: Deconstruction's Final Solution to the de Man Problem." *Salmagundi,* Vol. 92, no. 4, 160–173.

Macksoud, John. (1964). *The Literary Theories of Kenneth Burke and the Discovery of Meanings in Oral Interpretation.* PhD. Dissertation. University of California Los Angeles.

Macksoud, John. (1968). "Anyone's How Town: Interpretation as Rhetorical Discipline." *Speech Monographs.* Vol. 35, 70–76. https://doi.org/10.1080/03637756809375566.

Macksoud, John. (1969). "Kenneth Burke on Perspective and Rhetoric." *Western Journal of Speech Communication.* Vol. XXXIII, 167–174. https://doi.org/10.1080/10570316909384574.

Macksoud, John. (1971). "Phenomenology, Experience, and Interpretation." *Philosophy and Rhetoric.* Vol. 4, 139–149.

Macksoud, John. (1973a). "Ludwig Wittgenstein, Radical Operationism, and Rhetorical Stance." In *Philosophers on Rhetoric.* Donald G. Douglas, Ed. Skokie, IL: National Textbook Company.

Macksoud, John. (1973b). *Other Illusions: Inquiries Toward a Rhetorical Theory.* Binghampton, NY: Self-published.

Macksoud, John. (2009). *John Macksoud's Other Illusions.* Craig R. Smith, Ed. Gregory Desilet, Afterword. West Lafayette, IN: Purdue University Press.

Macksoud, John, and Ross Altman. (1971). Voices in Opposition: A Burkeian Rhetoric of Saint Joan. *Quarterly Journal of Speech.* Vol. 57, 140–146. https://doi.org/10.1080/00335637109383054.

Macomber, W.B. (1967). *The Anatomy of Disillusion: Martin Heidegger's Notion of Truth.* Evanston, IL: Northwestern University Press.

Madry, Alan R. (1995). Analytic Deconstructionism? The Intellectual Voyeurism of Anthony D'Amato. *Fordham Law Review,* Vol. 63, 1033–1067.

Margolis, Joseph. (1994). "Vs. (Wittgenstein, Derrida)." In *Wittgenstein and Contemporary Philosophy.* Souren Teghrarian, Ed. Bristol, UK: Thoemmes Press. 161–184.

Mark, J. (1989). "Wittgenstein, Theology and Wordless Faith." *New Blackfriars,* 70 (831), 423–433. Retrieved December 31, 2020, from http://www.jstor.org/stable/43248732.

Marsh, Jack E., Jr. (2009). "Of Violence: The Force and Significance of Violence in the Early Derrida." *Philosophy & Social Criticism.* Vol 35, no. 3, 269–286. https://doi.org/10.1177/0191453708100231.

McDougall, Derek A. (2008). "Pictures, Privacy, Augustine, and the Mind: A Unity in Wittgenstein's *Philosophical Investigations.*" *Journal of Philosophical Research,* Vol. 33, 33–72. https://doi.org/10.5840/jpr_2008_15.

McFee, Graham. (2015). *How To Do Philosophy: A Wittgensteinian Reading of Wittgenstein.* Newcastle, UK: Cambridge Scholars Publishing.

McGinn, Marie. (2013). *The Routledge Guidebook to Wittgenstein's Philosophical Investigations.* New York: Routledge.

McNally, Thomas, and Sinéad McNally. (2012). "Chomsky and Wittgenstein on Linguistic Competence." *Nordic Wittgenstein Review.* Vol. 1, 131–154.

McQuillan, Martin. (2001). *Paul de Man.* New York: Routledge.

Merrell, Floyd. (1985). *Deconstruction Reframed.* West Lafayette, IN: Purdue University Press.

Moati, Raoul. (2014). *Derrida/Searle: Deconstruction and Ordinary Language.* Timothy Attanucci and Maureen Chun, Trans. New York: Columbia University Press.

Monk, Ray. (1990). *Ludwig Wittgenstein: The Duty of Genius.* New York: Penguin Books.

Monk, Ray. (2001). "Ray Monk's Top Ten Philosophy Books of the 20th Century." *The Guardian.* Oct, 31. Online access January 2022.

Monk, Ray. (2005). *How to Read Wittgenstein.* New York: W.W. Norton & Company.

Moore, Ian Alexander. (2017). "Heraclitus and the Metaphysics of War." In *Blood Meridian.* In *Philosophical Approaches to Cormac McCarthy: Beyond Reckoning.* New York: Routledge.

Moore, Ian Alexander. (2020). "The Promise of Pain: (Di)spiriting the *Geist* of Heidegger's Trakl." DOI: https://doi.org/10.3998/pc.12322227.0014.002.

Moran, Shane. (1995). "White Mythology: What Use Is Deconstruction?" *Alternation,* Vol. 2, no. 1, 16–36.

Morin, Marie-Eve. (2006). "Putting Community Under Erasure: Derrida and Nancy on the Plurality of Singularities." *Culture Machine,* Vol. 8, 1–9.

Moringiello, S. (2003). Kataphasis, Apophasis and Mysticism in Pseudo-Denys and Wittgenstein. *New Blackfriars,* 84(987), 220–229. Retrieved December 31, 2020, from http://www.jstor.org/stable/43250714.

Morriston, Wesley. (1972). "Heidegger on the World." *Man and World: An International Philosophical Review.* Vol. 5, no. 4, 452–467.

Mulligan, Kevin. (1978). "Inscriptions and Speaking's Place: Derrida and Wittgenstein." *Oxford Literary Review.* Vol. 3, no. 2, 62–67.

Nietzsche, Friedrich. (1954). *The Portable Nietzsche.* Walter Kaufmann, Ed. New York: Penguin Books.

Norris, Christopher. (1982). *Deconstruction: Theory and Practice.* New York: Methuen.

Norris, Christopher. (2014). "Truth in Derrida." In *A Companion to Derrida.* Malden, MA: John Wiley & Sons, Ltd. 23–41.

Overgaard, Søren. (2006). "The Problem of Other Minds: Wittgenstein's Phenomenological Perspective." *Phenomenology and the Cognitive Sciences.* Vol. 5, 53–73.

Peeters, Benoît. (2013). *Derrida.* Andrew Brown, Trans. Malden, MA: Polity Press. (First published in France 2010).

Penco, Carlo. (2020). "Wittgenstein's Thought Experiments and Relativity Theory." In *Wittgensteinian (adj): Looking at the World from the Viewpoint of Wittgenstein's Philosophy.* Shyam Wuppuluri and Newton da Costa, Eds. Cham, CHE: Springer.

Pericles, Peter Trifonas, and Michael A. Peters, Eds. (2005). *Deconstructing Derrida: Tasks for the New Humanities.* New York: Palgrave Macmillan.

Perissinotto, Luigi, and Begona Ramon Camara, Eds. (2013). *Wittgenstein and Plato: Connections, Comparisons, and Contrasts.* New York: Palgrave Macmillan.

Plotnitsky, Arkady. (1994). *Complementarity: Anti-Epistemology After Bohr and Derrida.* Durham, NC: Duke University Press.

Potter, Jonathan. (2001). "Wittgenstein and Austin." In *Discourse Theory and Practice: A Reader.* M. Wetherell, S. Taylor, and S. Yates, Eds. London: Sage Publications. 39–46.

Priest, Graham. (2002). *Beyond the Limits of Thought.* New York: Oxford University Press.

Ricœur, Paul. (2014). "The Later Wittgenstein and the Later Husserl on Language." *Ricœur Studies.* Vol. 5, no. 1, 28–48. (Edited version of lectures given at Johns Hopkins University in April 1966). DOI: 10.5195/errs.2014.245.

Rorty, Richard. (1979). *Philosophy and the Mirror of Nature.* Princeton: Princeton University Press.

Russell, Bertrand, and A.N. Whitehead. (1910). *Principia Mathematica, Vol. I.* London: Cambridge University Press.

Russell, Bertrand, and A.N. Whitehead. (1912). *Principia Mathematica, Vol. II.* London: Cambridge University Press.

Russell, Bertrand, and A.N. Whitehead. (1913). *Principia Mathematica, Vol. III.* London: Cambridge University Press.

Sands, Danielle. (2008). Thinking Through Différance: Derrida, Žižek and Religious Engagement. *Textual Practice,* Vol. 22, no. 3, 529–546, DOI: 10.1080/09502360802263774.

Sasidharan, P.K. (1999). "Derridean Overtures of Wittgenstein Critique." *Indian Philosophical Quarterly.* Vol. 26, no. 2, 199–206.

Schönbaumsfeld, Genia. (2019). "Meaning Scepticism and Scientism." In *Wittgenstein and Scientism.* Jonathan Beale and Ian Kidd, Eds. London: Routledge.

Schroeder, Severin. (2006). *Wittgenstein: The Way Out of the Fly-Bottle.* Malden, MA: Polity Press.

Searle, John. (1977). "Reiterating the Differences: A Reply to Derrida." *Glyph 1: Johns Hopkins Textual Studies.* Baltimore: Johns Hopkins University Press. Vol. 1, 199–210.

Searle, John. (1993). "The World Turned Upside Down." In *Working Through Derrida.* Gary B. Madison, Ed. Evanston: Northwestern University Press.

Searle, John. (1994). "Literary Theory and Its Discontents." *New Literary History.* Vol. 25, 637–665.

Segal, Alex. (2017). "Deconstruction, Literature, and Wittgenstein's Privileging of Showing." *Advances in Language and Literary Studies.* Online access February 2019.

Shain, Ralph E. (2005). "Derrida's References to Wittgenstein." *International Studies in Philosophy.* Vol. 36, no. 4, 71–104.

Shain, Ralph E. (2007). "Derrida and Wittgenstein: Points in Opposition." *Journal of French Philosophy.* Vol. 17, no. 2, 130–152. DOI: https://doi.org/10.5195/jffp.2007.217.

Shain, Ralph E. (2018). "Derrida on Truth." *The Philosophical Forum, Inc.* Vol. 49, no. 2, 193–213. DOI: 10.1111/phil.12183.

Shannon, Claude E., and Warren Weaver. (1964). *The Mathematical Theory of Communication.* Urbana: University of Illinois Press.

Shotter, John. (2007). "Wittgenstein and His Philosophy of First-Time Events." *History & Philosophy of Psychology.* Vol. 9, no. 1, 1–11.

Silby, Brent. (1998). "Wittgenstein: Meaning and Representation." https://www.academia.edu/72993656/Wittgenstein_Meaning_and_Representation. Accessed January 2022.

Silverman, Hugh J., Ed. (1989). *Derrida and Deconstruction*. New York: Routledge.

Sonderegger, Ruth. (1997). A Critique of Pure Meaning: Wittgenstein and Derrida. *European Journal of Philosophy*. Vol. 5, no. 2, 183–209. https://doi.org/10.1111/1468-0378.00035.

Staten, Henry. (1984). *Wittgenstein and Derrida*. Lincoln: University of Nebraska Press.

Stone, Martin. (2000). "Wittgenstein on Deconstruction." In *The New Wittgenstein*. Alice Crary and Rupert Read, Eds. New York: Routledge.

Taylor, Mark C. (2004). "What Derrida Really Meant." *The New York Times*. October, 14.

Thomas, Michael. (2006). *The Reception of Derrida: Translation and Transformation*. New York: Palgrave Macmillan.

Tompkins, Phillip K. (2021). *Open Communication and Replication as Methods for Finding Truth*. Denver, CO: Outskirts Press, Inc.

Truong Rootham, Mireille M. (1996). "Wittgenstein's Metaphysical Use and Derrida's Metaphysical Appurtenance." *Philosophy and Social Criticism*. Vol. 22, no. 2, 27–46. https://doi.org/10.1177/019145379602200202.

Vaughan-Williams, Nick. (2007). "Beyond a Cosmopolitan Ideal: The Politics of Singularity." *International Politics*, Vol. 44, 107–124. DOI: 10.1057/palgrave.ip.8800161.

Venturinha, Nuno. (2015). "The Epistemic Value of Holding for True." *Journal of Philosophical Research*. Vol. 40, 155–170. https://doi.org/10.5840/jpr2015111046.

Wendland, Aaron James. (2019). "Philosophy Must Be Dragged Out of the Ivory Tower and into the Marketplace of Ideas." *New Statesman*. Online access January 9, 2019.

Werhane, Patricia H. (1992). *Skepticism, Rules, and Private Languages*. Atlantic Highlands, NJ: Humanities International Press, Inc.

Wheeler III, Samuel C. (2000). *Deconstruction as Analytic Philosophy*. Stanford: Stanford University Press.

Whitehead, A.N. (1978). *Process and Reality*. New York: The Free Press. (First published 1929).

Williams, Meredith. (2010). *Blind Obedience: Paradox and Learning in the Later Wittgenstein*. New York: Routledge.

Wilson, George M. (1998). "Semantic Realism and Kripke's Wittgenstein." *Philosophy and Phenomenological Research*. Vol. 58, no. 1, 99–122. https://doi.org/10.2307/2653632.

Winspur, Steven. (1989). "Text Acts: Recasting Performatives with Wittgenstein and Derrida." In *Redrawing the Lines: Analytic Philosophy, Deconstruction, and Literary Theory*. Reed Dasenbrock, Ed. Minneapolis: University of Minnesota Press. 169–188.

Wirth, Uwe. (2003). "Derrida and Peirce on Indeterminacy, Iteration, and Replication." *Semiotica*. Vol. 143, no. 1, 35–44. https://doi.org/10.1515/semi.2003.011.

Wise, Christopher. (2011). *Chomsky and Deconstruction: The Politics of Unconscious Knowledge*. New York: Palgrave Macmillan.

Wittgenstein, Ludwig. (1953). *Philosophical Investigations*. G.E.M. Anscombe, Trans. New York: The Macmillan Company.

Wittgenstein, Ludwig. (1958). *The Blue and Brown Books*. New York: Harper & Row, Publishers. (From dictations to students at Cambridge 1933–1935).

Wittgenstein, Ludwig. (1961). *Tractatus Logico-Philosophicus*. D.F. Pears and B.F. McGuinness, Trans. London: Routledge & Kegan Paul. (First published in English 1922 and in German 1921).

Wittgenstein, Ludwig. (1967a). *Lectures and Conversations on Aesthetics, Psychology, and Religious Belief*. Cyril Barrett, Ed. Berkeley: University of California Press. (Compiled from notes taken by Yorick Smythies, Rush Rhees, and James Taylor, summer 1938).

Wittgenstein, Ludwig. (1967b). *Remarks on the Foundations of Mathematics*. G.E.M. Anscombe, Trans. G.H. von Wright and Rush Rhees, Eds. Cambridge, MA: MIT Press. (From notes written between 1937–1944).

Wittgenstein, Ludwig. (1967c). *Zettel*. G.E.M. Anscombe, Trans. G.E.M. Anscombe and G.H. von Wright, Eds. Berkeley: University of California Press.

Wittgenstein, Ludwig. (1969). *On Certainty*. Denis Paul and G.E.M. Anscombe, Trans. New York: Harper & Row, Publishers. (From notes written during the last years of Wittgenstein's life 1949–1951, the last entry made two days before his death).

Wittgenstein, Ludwig. (1974). *Philosophical Grammar: Part I, The Proposition and Its Sense, Part II, On Logic and Mathematics.* Anthony Kenny, Trans. Rush Rhees, Ed. Berkeley: University of California Press.

Wittgenstein, Ludwig. (1975). *Philosophical Remarks.* Raymond Hargreaves and Roger White, Trans. Rush Rhees, Ed. Chicago: University of Chicago Press.

Wittgenstein, Ludwig. (1976). *Wittgenstein's Lectures on the Foundations of Mathematics.* Cora Diamond, Ed. Chicago: University of Chicago Press. (From the notes of R.G. Bosanquet, Norman Malcolm, Rush Rhees, and Yorick Smythies).

Wittgenstein, Ludwig. (1980). *Culture and Value.* Peter Winch, Trans. G.H. von Wright in collaboration with Heikki Nyman, Eds. Chicago: University of Chicago Press.

Wittgenstein, Ludwig. (1980). *Remarks on the Philosophy of Psychology, Vol. 1.* G.E.M. Anscombe, Trans. G.E.M. Anscombe and G.H. von Wright, Eds. Chicago: University of Chicago Press. (From notes written primarily between 1946–1949).

Wittgenstein, Ludwig. (1980). *Remarks on the Philosophy of Psychology, Vol. 2.* C.G. Luckhardt and A.E. Aue, Trans. G.H. von Wright and Heikki Nyman, Eds. Chicago: University of Chicago Press.

Wittgenstein, Ludwig. (2009). *Philosophical Investigations.* G.E.M. Anscombe, P.M.S. Hacker, and Joachim Schulte, Trans. Malden, MA: Blackwell Publishing Ltd.

Wood, David, Ed. (1992). *Derrida: A Critical Reader.* Cambridge, MA: Blackwell Publishers Ltd.

Wuppuluri, Shyam, and Newton da Costa, Eds. (2020). *Wittgensteinian (adj): Looking at the World from the Viewpoint of Wittgenstein's Philosophy.* Cham, CHE: Springer.

Zabel, Gary. (1979)." Wittgenstein's View of Metaphysics with Reference to the Problem of Solipsism." Boston: University of Massachusetts. Unpublished paper. (Previously on academia.edu but no longer available).

Index

205

Milton Keynes UK
Ingram Content Group UK Ltd.
UKHW010330130424
440672UK00017BA/127